INDIA
SEARCHING FOR THE PRESENT IN THE PAST

INDIA
SEARCHING FOR THE PRESENT IN THE PAST

PROSENJIT DASGUPTA

First published in 2020 by CinnamonTeal Design and Publishing

Copyright © 2020 Prosenjit Dasgupta

ISBN 978–93–87676–84–8

BISAC: HIS017000/HISTORY/Asia/India & South Asia

HIS000000/HISTORY/General

Cover design and Typesetting: CinnamonTeal Design and Publishing

CinnamonTeal Design and Publishing
Plot No 16, Housing Board Colony
Gogol, Margao
Goa 403601 India
www.cinnamonteal.in

Dedicated to my parents,
late Karunakumar Dasgupta and late Jyotsna Dasgupta

"Yena-aham na-amritasyam kim-aham te-na kuryam?"

(What use have I for that which does not give me an intimation of immortality?)

> ~ Maitreyi to the sage, Yajnavalka, in the
> Brihadaranyaka Upanishad

"Where the mind is without fear and the head is held high,

Where knowledge is free,

Where the clear stream of reason has not lost its way into the dreary desert sands of dead habit,

Into that heaven of freedom, my Father, let my country awake."

> ~ Rabindranath Tagore ("Naibidya", 1901)

"I do not want my house to be walled in on all sides and my windows to be stuffed. I want the culture of all lands to be blown about my house as freely as possible. But I refuse to be blown off my feet by any."

> ~ Mohandas Karamchand Gandhi

Contents

Preface

In India, possibly more than in most other countries, there is what Leonid Plotkin in his book of the same title (Niyogi Books, 2018) has called the "Nostalgia for Eternity". This fascination for the *anadi, ananta*, that which is without beginning or end, and which "is" and has always been, has marked the Indian thinking for ages. Of course, in rather an obvious way, the distant past and the immediate present are inexorably linked by time, much as day follows night, just as rational thoughts and not-so-rational beliefs are so intimately interwoven in each human being. This is an intriguing and interesting intellectual issue, and paradox, that we often have to confront. When one is closely preoccupied with the problems of day-to-day life and livelihood, these issues are all too often overlooked. But, in solitude, when one is walking by oneself along the seashore, or reading a book on a sunny terrace, suddenly, from nowhere, these thoughts take hold of one. Like most people, I have also had this experience, and have sought the answers in books, the most convenient panacea and, in the experience, thoughts and knowledge of so many scholars and sages.

As science has it, we, human beings, are members of the still-surviving and still-evolving species known as *Homo sapiens*, or "wise man". Whether we are really wise or not is a moot point. But, at least, we are thinking men and women, and are possibly capable of becoming wise after a fashion. This, then, is an attempt confined to a study of Indian history in both the far and the immediate past, so as to provide a perspective in discussing and understanding some aspects of the present. The primary focus is on the speculation and thoughts on life and human affairs that have emerged and developed in India over the millennia, and which give it that special fascination and charm. This is, in itself, a pretty large canvas to cover. But, of course, such an attempt needs to be supplemented by studies on the Indian economy, sociology, literature, arts, aesthetics, etc., which is beyond the scope of this work.

Basically, the purpose of this work is to inquire, state, discuss and argue (hopefully, with reason and rationality) about the past and the present, about the evolution of these thoughts and beliefs, in keeping with the basic tradition in India. And that is part of a great tradition, dating back to the dialogue between sage Yajnavalka and his wife Maitreyi as documented in the *Brihadaranyaka Upanishad*, or to the furious debates that Adi Shankaracharya engaged in during his travels throughout India to propagate his thoughts on *Advaitavad*, or "non-dualism". Hopefully, this work would help to widen one's knowledge and perspective and provide a modicum of understanding.

The ancient Sanskrit sacred texts, commencing from the *Rigveda*, through their associated *Brahmanas* and *Aranyakas*, to the *Upanishads* and the *Bhagavad-gita*, the epics *Mahabharata* and the *Ramayana*, the *Manusmriti* and the *Puranas* of later eras provide the basic foundation to practically all of Indian thought and culture. No doubt, over the past four or five millennia of Indian history, there have been many occasions and instances of interaction between more than one ethnic group, and other languages and cultures, which have culminated over the years into what India is today. This is not unique to India: Iran, Turkey, Afghanistan, and many other countries have witnessed this to a greater or lesser degree.

It is not at all easy to follow through these numerous strands of time and change. References to the sacred texts help to an extent, as do the results of systematic paleontological, geological, archaeological, anthropological, epigraphical, linguistic, and philological researches into Indian history and culture that so many scholars have pursued over the last two centuries and more. Stone implements used by ancient

Prosenjit Dasgupta

man, and the rock paintings, pottery remains, seals, coins, and inscriptions unearthed from a large number of sites in India, each tell their own story to anyone who is sufficiently interested. The boundaries of knowledge are, therefore, ever-expanding and extending, and thus changing the way we look at and understand persons, things and events. Ignorance is bliss, as the old saying goes; but surely, knowledge and emancipation of the mind are not to be sneered at.

To keep things simple, this work has italicized the first references in the text to non-English words so as to alert the reader. Sanskrit and other words are spelled in simple phonetic, Roman script. The work gives necessary references as required in the body of the text itself for those who may wish to pursue further enquiries on their own. The Bibliography at the end should assist the more serious readers. I sincerely hope that they will enjoy that effort just as I have enjoyed mine.

Prosenjit Dasgupta, Kolkata, 30th December 2019

Chapter 1

Glimpses of Pre-history

One necessarily has to begin at the beginning. In the beginning, as the *Nasadiya Sukta* of *Rigveda* (Book 10, hymn 129) has it–

"*Na asat asit na u sat asit tadanim*"
(It was not that the non-existent existed, nor did the existent exist then).

Intrigued by the rhythm of life all around them and gazing at the stars in the night sky, the sages asked themselves -

"*Yádi vā dadhé yádi vā ná*"
If He has created it, or if He has not.

Significantly, the hymn goes on to suggest -

"*Kamastagre samavartatadhi
manaso retoh prathamam yadasit*"

This, Dr Karan Singh translated in his book, as:

"Thereafter, rose Desire in the beginning; Desire, the primal seed and germ of spirit?"

Adding -
"He, the first origin of this creation,
Whether He formed it, or did not form it,
He verily knows it, or perhaps He knows it not."

It is, in one part, a lyrical verse, and on the other, a metaphysical speculation of the highest order, and utterly truthful to itself. That was the basis of the cosmogony, that is, thoughts on the origin of the cosmos and the creation of life on Earth as Indian sages at that threshold of history had thought of it. It is difficult to see how any other more definite concept of the origin of creation could have been posited at that horizon of time, when many, even in the present times, find it difficult to comprehend the extent and nature of the cosmos. It was again a most natural inclination for the sages to have believed that the Ultimate Reality came to have a desire for creation, and the idea of *Hiranyagarbha* (or the golden germ or womb) came to their mind. Thus, one is led to the *Purusha Sukta* of the Rigveda that discusses at some length the various aspects of creation of life on Earth as we now know it.

These features of cosmogony as propounded by the thinkers and sages of ancient India may be said to have been just as valid (or invalid) as the generally accepted theory in scientific circles that the formation of the Earth was the result of some galactic "Big Bang", and the progressive association of space debris and gases into an increasingly compact mass. It is just that the Indian thinkers posited a "desire" by Him (*tadekam*, the One and Absolute), while science puts forward the idea of the Big Bang, without being quite able to put a finger on the definitive cause of such a sudden and cataclysmic event. But from theorizing or philosophically speculating on the origin of the cosmos, one has to come to terms with the planet that we inhabit.

Here, we seem to be on more firm ground as geological sciences consider that Earth came to be formed some 4.5 billion years ago. Most scientists currently believe that at that time there was no life on Earth; for, there was no oxygen, and the nascent Earth was largely surrounded by methane, ammonia and some other gases. Again, available scientific evidence suggests that the constant bombarding of this atmosphere with asteroids and meteorites led to some complex sequence of temperatures and pressures that helped generate the amino-

                    Prosenjit Dasgupta

acids that are universally found in the living process as we have it today. This is said to have occurred more than 3 billion years ago. This is scientifically known as abiogenesis (i.e., biological growth in the absence of living cells or tissues) or the beginning of early life on Earth. A simulation of the Big Bang, leading to a process for abiogenesis, was experimentally tried out in 1952 by the scientists Stanley Miller and Harold Urey at the University of Chicago, later repeated at the University of California, San Diego. They were largely successful, as were similar experiments by other scientists later.

Living tissue grows (in fact, growth itself is a sign of life), and in time, dies. So, microbial fossils have been discovered in more than one part of the world by palaeontologists, dating back to about 3.5 billion years, while evidence of plant life has been found to date back to about 2.5 to 3 billion years ago. This approximate dating is not a matter of conjecture; but is the result of scientifically designed tests by way of radiocarbon dating and other methodologies, such as uranium-lead or potassium-argon dating, magneto-stratigraphy, optically stimulated luminescence, and so on. These are highly sophisticated techniques developed by hundreds of scientists and scholars working to extend and refine this area of knowledge, and are widely accepted. Similarly, DNA testing has become quite the standard in researches on animal and human tissues. In point of fact, the field of DNA testing has been further extended to the study of Y-DNA linkages through successive generations of the male line and the "mitochondrial" linkage over many generations through the female line. Of course, there are occasional controversies about this or that dating, but these are more concerned with the interpretation of data than with the methodologies themselves.

Within this overall framework, geologists agree that the Indian sub-continent was many millions of years ago a part of a supercontinent called Pangaea, with India linked by land to what is now Africa and Australia. During the Jurassic Period that goes back to about 160 million years ago, geological forces caused Pangaea to break apart into two large land masses, called Gondwana (to the south) and Laurasia (to the north). There was a further geological tectonic movement about 125 million years ago, in what is called the Cretaceous Age, when the Indian sub-continental plate broke off from Pangaea and started to drift northwards, nearer the Eurasian plate. This process continued till about 50 million years ago, when the collision of the Indian sub-continent with the Eurasian continent led to the drainage of the huge Tethys Sea (that had separated Gondwana and Laurasia) and the emergence of the Himalayas, the Alps and the Caucasus mountain ranges. Remnants of the ancient Tethys Sea are what are today the Mediterranean, the Caspian, Black and Aral Seas. Relicts of the Tethys may also be seen in India in the Rann of Kutch in Gujarat and the Tso Moriri and Pangong lakes in Ladakh. The evidence of these geological changes in the Jurassic and Cretaceous (that is 125 to 150 million years ago) are also to be found in many places in India, e.g., the Rajmahal Hills in north-eastern Jharkhand, and the numerous hot springs, such as at Manikaran, Bhimbandh, Bakreswar, and elsewhere, and the fossils of ancient sea-dwelling creatures in many parts of the country (notably in the Rann of Kutch and in the Pin valley in Himachal Pradesh). Another notable site is a crater made by the collision of a large meteor with Earth, having a diameter of about two kilometres at Lonar, which is approximately 120 kilometres south of Akola in Maharashtra.

It is only when one has the opportunity to hold a "geode" (a volcanic bubble) in one's hand and see the amethystic crystal formations inside, that one may be led to visualize the long-past ages and the forces at play at that time. Similar is the case when one comes across ammonites, crab and bi-valve fossils, or the remains of petrified trees (dating back to the Jurassic or Cretaceous periods) from the Rann of Kutch, Rajmahal or the Pin valley in Himachal. It would indeed be unusual for

　　　　　　　Prosenjit Dasgupta

a person to find such fossils and yet be unmoved that one is holding perhaps 75 million years of time in the palm of one's hand.

H.D. Sankalia, a noted scholar of Indian pre-history and proto-history (see Bibliography), has opined that Early Palaeolithic (Palaeolithic means the early historical times when mankind relied on stone implements) remains in India dating back to 150,000 BCE and Middle Palaeolithic remains of about 25,000 BCE may be found at several sites in both Northwest and Peninsular India. Upper Palaeolithic (a later period, related to stratigraphic positioning) remains of about 6000-5000 BCE and Neolithic finds of about 3500-3000 BCE are to be found at Panchmarhi in Madhya Pradesh, near Bundi in Rajasthan, Nagarjunakonda in Andhra Pradesh, and Brahmagiri in Karnataka. The Chalcolithic period (that is, the time by which man had started using copper and bronze-based implements), around 2500-2000 BCE, is well represented in the Indus Valley Civilization sites (and there are at least 1500 such sites), at Nevasa in M.P. and Navdatoli in Maharashtra. Iron implements seem to have been introduced by about 1000 BCE, judging from the relicts found at a large number of archaeological sites.

A visit to some of the Indus Valley Civilization (IVC) sites in India, dating back to about 2500 BCE, such as Kalibangan in Rajasthan or Dholavira in Gujarat, is equally instructive for a visitor. Here is a fireplace, there the remnants of a large jar, there a grinding stone, and, to one side is a well. One finds reflections, however crude, of life much as rural India has it even today. Then, what seemed for a time like a conjecture or a play of imagination resolves itself into palpable reality. To deny this reality would be really denying oneself the faculty of sight, as also the capacity for rational thought.

Following upon the pieces of geological and fossil evidence dating back to the infancy of the Indian sub-continent, one then comes upon other material evidence, such as stone implements dating back to fifteen thousand or even twenty thousand years ago that ancient man used to get food, always one of the prime concerns of mankind. Stone axes and arrowheads, sharp-edged stones for scraping flesh from bone, and fish-hooks made from deer antlers and bone help to create an impression of what man in ancient India made use of to get food, besides providing evidence, via radiocarbon dating and other methods mentioned earlier, as to the possible age of such implements. There are numerous sites in India where such stone implements as fist-sized scrapers or much smaller microlith implements have been found. Many of them are in Andhra Pradesh, Tamil Nadu and Karnataka where Robert Bruce Foote of the Geological Survey of India in the 1860s decided to devote the rest of his life searching for such evidence, with great success. There are many other sites, such as Panchmarhi (near Jabalpur), Bhimbhetka (near Bhopal), Bundi in south eastern Rajasthan and even in the Kangsabati river valley in West Bengal where such stone implements have been found.

Other evidence that ancient man in India has left for us are the rock paintings at numerous sites, ranging from those near Almora in Uttarakhand to Bhimbhetka near Bhopal, at Mirzapur near Benaras, and close to Bundi in south-eastern Rajasthan, as well as those near Hazaribagh in Jharkhand and near Sundergarh in Odisha (there are many other sites). The rock shelters that occur in many places in these sandstone cliffs and outcrops were used by people residing in India in the pre-historic days; that is, long before the time when any form of written script (whether on clay, stone, bark or palm leaves) was used. These rock paintings, made with bare fingers or possibly twigs, in red, green or white in mineral and vegetable colours of interesting geometrical designs, or paintings of buffalos, deer, elephants, tigers, some fantastic creatures not properly understood, horse-riders, warriors bearing lances, and dancing groups hint at the concerns and activities of men

     Prosenjit Dasgupta

in those early times, dating back to six to eight thousand years before the present ("Before the Present" or BP, is reckoned from 1950). These paintings possibly served some ritualistic or magical purposes.

Another aspect that the Indian society has for long been fascinated and dominated by is time. Most, or at least many things had to be done at prescribed times, such as the various Vedic rituals (more on that later), marriages, *shraddhs* or funerals, *upanayana*, or the "thread ceremony" for the initiation of a young Brahmin boy into *brahmacharya*, or *jata karma* or the formal presentation of a new-born child in the family, *anna-prasanna* or the first rice-eating by a baby, or the many *vratas* or vows that widows, in particular, and women, in general, had to comply with. For many of these, there may or may not have been cogent scientific reasons for the introduction of such practices; but, then, many other social and religious practices do not seem to have had any such basis.

Traditionally, the division of time in India has been the *nimesha*, or the blink of an eye; but that has two commonly-accepted definitions. One that is 106.7 milliseconds and another that is 430 milliseconds. Then there is *pala* (in sidereal time), which is 24.1055 seconds; while the *kshana* is taken as 0.82 seconds; the *danda*, or a pause or period, is 24 minutes; while a *muhurta*, or a slice of time, is 48 minutes.

The lunar month is common in India. In North Indian tradition, it is counted from *Krishna paksh*, or the first day of the dark fortnight, to the *Purnima*, or full moon, while the South Indian tradition is just the opposite, taking it from the full moon to the last day of the dark fortnight. Not content with this, many Indian scholars have worked out time spans by their own light to measure the historical periods given in the *Vishnu Purana* as 1.728 million years comprising the *Satya Yuga*, 1.296 million years for *Treta Yuga*, 0.864 million years for the *Dvapara Yuga*, and 0.432 million years for the current and running *Kali Yuga*.

While this provides a reference framework and context to the Puranas (again, more on that later) and a sense of great antiquity, it again depends on a human construct of one human year being just a day in the life of a deity, or a blink of Brahma's eyes as being so many million years. As to why such claims of antiquity can, or should, provide merit or sanctity to what is essentially a human and subjective judgement of a much later stage is not immediately understood and may be debated interminably. After all, scientific evidence so far seen does not provide for human beings or *Homo sapiens*, as distinct from the hominids that predated the humans by over a million years, as is currently known, like *Australopithecus*, *Ramapithecus*, etc. Human belief then confronts ultra-human scientific data. And, while to be human is only natural, there is also the very human impulse to try and know more about ourselves and the world around us. If there had not been such conscious and contemporary attempts in the past to understand the human condition and the physical world around us by the Indian sages of yore such as Uddalaka Aruni or Yajnavalka, or later by the Jaina *tirthankaras* or by Gautama Buddha, and much later by the great teachers like Adi Shankara, Kabir and Nanak-ji, much of Indian history would have been a matter of just "marking time". So also would have been the history of the West, from the time of Socrates and Plato, to the teachings of Jesus Christ and Prophet Mohammad, to the work of Copernicus, and even later of Sir Isaac Newton.

If one uses the imagery of time as a flowing river, having its source in some Himalayan heights at the origin of the cosmos, or at least that of the Earth that we all inhabit and moving towards the other end of eternity, one has to take into account that this flowing river is not just one sheet of water but includes several twists and turns in its course. There are other streams joining it at different places and different times, there are rapids and sheer falls, and backwaters and all that.

It is generally believed in scientific circles that early man,

        Prosenjit Dasgupta

i.e., man as we presently know him, walking erect on two legs and able, to an extent, to use the various tools made of wood or stone, living as a family or in small communities largely dependent on hunting or gathering food from the forests, lived in India from about 65,000 to 75,000 years ago. Similarly dated to about one million years are the fossils of hominids, or resembling humans, such as the *Ramapithecus* and the *Sivapithecus*, the remains of which have been found in the Sivalik Hills and elsewhere. Whence they came from, or were they native to the soil of India, cannot be said with any firm degree of certainty. But there are fairly strong grounds for the scientists to hold that "early man" in India (as also in other parts of the world) may have originated from somewhere in Eastern Africa and had come in groups over several centuries, mainly along the coastal areas ("beach-combing" as it were), into India. But they were apparently not "unmixed" types; for there is scientific evidence that there may have been some inter-mingling in North Africa and the Middle East with other hominid and human species or tribes, including the Neanderthal Man of Eastern Europe. Evidence of the use of fire is also found in a number of rock shelters at several sites in India, dating back to about 100,000 years. All this knowledge and understanding has not come in a day, but over the last two hundred years or so, as more and more archaeological and anthropological researchers reached more and more places, and the science of genetics and DNA (i.e., knowledge about deoxyribonucleic acid in human and other once-living tissues) came of age.

Thus, it may be said with a degree of confidence that the sciences of palaeontology, paleogeology, paleo-botany and archaeology, together with the dating methodologies mentioned earlier, give us a reasonable picture of the geological evolution of the Indian sub-continent and early man in India over the past many millennia. Of course, it is open to anyone to reject the results of scientific research as outlined above and to rely on imagination and traditional beliefs to create a parallel thesis about the creation of the world and about human life on the sub-continent. But then, no one has a monopoly on the play of imagination or the development of belief systems, and mere assertion of a hypothesis cannot, *per se,* elevate it to the status of "law", like the laws of thermodynamics, and any one of them may be taken to be as true as any other.

That should bring us back to the fundamental question posed at the beginning, as to the flow of time from the past into the present and the interaction and inter-relationships, if any, between thoughts and beliefs, and whether one could strike a balance between the two.

 Prosenjit Dasgupta

Chapter 2

Stories the relics tell

With this brief introduction to the geological origins of the Earth on the one hand and the cosmological thoughts in Rigveda on the other, it would be difficult for an interested person to look over the Jurassic remains of hundred million years or the stone implements that are more than twenty thousand years old, or the rock art paintings of a mere ten thousand years without getting bowled over. Even now, one can find such Jurassic fossil remains in the Rann of Kutch or the Rajmahal Hills, dating back to more than a hundred million years, or the stone implements found at several sites in India, which date back to a more manageable forty or fifty thousand years ago, to yet more "recent" finds of rock paintings and cupules (i.e., marks left by striking a round stone against a rock face, resulting in a cup-like outline) that are about ten to fifteen thousand years old. Of course, such lengths of time are mind-boggling to a common person, as one often has difficulty in recalling events just about ten years ago. But the mind must quickly adjust to, and accept what is right there before the eyes. To deny such facts would be like denying one's cognitive faculties.

It is only when one stands on the shores of "history" where ancient man has left some signs of his life and concerns by way of clay images, pottery and inscriptions on clay tablets and stones that one finds oneself surrounded by a cacophony of voices, each wanting and waiting to be heard for the history of man to be understood and appreciated. If some form of primitive cognition by primitive man was there in the shaping of a stone implement or in a rock painting, now there is a veritable eruption of myriad thoughts by about the fourth millennium

BP, once man found language and a script to express him or herself in a textual work such as this. Today, it takes only a few taps on a keyboard to type twenty-thousand instead of one-hundred-thousand. But it took many, many thousands of years for mankind to progress from sign language or grunts, croaks and squeals to communicate with one another to some kind of written script that forms the bedrock of history as one understands it today.

In ancient Egypt, the hieroglyphs came to be used to record and communicate by about 3200 BCE and the cuneiform script developed in ancient Sumeria has been dated to 3100 BCE. In India, the Harappan seals associated with the Indus Valley Civilization (IVC) have been dated to about 3000 to 2600 BCE, i.e., 4600 to 5000 years BP. It is to be mentioned that sites resembling the Harappan Civilization have been extensively found in the Ghaggar-Hakra river valley region of north western Rajasthan, lying between the Indus and Sutlej rivers. This area has been identified by several scholars with the Saraswati River that finds mention in the Rigveda. Archaeologists have also found evidence of human civilization by way of pottery remains in Baluchistan going back to about 6500 BCE.

When people often find it difficult to recall events that had taken place just about ten years back without a diary entry or a newspaper cutting, one can well imagine the immense difficulties in re-constructing or just envisioning the situation as it prevailed five thousand or six thousand years ago. It was Daya Ram Sahni in 1921 who was the first to work on the Harappan site in the Indus Valley, while Rakhaldas Banerjee made the initial discoveries at Mohenjo-Daro in 1922. It was the first evidence that India had a civilization that was contemporaneous with that of ancient Egypt and Mesopotamia, and one that far predated the rise of Buddhism and the onset of the Mauryan Empire. It is worth noting that in the decades preceding these discoveries, a good deal of clay bricks (and possibly other remains as well) were used as ballast for extension of the railway lines in the area. Moreover, in the initial excitement of the finds, careful stratigraphic records, so essential in any archaeological work, were not duly maintained. This has affected to some extent the findings from such works. In any case, the subsequent decades saw an enormous amount of archaeological activity, principally by the Archaeological Survey of India, many scholars from abroad and, after Independence in 1947, by a growing number of Pakistani researchers. Progressively, the archaeological work was extended farther afield to Baluchistan and even Afghanistan, to the Ghaggar-Hakra river systems lying to the extreme northwest of Rajasthan, and thence to Gujarat, Punjab and elsewhere. The boundaries of knowledge of the IVC have been ever-expanding till it seems almost to overwhelm any casual student.

Besides the relics of pottery, terracotta figurines, copper implements, etc., the Harappan seals, as they are commonly known, bear the earliest extant written script found in India, dating back to around 2600 BCE. Numerous scholars such as S.R. Rao, I. Mahadevan, Asko Parpola and others have put in decades of research to try and decipher the script; but, alas, despite extensive research by many scholars, this has not been successful so far. The problem is that most of the seals just have five or six of the symbols and the total number of symbols are no more than about three hundred and fifty. Further, the lack of any long inscription running into two or three lines and the absence of cursive or continuous writing suggests that both language and script had not significantly developed in the IVC at that point of time about 5000 years BP. This necessarily casts a shadow of doubt on claims of some of the sacred texts as pre-dating the IVC.

Many of the Harappan seals (so-called because they were initially found in large numbers at the Harappa and Mohenjo-Daro sites – more than 2000 seals have been found) are in the nature of small seals (just a few inches square). Yet, in their depictions, they give a reasonable indication about the life and concerns of the IVC. The bulk of the seals show a bull or a tiger or some such animal shown in profile in front of a manger, receptacle or lamp. Many depict multiple animals such as a humped-and-dewlapped bull, buffalo, ox, tiger, elephant, antelope, rhinoceros, crocodile, and so on, and every seal bears a few symbols from the so-called Harappan script. So, it is but natural to surmise that oxen, tigers, etc., were commonly found in those areas in those days, going back to about 5000 years BP.

While most of the seals, with a perforated ring at the back, seem to be only for "sealing" purposes and bear the images of various animals, W. Fairservis, in "The Roots of Ancient India" (see Bibliography), has discussed at some length in the chapter on "Artefacts" about the images to be found on many of the other Harappan seals and the stories they have to tell. He remarks on the number of seals that show scenes of ritualistic sacrifice and prayers to a deity. Also, some of the Harappan terracotta figurines depict royal figures or deities with diadems and throat ornaments, and one of them is a bearded male figure with a cloak or shawl (with trefoil patterns) over his shoulders. There are also some Harappan seals showing some sort of offerings, and most importantly, a cross-legged seated male figure in what seems to be a "yogic" posture, with what appears to be horns on either side of his head with several animals, including a tiger around him. This figure has been taken by many scholars as depicting an image of *Pashupati* or *Siva*, the great god of the Indian pantheon. The terracotta figurines found at the IVC sites, especially of ladies with their elaborate headdresses, necklaces and jewellery (that were separately made and stuck on, and not sculpted in the clay) are striking. They also suggest similarities with the figurines found around the same dating (say 2000 BCE) in Mesopotamia and Iran.

　　　　　　　　Prosenjit Dasgupta

Irfan Habib (see Bibliography) has noted that the posture of the horned deity (or Siva) is akin to those found in some proto-Elamite seals (3000 to 2750 BCE) found at Susa in Iran. Habib has also drawn attention to tablets found at Bogazkoy in Turkey, which bear Hurrian texts of about 1400 BCE that have a number of words spoken by the Mittani tribes, which seem to be of Indo-Aryan nature and similar to the language of the Rigveda. Fairservis has also remarked on what he considers are some similarities with the tablets found in Mesopotamia and Crete. There are repeated symbols of trees on the seals, especially the *pipal* tree (*Ficus religiosa*), with stylized leaves and some fantastic animals below it. There are several showing water buffaloes with sweeping horns, either being killed or chased by humans, and in one, setting the chasers to flight. Fairservis has also noted the finds by S.R. Rao and John MacKay of seals depicting ships or boats, which clearly indicate ocean-borne (or, at least coastal) trade by sea.

Evidence has also been found in the IVC of "non-seal" sculpting (though very few in number) in both terracotta and sandstone. There is one exceptionally well-sculpted male torso in red sandstone, a seated figurine (also in stone that Fairservis finds similar to some Sumerian figures), one ram resting on a plinth made of limestone (reminiscent of ancient Egyptian sculptures), and terracotta bull and tiger heads. As mentioned above, there is the famous figurine (in steatite) believed to be of a priest that shows a bearded person with a head-band and a shawl (with trefoil designs) thrown over his shoulder, and another similar one with hair gathered in a knot at the back. One of the intriguing aspects of the IVC is the significant lack of sculptures or sculpted panels that one finds in other ancient sites, be it in Luxor or Abu Simbel in Egypt or Bogazkoye in Anatolia or the many Assyrian sites of similar vintage. It is not as if stones were not to be found in the vicinity; Baluchistan hills are not far off, nor the Afghan foothills. In Egypt, blocks of stone were brought from as far as the Ethiopian or Nubian mountains to build the pyramids. The IVC had oxen-drawn carts and could well transport stones from thirty or forty kilometres away, if so required. So far as is known there is just one sculpture of a torso made of stone, and one of copper-bronze of the "Dancing Girl". However, many terracotta figurines of female deities have been found that quite resemble those found in the Middle East, in addition to about 2000-odd IVC seals with their depictions of animals, deities, plants, etc., which tell their own story of sorts.

There are numerous other finds that may be taken to reflect the commonplace day-to-day life in the IVC: toy carts, small figurines in terracotta of bulls, rams and tigers that children would have enjoyed playing with, rattles, stone spindles for spinning flax or cotton, grinding stones for wheat or barley, stone axes, etc. Of course, pottery remains have been found in plenty, typically with a red background, painted over in black with geometric and natural motifs (trees, leaves, birds and animals), including beakers, vessels with stands, wide-bellied pots, cups with a narrow bottom, etc. The pottery is generally found to be quite robustly made and heavy. On the other hand, the copper and bronze weapons (such as lances, spears or arrow-heads) found at IVC sites are not robust and impressive, being somewhat small and light. The heavier ones, Fairservis has noted, were found in the upper layers of the excavations, suggesting later developments. K.N. Dikshit has opined in his article in the "Frontiers of the Indus Civilization" (see Bibliography) that the full impact of more robust weapons and implements made of iron has not been noted in Northern India prior to 800 BCE.

As one reads about the Pre-Indus Valley civilization in Baluchistan (i.e., dating back to about 6500 BCE) at sites such as Mehrgarh, Mundigak, Kile Gul Mohammed, and then the later Harappan sites of around 2600 BCE, one is left with impressions that clearly suggest some signs of early urban agglomeration, with some pastoralism combined with

 Prosenjit Dasgupta

agriculture that was obviously not just at subsistence level, but generating some amount of surplus as suggested by the presence of granaries. Close by, at Sistan, which forms the border between the northwest of the sub-continent and Iran, linseed that provided both oil and flax were grown, as also grapes and melon. It would not be unusual that such practices were also current in the neighbouring IVC. There is evidence of weaving, pottery, some smelting of copper, making of fired as well as baked bricks for house construction, and making of jewellery (including gold jewellery). The excavations have shown up that there were fine streets, neat houses with fireplaces, storage jars, drainage channels, wells, baths, walls with towers, and even workshops for making beads of carnelian or glass frits that was commonly worn by the ladies. The houses were soundly built of both fired and sun-baked bricks of standardized sizes. Fragments of bones and other remains of food suggest that IVC people often ate deer, sheep, and possibly some horse-like creatures, and their main cereals were barley and wheat. From remains of small clay carts at the IVC sites, one may guess that they were aware of solid-wheeled carts. They used articles made of metals, but only of copper and bronze (alloy of copper and tin, and at times zinc). Of course, pottery remains at such sites have been substantial and they indicate a degree of sophistication in the preparation of the clay mix and fabrication, besides the designs on them, from simple comb-drawn geometric patterns on the outer surface to drawings of animals like deer, ox, fish, etc.

Durrani (see Bibliography) and others have drawn attention to the figurines that suggest some sort of a fertility cult at few of the sites (figurines from some IVC sites from about the middle of the second millennium BCE showing affinity with Central Asian figurines), as also of phallus worship (the Rigveda is later found to remark severely about *sisna-devas* or phallus worshippers). The terracotta figures, the seals and the paintings on pottery at such sites suggest that the people of the

IVC worshipped animal-like or zoomorphic deities. Fairservis, in "Frontiers of the Indus Civilization" (see Bibliography), has opined that he finds stylistic affinities between the relicts from some of the Baluchistan sites and those of eastern Iran, and also to an extent with south Turkmenistan from the excavations made by Viktor Sarianidi. Fairservis has drawn attention to the fact that the symbols on the Harappan seals were very possibly mutually intelligible to the people in the Middle East with whom the Harappan cities had trading links. Despite the fact that the IVC, from its flowering about 3000 BCE to its decline around 1500 BCE, shows ups and downs, and pauses, there is nonetheless the overall impression of a reasonably functioning economy with part pastoralism and part agriculture, a growing division of labour, a good deal of both inward and outward trade, and an incipient trend towards urbanization. Overall, the houses and citadels suggest that the people had some social and economic stratification among themselves, with what may be considered chiefs and priests co-existing with artisans, agriculturists and others. Durrani has added the important point that by mid-4th millennium BCE, "there existed a mosaic of regional cultural groups"— and not uniformity—at sites ranging from Mehrgarh, Kuli, Rehman Dheri, Damb Sadat (all in the Baluchistan area), to the Harappan sites in Sind and the Ghaggar-Hakra (Saraswati) areas following a few centuries later.

B.K. Thapar, the noted archaeologist, has mentioned in his article (also in "Frontiers....") that remains in the Amri-Nal area of Baluchistan and Sind suggest some affinities with the Zhob culture of early Iran, as well as with Elam in Mesopotamia. He has indicated the "chronological horizon" of the IVC as ranging from about 2500 BCE for Mohenjo-Daro to about 2300 BCE for Kalibangan in Rajasthan and Lothal (in Gujarat). While the material culture by way of manner of house construction, layout, etc., was broadly similar, Thapar has pointed out that the people apparently followed somewhat

Prosenjit Dasgupta

different religious practices: some used fire altars, and others used goddess figurines. He avers (on page 18) that excavations at Tepe Yahya and Shahr-i-Shokta point towards eastern Iran being the focus of a formative influence on the various components of the IVC.

V.N. Mishra, in an important article (also in the "Frontiers…"), holds that the farm-based economy of the Indus and Hakra region in all probability was derived from the incipient agricultural practices of northern Baluchistan (at Mehrgarh in 7th millennium BCE, and later at the sites of Kile Gul Mohammad and Damb Sadat). Mishra considers that the large-scale growth of sites (numbering about 66) closely resembling the IVC, usually known as "the late Harappan sites" (Mishra has called the sites at Bulandshahr and Meerut, "degenerate"), came up in the upper Yamuna-Ganga Doab, possibly on account of large-scale immigration into that area as the Indus and the Ghaggar-Hakra river system shifted course and/or dried up sometime in the mid-2nd millennium BCE. He is of the view that in the earlier times, both the Sutlej and the Yamuna contributed some of their waters to the Ghaggar-Hakra, and the shift in the courses of these rivers caused serious depletion in the flow of the Ghaggar-Hakra. All said and done, the IVC culture covered an area of about 700,000 square kilometres. As Durrani pertinently suggests, such "nucleated regional centres" through inter-regional and intra-regional trade grew over time to become large and powerful metropolises. Note that the Harappa site covered 150 hectares when many other sites were hardly more than 10 to 20 hectares each.

But what of the people themselves? Were they short or tall? Did they have round or long faces? Were they robust in stature, or finely boned? Strangely enough, considering the large number of the IVC sites and their size (the number of sites is said to exceed 1500, and Harappa, with its 150-hectare extent, is estimated to have had 60,000 inmates at one time),

the number of skeletal remains found at such sites is relatively
small. This may be because the burial sites were at a distance
from the townships — some sites such as Lothal in Gujarat
suggest this -— and these may not have been yet located. Or
it could be that a relatively high underground water table
destroyed such relicts, or just that enough effort has not yet
been put into finding such grave sites, or they could have gone
under some canal system (especially true in Sind and Punjab)
or later urban growth.

According to an exhaustive study of seventy-two skeletal
remains, B.K. Chatterjee (see Bibliography) opines that the
population, at least at Harappa, was racially mixed in nature,
comprising what he has called (a) long-headed, rugged proto-
Nordic type, (b) smaller, long-headed proto-Mediterranean
type, (c) medium-headed Alpino-Armenoid type, and (d) low-
headed dolicho-cranial type akin to Australoid people. The
average height for males was found to be about 167.48 cm and
of females, about 154.56 cm. The majority of the specimens
studied had medium to broad, flattish noses; although there
were a few with finer features. Chatterjee opines that these
people were Indo-Iranians or Indo-Europeans from the Aral-
Caspian Sea basin (Chatterjee, pages 20-21). Whether such
ethnic types prevailed from the days of Mehrgarh (about 7000
BCE), or from the pre-Harappan period of about 3500 BCE
is not clearly known; but at least that was the data from the
mature Harappan period of about 2500 BCE. That several
ethnic groups co-existed with some numbers of traders from
different neighbouring areas and a gradual inflow of migrants
cannot be entirely ruled out. Chatterjee further observes
unequivocally that the damages to the skulls or other bones
were not the result of any armed attack or "an invasion", which
archaeologists such as Mortimer Wheeler at one time held, but
were from other causes, including ailments, or occurred due
to the natural erosion of bone tissue over time.

Again, from the remains at the IVC sites, one may guess that

                        Prosenjit Dasgupta

there was some amount of trade with neighbouring areas such as Afghanistan, Kashmir, and farther north, and possibly even with Sumeria in the Middle East, for import of metals, and semi-precious stones like lapis lazuli used in ornamentation. There is reason to believe, at least from the IVC site of Lothal in Gujarat, that there was some degree of sea-borne trade, and there have been collateral finds from Muscat and Oman in the Middle East to substantiate this. As to why the IVC declined, and practically vanished, for nearly nothing resembles it in the rest of ancient India, is not clearly known. It is, however, widely believed among archaeologists that this was because of the shifting of river courses (especially of the Ghaggar-Hakra, and to some extent, the Indus and the Sutlej) and some other environmental reasons.

Very recently, however (as reported by Shubashree Desikan, in "The Hindu", 11-08-2018), Prof. A.K. Sanghvi of the Physical Research Laboratory, Ahmedabad, and Dr A. Singh of IIT, Kanpur, have studied the mineralogy of the river sediments in the region between the Sutlej and the Yamuna river systems for signs of shifting of course or otherwise drying out that apparently led to the decline of IVC sites at or near the Saraswati and Drishadvati river systems, as believed for several decades. The study has concluded that shifting of courses and changes in the flow of the Indus, the Sutlej and the Yamuna rivers in that area took place about 24,000 to 45,000 years ago and, therefore, long pre-dated the IVC. This has led the scientists to conclude that factors other than perennial river waters dictated the location of the Harappan settlements. Concurrently, evidence was also found of water harvesting techniques of Harappans and their cropping patterns that suggested their dependence on seasonal monsoon rains rather than a perennial supply of river water for irrigation. This has, no doubt, added another element of uncertainty about the possible causes for the decline of the IVC. One cannot entirely rule out the possible influences of some later ethnic and cultural pressures that may have come to overlay the IVC, not only in the traditional areas in and around the Indus and the Ghaggar-Hakra but also the later sites at Kalibangan, Lothal, Dholavira, Ropar and elsewhere.

Perhaps even from this brief and bare description of the IVC (more detailed references will be found in the Bibliography), some ideas and impressions would have been gained about man and his culture and civilization as it existed in that region of India between about 3000 BCE to about 1500 BCE. Much of this has been very simply put in these pages, avoiding the many questions and controversies that still persist, despite the decades of archaeological work and research. Just to give one example, it is a moot point whether the fireplaces found at many IVC sites were for cooking or sacrificial fire. Another is the burial practices; some of the dead were buried, and at some places, they were cremated. What is one to make of that except to appreciate that there were already people at the IVC stage who were ethnically and possibly culturally differentiated but living together (much as India does today in Mumbai or Kolkata) in those early semi-urban agglomerations?

　　　　　　　Prosenjit Dasgupta

Chapter 3

The Neighbourhood "gossip"

Whether one takes modern India or pre-historic India, it is somewhat of a truism that one is affected and even possibly influenced by one's neighbours. In ancient times, such influences were no doubt quite feeble and sporadic, for the simple reason that transport and communication were very primitive, if not non-existent, and it took decades or perhaps a couple of hundred years or more for the impact of such influences to become visible.

The development and use of copper implements was a defining moment in the history and culture of mankind in general. With a hoe and a sickle, mankind could take the first steps towards the development of agriculture, as both cultivation and harvesting of crops could now be done on a wider scale and in a shorter time span, and the diet could be more varied. It is seen that copper and bronze implements (bronze requiring some alloying of copper with tin and zinc and, at times, arsenic) came to be used by the onset of the 2nd millennium BCE around the Black Sea, down to the south of the Ural Mountains and into the adjoining areas. The smelting of iron and its fashioning into implements and weapons of war took a little more time, and it seems to have come about by the commencement of the 1st millennium BCE in the south of the Urals, towards the Aral Sea. By this time, the domestication of the horse for drawing chariots seems to have come about. Earlier, the horse seems to have been used primarily as a source of meat. "Massive" horse-bone remains have also been found in the Azov area of the Black Sea and in northern Kazakhstan. The earliest evidence (so far) of a spoked-wheel chariot has been found at Sintashta (just north of the Aral Sea, close to the southeast end of the Ural Mountains), dated about 2000 BCE. These archaeological "markers" have some bearing on the developments following the Indus Valley Civilization in India, as also the use of iron implements and horses that are central to any discussion of the text of the Rigveda, about which more later.

The "Encyclopaedia of Archaeology" (see Bibliography) has it (Vol. I, page 539) that the early Iron Age nomads spoke a type of Indo-Iranian language and were ethnically Caucasoid with some later Mongolian admixture. The "Encyclopaedia of Indo-European Culture" (see Bibliography) also has information that is both interesting and relevant. Besides providing several long lists of words of Proto-Indo-European origin (that is, showing affinities with the languages spoken in a wide swath of countries from India, via Iran into Europe) and corresponding words from some more modern languages that are obviously similar in pronunciation and meaning, it mentions that the Indo-European languages manifested themselves in written script in the Akkadian seals of Anatolia (modern Turkey) around 1900 BCE, Mittani seals and inscriptions of Syria by about 1600 BCE, Greek and Mycenaean inscriptions of around 1300 BCE, and in Thrace, Balkans and Iran by about 700 BCE.

One would have thought that similar seals and inscriptions in Sanskrit (which is also considered by many scholars to have had an Indo-European origin) of earlier or similar provenance would have been found on the Indian sub-continent; but that hope has been belied (about which more later). The publication also refers to evidence of cattle herding and to the *soma* ritual (that is, ritualistic sacrifices in which the juice of the herb "soma" was used) in south Turkmenistan near the River Oxus (*Amu Darya*). It considers that the most widespread model of an Indo-Iranian cultural pattern finds it source from the peoples and cultures of the Southern Urals and Kazakhstan, including the domestication of the horse and the use of spoked-wheel chariots. The Encyclopaedia also mentions that the

　　　　　Prosenjit Dasgupta

term "Iranian" was used initially to refer to several population groups believed to have arrived at the Iranian plateau around 1500 BCE, perhaps from a homeland east of the Caspian Sea. They were a branch of Indo-European language speaking variants of peoples who, from about 3000 BCE, dispersed from time to time throughout many parts of the Middle East and East Europe, speaking ancient Persian, Avestan, Scythian and Median languages. The word "Iran" derives from the Old Persian "Ariyanan", which in turn came from "Ariya", meaning noble or lordly (page 336 of the Encyclopaedia).

S. P. Gupta, who died in 2007, was a noted archaeologist who had worked at Harappa and in several overseas countries. He has rendered a very useful service in bringing to the fore archaeological researches in Soviet Central Asia (as it existed prior to 1980s, mostly by Russian researchers like Maruschenko, Y. Kuzmina, Masson and Sarianidi) and the Indian borderlands (in the book of that title – see Bibliography). His basic thesis is that south Turkmenia, Bactria and south Tajikistan had contacts with, and, to an extent, influenced the cultures of Afghanistan, Baluchistan, Sistan and the Indus region through trade or limited migration, or both (Preface to this book, page xiv). He has emphasized the geography of a place as providing the context for the differentiation of cultures even in a fairly close neighbourhood. Gupta observes that the clay and salt marshes separated by deserts, such as the Kara Kum, and the mountains of Kopet Dag, and those of Kirghizia, Ferghana and Turkistan provided the basis for several foci of development in relative isolation. He goes on to suggest that similarities in stone and bone implements, pottery, etc., can be found in locations such as Mehrgarh and Kile Gul Mohammad (both in Baluchistan), Ak Kupruk in Afghanistan, Sarai Khola near Taxila and Burzahom near Srinagar in Kashmir. Such evidence leads Gupta to state that: "Broadly speaking, southern Soviet Central Asia, north western Iran, Baluchistan and Afghanistan formed one large cultural-geographical area in the 4th millennium BCE" (page 88).

Further, at Shahr-i-Shokhta in Iranian Sistan, a clay tablet was found with a proto-Elamite inscription dating back to about 3200 BCE that suggests that people from south Turkmenistan and Mundigak in south Afghanistan moved and colonized the delta region of the Helmand River in southern Afghanistan. Thus, Gupta takes the view that: "The first half of the 3rd Millennium BCE ushered in a new era in the movement of people and ideas in the north western region of the Indian sub-continent in which Central Asia played a prominent role (page 130)...The culture-interaction zone extends from Central Asia up to the Indus Valley, covering north eastern Iran, southern Afghanistan, Sistan and northern Baluchistan" (page 171). He goes on to state, "Although opinions differ on the very vital issue of the original home of the people responsible for it (the onset of the Iron Age – parentheses added), nevertheless, it is generally agreed that at least some of them came from northern Iran" (page 223). He concludes by saying: "We firmly believe that the phenomenon of cultural diffusion and area-colonization have been as much the fact of history as autochthonous development of cultures" (page 284).

If there is anything truly remarkable about Gupta's exposition of his researches and findings in this book, it is his constant self-questioning. Every now and then, he is asking himself, "Why this? ... Why not that?", "How could this have happened without that also occurring?". There is a refreshing lack of assertions, unless he is reasonably satisfied with the evidence in hand, which seems to mark him out amongst many other Indian archaeologists.

One cannot leave the neighbourhood of north-western India without at least a reference to the work of Marja Gimbutas and fellow archaeologists in the central Asian region. If for nothing else, the very range of her work is both interesting

     Prosenjit Dasgupta

and exciting and, indeed, much useful information has been gathered about the region and its history that is of more than a passing interest to those concerned with the ancient history of India. Unfortunately, this work has got mixed up with the question of *Urheimat* (or, the original home) of the peoples speaking one form or the other of the Indo-European group of languages. That has raised the hackles of several scholars; although, at no stage, was anybody obliged to accept Gimbutas' findings. She has highlighted the typical *kurgan* or the partly subterranean burial mounds that in one form or the other mark out the ancient history of that area. Such burial mounds have not been found in much numbers in India; but there have been instances at Burzahom in Kashmir and in some other places. Gimbutas has taken the kurgan as a marker, and traced its spread from central Asia across other parts of the continent. In the absence of any written records, it has at least provided something to think about and to go ahead on.

The work of Gimbutas and Sarianidi is not widely known in India. But understanding pre-history requires the development of a greater breadth of knowledge and ought not to be closely confined. To criticize and then to sit on one's hands does not seem a particularly useful thing to do. One has just to refer to the "Encyclopaedia of Archaeology" to learn about the advances made in the sub-branches of this field of knowledge, such as paleo-botany, paleo-climatology, bio-molecular archaeology, behavioural archaeology, cognitive archaeology, and last but certainly not the least, experimental archaeology. This last is a highly interesting branch that is deserving of greater attention, in that it tries to replicate experimentally the making of stone implements, copper and iron smelting and making of metal implements, making of houses with stone and/or grass, building boats, creating burial pits, and so on. Thus, a bridging of the theoretical with the empirical is attempted, and that is all to the good. One can think of many sites, starting from the Jurassic remains in the Rajmahal Hills of Jharkhand or those in the Pin Valley in Himachal, to the rock art site at Bhimbhetka or the IVC site at Dholavira, where one may well create "open air" museums and class-rooms to initiate studies in experimental archaeology. There is much work yet to be done in further widening and deepening archaeological research in India, and the nation will have to find the necessary time and resources for this.

Prosenjit Dasgupta

Chapter 4

Surya, Agni, Ushas and the "hotri"

By and large, many, if not most, of the scholars consider that the oldest extant sacred text of India, the Rigveda, was compiled around 1500 to 1200 BCE. This observation is based on various factors, such as linguistic patterns, philology, etc. As mentioned in the Acknowledgement to this work, the Rigveda, as we presently have it, was recovered from the Nirukta of the scholar Yaska in the 6th century BCE and from the commentaries that followed, culminating in the commentary, "Vedartha Prakash", by Sayanacharya of Vijayanagar in the 14th century CE.

Here, one must take note of the observation by Prof. Bishnupada Bhattacharya (see Bibliography) that according to Prof. Bhagavaddatta, in the "History of Vedic Literature", Rathitara and Bharadwaja Vaskali were redactors of different recensions of the Rigveda, and, it may be that, Sakalya on the one hand and Yaska on the other may have been following one or the other versions (page 12).

The Nighantu, or the list of words, apparently existed long before Yaska's commentary was written. Bhattacharya also mentions that according to Prof. R.D. Karmakar, the Nighantu was not the work of just one author. Yaska has himself referred in his commentary to the various interpretations of the Vedas by the *aitihashika* (that is, the historians), the *atmavadin* (those considering spiritual aspects) and the *naurukta* (etymologists/philologists) categories of scholars. Prof. Lakshman Sarup (see Bibliography) has cautioned that there is no doubt that the text had already seen earlier modifications and that one should be cautious in making Yaska responsible for some passages in the text and the "absurd derivations therein" (page 1). It would not be too much to come to the conclusion that the Rigveda is a compilation of ancient thoughts, and is not an integrated, comprehensive work by any one individual. While it is rich in metaphysical thought, due care must be taken in considering any historical references and geographical descriptions in the Rigveda as being contemporary and definitive.

The derivation of the word, "*Veda*", is from the root, "*vid*" (to know), and incorporates the wisdom of the sages as it developed over a considerable span of time while they pondered over the issues of creation, life and death, and the natural phenomena around them. The significance of the Rigveda (and its associated texts, the *Yajurveda, Atharvaveda* and *Samaveda*) is manifold. It is the first known expression of theistic and metaphysical thought in the Indian Sub-continent, besides casting some light on the contemporary rituals and practices, and on the Indian society in general, at least in the region of the Indus and the Helmand rivers in Afghanistan and neighbouring north-west India as it was around 1500 BCE or thereabouts, as believed by many scholars.

The proximate and customary source of the Rigveda is the translation into German that Max Muller, then teaching at Oxford, made in 1869, of the commentary, "Vedartha Prakash" (i.e., expression of the meaning of the Vedas), written in the 14th century by Sayanacharya, a scholar in the Vijayanagar kingdom. There has been criticism of Max Muller's work on several counts, but his work remains one of the major sources for the study of the Vedas; although, the work of John Muir, and later of Monier Monier-Williams and R.T.H. Griffiths, other renowned Sanskrit scholars who were almost the contemporaries of Muller, are often relied upon as source material for studies on the Rigveda. That it was not just an open-and-shut case, would be understood from the fact that prior to Sayana, the Rigveda had been studied only indirectly for about two thousand years before him. It was then confined to the Nirukta or the etymology (together with

     Prosenjit Dasgupta

some commentaries) of some of the difficult and rare words in the Rigveda, as written by Yaska around the 6th century BCE. Yaska, in turn, had relied to some extent on the Nighantu or a dictionary of words from the Vedas, compiled even earlier. Unlike the *Mahabharata* (about which more later), no commonly acceptable "standard edition" of the Rigveda has so far been compiled based on the several variants extant.

What does the Rigveda have to say? Plainly put, the Rigveda comprises ten books or *mandalas*, with 1028 hymns extending to 10,600 verses, which, in different ways, consider or speculate about metaphysical issues, such as the origins of the cosmos and life on Earth, the nature of god, praise for deities, including *Varuna* (water), *Agni* (fire), *Surya* (sun), *Ushas* (dawn), *Indra*, and *Soma* rituals (a herbal drink) in the main. There is repeated questioning as to the nature of the gods to whom the sacrifices were being offered. Were they there, were they for real? This is expressly asked in Book 10, hymn 121 - "*Kasmai devaya havisa vidhema?*" that translates to "What god shall we honour by this sacrifice?"

There are instructions about the arrangements to be made for fire sacrifices (including the categories of persons, e.g., the *hotri*, the *adhvaryu*, the *udgartri*, the *agnidhra* and the *Brahmana*, who are required to make such arrangements) to such deities to gain some benefits for the sacrificer (usually the householder), such as long life, larger herds of cattle, many sons, etc. The prescriptions for the rituals are expressly given in the Yajurveda, which comes later than the main text of the Rigveda, while the Samaveda lays down the text and the manner of chanting the hymns that accompany the sacrifices.

There are, additionally, references to other people who were considered inimical by the composers of the Rigveda, as also interesting geographical details about the land of the *Sapta Sindhu* or the seven rivers. The Rigveda mentions four regions, these being the *Sapta Sindhava, Panchanada, Madhyadesa* and *Praki*, from which one may conjecture that the references are being made to the land where seven rivers and then five rivers flowed, and the land in between. There is specific mention of other rivers, too, such as the *Kubha* (believed to be the Kabul river), the *Suwastu* (or the Swat river) and the *Gomati* (or the Gomal river). The *Nadistuti Sukta* of RV goes on to praise several other rivers, such as the *Parushni* (which scholars have identified as the Ravi), *Shatudri* (or the Sutlej), *Saraswati* (identified with the Ghaggar-Hakra river system in northwest Rajasthan), the *Ashikni* (or Chenab), and the *Vitasta* (or Jhelum) ending with the Yamuna (first) and then the Ganga. Looking at the geography of the extreme northwest of the sub-continent, one finds rivers such as the Amu Darya, the Helmand, and the Arghandab flowing from the snowy reaches of the Hindu Kush; then, after a gap, the Indus, the Jhelum (from the Pir Panjals), the Chenab, the Ravi, the Beas and the Sutlej flowing down from somewhere near Mount Kailash in Tibet, or the Dhauladhar and the Kinnar Kailash mountain ranges. The sources and courses of the Yamuna and the Ganga are farther to the east in Uttarakhand. The major IVC settlements of Mohenjo-Daro and Harappa, with whom the Indo-Aryans may have had interactions (as reflected in the Rigveda), are considerably to the west, primarily in the Indus and Ghaggar-Hakra river valley systems.

Several of the books of the Rigveda are said to be the works of sages and their respective clans, such as Angirasa, Atri, Vashistha, Vishvamitra, Bhrigu, Kanva and some others. Apparently, considerable additions and alterations, and attempts to iron out the vagueness or textual differences (technically known as "redaction"), have taken place over the centuries since the compilation of the original text. Further, some scholars believe that certain words, at times, had to be modified to suit the *anustubh* or the *gayatri* style of versification used mostly in the Rigveda. But, overall, the text was not committed to writing, thus raising the question whether Sanskrit in its *Devanagari* script had come into being by the

   Prosenjit Dasgupta

15th/14th century BCE (Panini's Sanskrit grammar came much later, around 5th century BCE). The unwritten verses were passed down, across generations through memorization from scholar to scholar. Consequently, the Vedas later came to be known as *Shruti* (that which is heard) and considered as revealed or *apaurasheya* (i.e., beyond human origin). But this process of bringing the RV down to earth to be read and studied by ordinary mortals came much later, in the 6th century BCE or thereabouts, by Yaska in his Nirukta, or his work on the etymology of the RV words. Much of the associated Vedas, being the largely ritual-oriented Yajurveda, the recital-based Samaveda, and the magic-based Atharvaveda, comprise large numbers of hymns taken from the Rigveda itself.

Interestingly, the next phase in the history of India, being the age of the Vedas (primarily the Rigveda), around 1500 to 1200 BCE, almost dovetails into the decline of the IVC. That was coincidental, and surely not causative. But there is one very important difference: the corpus of the material relicts of the IVC is much greater than those of the RV. It is significant to note here that the material remains of the Rigvedic people, by way of dwellings, grinding stones, remains of fire and food, ornaments, sacrificial fires, skeletal remains, burial sites, and implements for both war and peace are few and far between. The hiatus in historical evidence between the profusion of remains of the IVC of 2500 BCE on the one hand and those of the Buddhist and Jain era of 500 BCE on the other is both striking and difficult to explain. There is only the text of the Rigveda as it has come down to us and its associated etymological, philological and linguistic studies that provide the basis for research. Coming to that, it seems very difficult, if not well-nigh impossible, that the verses of the Rigveda had been composed by the sages concerned in practically a "word-perfect" manner and were immediately memorized, as they emerged from the lips of the sages, and transmitted without the medium of a written script to other disciples or scholars.

This not only strains logic, but also imagination. Anyhow, judging by the outpouring of the learned books and research papers over the last one century or more, the differences in the interpretation of the Vedic texts seem, at times, almost diametrically opposed to one another, to the extent that the differences in the interpretation of material archaeological evidence do not appear to have generated. There the differences are more of degree, than of kind.

In their studies of the Rigveda, and in the absence of material evidence, scholars have had necessarily to rely more on linguistic, philological, syntactical and etymological analysis and interpretation of the texts. Colin Renfrew and other scholars, in fact, have referred to "linguistic palaeontology", that is, extending the knowledge of linguistics backwards, far into time, to "excavate", so to speak, into the buried strata of evolution of languages. There was now far greater reliance on the study of idiom and syntax, and even the pronunciation of individual syllables constituting a word. So, even if there was some degree of closeness in the interpretations to begin with, the differences seem to have widened — not closed — in the last sixty to seventy years. It has something to do with Sanskrit itself, the language in which the Rigveda in its present form was apparently composed. The word "*Sanskrit*" etymologically means something that has been reconstructed and refined, and it also evolved over time to be almost solely used for religious studies and rituals. There was increasing accretion of meanings and nuances with each stage of evolution and elaboration, till Panini in his *Astadhayayi* in the 5th century BCE considerably codified the Sanskrit of the day.

Prakrit, or the language used by the common people, developed in parallel to Sanskrit, found voice in the edicts, written in the Brahmi script at the time of the Emperor Ashoka in the 3rd century BCE, as well as in some places in the plays of the poet, Kalidasa. Thus, it is found that unlike other civilizations of similar antiquity, like that of Mesopotamia

     Prosenjit Dasgupta

(and that had its Akkadians, Assyrians and Sumerians), the Hittites in Anatolia, and the Egyptians, who have left behind numerous inscriptions and clay tablets with cuneiform script or in hieroglyphics, the composers of the Rigveda had left behind nothing in physical and verifiable form. Was it because Sanskrit, as it was then spoken, was still an orally transmitted language that had not at that point in time developed a script for itself? Interestingly, some portions of the Rigveda have been found to have been written in the Brahmi script, which was mainly used to write in the Prakrit dialect that mostly ordinary people used. There is a widely held thought among specialists that Brahmi script may be of Semitic (or Middle Eastern) origin. Be that as it may, the Sanskrit of the Rigveda, as is now commonly accepted, was much simpler (and, one may say somewhat colloquial) as compared to the more evolved Sanskrit that Panini dealt with in his famous Sanskrit grammar written in the 5th century BCE or the classical Sanskrit that Kalidasa used in the 4th century CE (mixing this occasionally with colloquial Prakrit and *apabhramsa* or corrupted words or pronunciation of some of the characters in his plays).

So, what does the Rigveda tell us of its principal concerns and contemporary times? Firstly, there is the word *"Arya"* itself, and the question may well be asked if it denotes any ethnic or racial group, or, as most scholars believe, that the word denotes a noble or respected person. The hymns are composed in Sanskrit, though of a much simpler structure as compared to the later classical Sanskrit that is considered to be an Indo-Aryan language. There is fulsome praise in the Rigveda of the deity Indra, as *Purandara* (or, destroyer of citadels), for having vanquished his enemies, the *Vratras* and *Dasyus*, clearly suggesting the existence of citadels or fortifications in the settlements. Bryant (see Bibliography) has drawn attention to the findings of P.T. Srinivasa Iyengar that the word "Arya" occurs 33 times in the Rigveda, while the word "Dasa" is mentioned 50 times and "Dasyu" about 70 times. Further, the word "Arya" is found 22 times in the hymns dedicated to god Indra, and 6 times in hymns dedicated to Agni, while "Dasa" occurs 50 and 2 times respectively (in the two sets of hymns), and "Dasyu" is found 50 and 9 times, respectively. Further, the Rigveda mentions the Dasyus as *avrata* and *anyavrata*, meaning, not following Aryan rites, or, following different rites (Notes of Iyengar, quoted on page 61 by Bryant). Whether or not the people referred to in the RV as Dasa or Dasyu were Dravidians or Austric or some other ethnic group is not fully clear. But many scholars point to the infusion of Austric words in different Indian languages, the use of turmeric and vermillion in numerous rituals, the idea of creation of the world from a primeval egg, counting of days by the phases of the moon, the cult of the phallus in ancient India, etc., as vestiges of such Austric influence. Moreover, there are a good number of Dravidian vocables in the names of several north Indian places, the presence of a number of Dravidian words in Sanskrit, as also traces of Dravidian influence on common Hindu religious practices (N.N. Bhattacharya, pages 12-14).

Sukumari Bhattacharji (see Bibliography), a scholar of renown, in her work on Indian theogony (which relies considerably on the Rigveda), has made a number of interesting observations that are of note. The first is that while orthodox Indian religion, as it stands today, contains much that seems to have been assimilated from primitive bases; Indian mythology, on the other hand, has little that is recognizably primitive or ancient. It could, in fact, be said to be quite noticeable from the closing centuries of the pre-Christian era. Obviously, this disjunct is both interesting and intriguing. She goes on say that the Rigvedic gods arose largely from awe, wonder and admiration of natural phenomena and remained close to the imagination of mortals, thus sharing a good bit of their faults and frailties, such as pride and anger. She stresses that three successive strata may thus be found in

     Prosenjit Dasgupta

the Indian pantheon, these being the Indo-European gods (as apparently extant before their advent in India), the Vedic-Brahmanical gods in large parts of north India, and the later non-traditional gods, who became prominent from about the 6th century BCE. While the pre-occupation in the Rigveda was part metaphysical and part ritualistic, it was more of ancestor-worship for the non-Vedic or pre-Vedic populace. With the Vedic society being largely patriarchal, Bhattacharji points out the gods were also largely male. It was in the later Vedic period, and around the time of the composition of the Brahmanas, that more of female gods were seen, e.g., Sachi, Rudrani, Lakshmi, Saraswati and others. Buddhism added tutelary gods, trees and other spirits, while yet later *Tantrism* combined features of *Shaivism* and Buddhism that were added to the list. But there were deletions from the pantheon as well. By the time of the Imperial Guptas in the 4th/5thcenturies CE, the gods who were personifications of natural phenomena, such as Agni, Vayu, Ushas, Varuna and Pusan had faded from the popular imagination. Bhattacharji observes that in the Vedic and the immediate post-Vedic times, the society in northern India was notably heterodox and amorphous in composition and, in terms of belief, without any pretensions to a centralized religious organisation. The society was, in fact, largely split up into different communities, each of which practised some common *shrauta* or prescribed rituals (page 17 in Bhattacharji).

One may not take leave of the Rigveda without taking note of one of the significant verses that have dominated the later Rigvedic period, and continues to dominate the present Indian scenario, as little else has. This is the *Purusha sukta* (verses 2 to 15 of hymn 10.90) that deals with ideas on the creation of life on Earth. The latter part of the hymn runs, thus: "When they divided Purusha, how many portions did they make? … What do they call his mouth, his arms, what do they call his thighs and feet? …The *Brahman* was his mouth, of both his arms was the *Rajanya* made, his thighs became the *Vaishya*; from his feet the *Shudra* was made."

Thus, the Brahmans were taken to be the scholars and teachers in society, while the Rajanyas were warriors, kings and administrators. The Vaishyas, or the merchants and traders, provided the economic and commercial services in society, and the feet were the Shudras, or the artisans and workers. While there is some controversy as to whether this verse was a later interpolation or not, it does describe a certain contemporary social, economic and political categorisation according to the capabilities and specialisation of functions then prevalent in society, and it indirectly underlined the interdependence of one upon the other. The warrior could not function without the support of the merchant; nor the merchant without the assistance of the artisans or workers. At least in those early days, it was quite possible for individuals to move between one category and another by the dint of their efforts and achievements; nobody found this improper or unacceptable. While the Brahmans had nominal superiority in ritualistic matters over the Kshatriyas, the latter wielded social superiority over the Brahmans, based on their material wealth and power. A member of the warrior category thus became one of the foremost Brahmanical *rishis*, and one has just to open some of the *Upanishads* (or, the sacred metaphysical texts) to find the role that some Kshatriya kings played in the discussions and deliberations. Even a millennium later, in the 2nd century BCE, guilds of artisans, such as weavers and ivory carvers, made donations towards the building of Buddhist *viharas* or scholastic monasteries or *stupas* to house the holy relics of the Buddha. It is very possible that artisans and merchants contributed likewise for the building of temples during the times of the Imperial Guptas in the 6th century. At the same time, some of the *Grihyasutra* texts (meant for day-to-day life, such as that of Gautama, Vasishtha and Boudhayana) do suggest something of an incipient alliance between the

Brahmans and the Kshatriyas, or at least the need for it. The Gautama Grihyasutra considers that trade and usury may be permitted to the Brahman under some circumstances, while the *Manusmriti* (a definitive text for social norms and practices that came somewhat later than the Grihyasutras), is even more permissive. As Ramendra Nath (see Bibliography) observes, the "gift-exchange" between the Kshatriya clients and the Brahman priests for the rituals performed on the former's behalf was progressively changing to a market-oriented social order. He adds that the Puranic passages (that is, texts relating to old genealogies and history, the Vishnu, Vayu and Matsya Puranas being dated between 3rd and 5th centuries CE) that refer to a shift from the *Dvapara Yuga* to *Kali Yuga* marked the relative decline of towns in that period and the growth of a village-based subsistence economy, with greater incidence of *varnasamskara* (i.e., the caste system) and diversification and regimentation of castes (page 13 in Nath). It is noted that some of the non-Kshatriya chieftains (e.g., Yavana, Shudra and even *mleccha* kings, i.e., those who did not speak the local dialects) were able, with the good-will of the Brahmans and the performance of certain rituals, to get elevated to regal status. For example, the Satavahana king who performed the Hiranyagarbha *Mahadana* (the "golden-wombed" sacrifice) gained the status of a Brahman (page 14 in Nath). The caste system in India, as presently understood and still practised in places, grew increasingly rigid only with time, that too, much later in history,

It is found that of the five tribes or the *pancha jana* mentioned in the Rigveda, the *Yadu-Turvasa* and the *Anu-Druhya* were settled in northwest Punjab (the land of Sapta Sindhu, so well-known from the Rigveda) as were the *Purus*, while the *Bharata* clan was caught up somewhere near Afghanistan, where their leader, Divodasa, was fighting Sambara, possibly a local tribal chief. Then the Bharata clan is seen to emerge on to the land of Sapta Sindhu, where their new chief, Sudasa, and the "ten kings" engage in a fierce fight on the banks of the Parusni River (identified as Ravi), before emerging near the Yamuna River, and finally settling towards the south-west of the Saraswati River, which most scholars hold to be the Ghaggar-Hakra river system, in the extreme north-western Rajasthan.

So far it is known from the Rigveda and is commonly accepted, the local populace (the Vratras) were inimical or opposed to the persons who are thought to have composed the Rigveda. This further suggests that the "people of the Rigveda" (if one can put it quite like that) came from elsewhere, as they have remarked on the citadels and the characteristics of the local people, the Vratras, just as much any outsider visiting Egypt would remark on the pyramids and Bedouins or someone visiting Germany would draw attention to the Gothic churches and the many blonde-haired Germans. That would be a common-sense way of looking at the content of the Rigvedic verses. It is very likely, as has been the experience world-wide in the last 70 or 80 years, that immigrants were looked upon with disfavour by the local people. Secondly, it is clear from the Rigvedic text that its composers or compilers held in high regard the various natural phenomena, such as the dawn (hence, the god *Ushas* - dawn), *Surya/Savitr* (sun), *Agni* (fire), *Parjanya* (thunder and rain, "roaring like a bull"), *Apas* (water) and *Vayu* (wind). There are also many references to *Mitra/Varuna, Dyaus Pita* ("the father in the sky"), *Pushan* and others, which show considerable similarity (and, in fact, specific mention) to deities known in the ancient times in the Persian and Anatolian regions. The Rigveda goes on to record repeated pleas to the gods for long life, many sons and large herds of cattle, and provides details of the sacrifices and rituals required to make this possible. Rigveda, in the 5th manadala, 54th sukta and 15th verse says that: "*Idam su Maruti haryata vacho yasya tarema tarasa satam hima.*" It translates into, "Be pleased, Oh Marut, with this hymn of mine, by the force of which may we pass a hundred winters."

    Prosenjit Dasgupta

Sayana, in one place, refers to the Rigveda as pertaining to *"Bhog vishaya .... ityadirupa vyavahariki"*, i.e., a prescription or manual for acquiring more resources or wealth for daily life. This would suggest that the Rigvedic society was at that time quite acquisitive, patrilineal in structure and that they obviously held cattle to be a major source of wealth. The text mentions in some places about mleccha or foreign-language speakers, the Dasyus. Further, the verses indicate that the Rigvedic people had to contend with, and perhaps, at times, came into conflict with the Dasyus or Asuras, who were differently complexioned. Some scholars have controverted this; but, Rigveda III. 34.9 (i.e., 3rd mandala, 34th sukta and 9th verse) mentions, *"Hatvi Dasyum pra Aryam Varnam Dvat"*, implying that the Aryans were of different complexion from that of the Dasyus. The word *Varnam* is generally taken to mean colour, though in some contexts it may mean type or category (for that, the typical word would be *"varga"*) as well. Anyway, the non-Aryans were "different".

But, if there is something particularly notable about the Rigveda, it is that many words resemble or are phonetically very close to those of the *Zend Avesta*, the sacred text of Iran. John Muir provides over fifteen pages of words that are very similar, e.g., *apa-ap*-water, *jihva-hizva*-tongue, *arya-airya*-respectable person, *sarva-harva*-all, *siksh-saksh*-learn, *smar-mar*-remember, *asmi-ahmi*-I, *asti-asti*-he is, and so on. Not only that, the history and the emergence of the Zend Avesta is strikingly similar to that of the Rigveda. A verse of the Zend is reproduced later in the text, and it would be an interesting exercise for any reader with some familiarity with Sanskrit to find similar (and familiar) words and sounds. The Zend was also lost for a long time in the sands of history; it is also in the form of hymns or *gathas* and deals with the creation of the world and of man. There are large sections that deal with the liturgy and rituals for sacrificial *haoma*, which sounds quite close to the Sanskrit word *homa*, or sacrificial fire.

At the same time, a good number of scholars have pointed out that Rigvedic Sanskrit also has a number of "loan words" from Proto-Dravidian language(s), e.g., phala, pinda, danda, khala, and that in terms of syntax (i.e., positioning of subject, verb and object in a sentence), it has borrowed from the Dravidian, which distinguishes it to an extent from the structure of several other Indo-European languages. Also, scholars have ascertained that there are more than 350 words, apparently of non-Indo-Aryan origin in Sanskrit. This is not the place, nor is it the intention, to enter into any consideration of the matter of such "loan words", or of any "sub-strata" of other languages that may or may not have influenced Rigvedic Sanskrit. Interested readers may refer to the works of Michael Witzel, F.J. Kuiper, as well as several other Indian scholars, such as V.S. Mishra and others for further details. Moreover, several scholars, such as N.N. Bhattacharyya, Benoy Sarkar and others have suggested that common beliefs and practices, such as the creation of the world from an egg, counting of days from the phases of the moon, the cult of the phallus, the use of vermillion and turmeric on auspicious occasions in India, are derived from very ancient Austric (largely Mundaric) and/or Dravidian practices.

But the Rigveda must not be understood as being relevant only for historical or geographical references, or just for linguistic and philological studies. It must not be reduced to that; for, the Rigveda is the first repository of Indian theological and metaphysical thought. The *Gayatri shloka* (Rigveda 3rd book, 62nd canto and 10th verse) that encapsulated the yearning of the sages for enlightenment is instructive (despite its transformation into a lilting song in some places in recent times) -

"Om bhūr bhuvaḥ svaha
Tatsaviturvareṇyam
bhargo devasyadhīmahi
Dhiyo yo naḥ prachodayāt"

          Prosenjit Dasgupta

This has been interpreted by several scholars as a fervent call to meditate on that glorious and divine light of the radiant Being who lights up our physical world and the cosmos, so that He may remove our ignorance and enlighten our minds and intellect.

The text of the *Brahmanas* (extensions of the Vedic texts) and the further extension of the Brahmanas into *Aranyakas* in prose (unlike the Rigvedic verses) laid down the procedures for major fire sacrifices and other rituals. Thus, the Rigveda and its associated texts, on the one hand, take one to the heights of metaphysical speculation about the creation and life, and on the other, deal with fairly mundane affairs of arranging fire sacrifices for the health and wealth of the householders. Rigvedic text also provides glimpses of the geography of India (mainly of the northwest) and shares some details about the local population and the deities that were important to the authors of the Rigveda. It would be too much to expect that its 10,600 verses would be any sort of an exhaustive documentation of the life, culture and history of India in those times. It is perhaps best to take the Rigveda as it is, to educate and elevate one's mind about life and creation as enjoined in the Gayatri mantra and speculated upon by thinkers in those distant times, without getting mired in controversies about the nitty-gritties of the interpretation of each word of the text.

Chapter 5

Much ado about controversies

This is as good a place as any to consider the question of the "Indo-Aryan Controversy". A great deal of time and effort has been invested by numerous scholars on this issue. Therefore, considerable reliance has been placed on the book, "The Indo- Aryan Controversy (Evidence and Inference in Indian History)", edited by Edwin F. Bryant and Laurie L. Patton (see Bibliography). Basically, the book mainly refers to studies and hypotheses, firstly, about the dating of the Rigveda, and secondly, the origins of the Indo-Aryans, who are considered to have been the composers or compilers of the Rigveda. There has been much speculation as to whether the Indo-Aryans were among the original inhabitants of India and emerged from India to spread out into Iran, Central Asia, Anatolia and elsewhere (the "Out of India" hypothesis), or, were people who migrated from somewhere near Iran and adjoining areas (possibly around the Amu Darya/Oxus River valley?) into India.

The dating of the Rigveda has been put by some scholars to be around 5000 BCE or even earlier, relying primarily on astronomical calculations based on some references in the Rigvedic text. As a second or third stage interpretation (in contrast to archaeological findings, which are direct, or first stage observations), attempts at historical dating based on astronomical references can be challenging and depend not only on the accurate recording of an astronomical event in a text but also the interpretation of that text. Therefore, any findings about historical events based largely or entirely on astronomical references would rest on the reliability of the respective text and the degree of accuracy of the account of

Prosenjit Dasgupta

astronomical phenomena associated with that historical event (e.g., a solar eclipse at the time of death of some king or warrior).

For instance, dating of the Rigveda to 2300 BCE based on a reference to the planet Pleiades as having *generally risen around that time* ("due East") without providing (presuming it was possible) the precise positioning of the planet at a specific point of time is quite likely to be influenced by a somewhat vague description by the composer of the hymn, relative to precise scientific references (if that was possible at the time). Moreover, each planet has a specific time cycle as to its rising and setting over the horizon (Venus has a cycle of 8 years). Then, there is the matter of the precession (or, tilt) of the Earth's axis (no doubt, a very slow process, taking 26,000 years to complete) which would affect the planetary positions viewed from a point on Earth, and the solstices and equinoxes, over time. According to most scholars, the verses of the Rigveda were composed or compiled by tribes or clans of some sages like Atri, Bhrigu, Vashistha and others. It is possible that the astronomical observations were not made by the sages themselves and that some of these references may have been recollected after a lapse of time or may have been based just on hearsay. No doubt India has produced several great astronomers like Aryabhata, Varahamihira and Bhaskara, but they were all from much later times, and their notions would not in any way have been reflected in the text of the Rigveda itself. Further, it was long the tradition in India to divide the solar year as being 360 days into 12 months, with each being of 27 or 28 days. This difference from the actual 365.25 days had to be adjusted for every five years or so. Also, the accuracy of the observations regarding the position of the planets with the naked eye (there is no mention of any device like a telescope or a sextant in the Vedic texts) is open to question. In any case, the position of the planets in the sky at a particular time or season would be relative to the location from which the observation was being made. Obviously, an observation made from Patna would differ from that made at Amritsar. Given that a one-degree shift in the position of a planet in transition would translate into 72 years, it is possible to have a glimpse of the likely problems in attempting any clear-cut dating of the Vedas, or some event mentioned in it, based exclusively on astronomical data. These variables need to be to be taken into account for any definitive assertion to be made, based on astronomical references. But most discussions on such findings based on astronomical data do not seem to have considered any *"contra"* factors and have just repeated the previous statements on the issue.

B.B. Lal, in his essay, "The Aryan Invasion of India – Perpetuation of a Myth" (in the book, "The Indo-Aryan Controversy", mentioned above) has adduced considerable evidence that the so-called Aryan invasion of India is a mis-reading of archaeological evidence, and has taken the historian R.S. Sharma to task for suggesting that the Rigvedic people entered the sub-continent from the northwest by the early second millennium BCE. Lal has thence gone on to press for the Rigveda as having been composed around 2000 to 1900 BCE, or even earlier, although how much earlier has not been defined by him. This he has tied up with the description of the Saraswati River in the Rigveda and the drying up of the Saraswati-Ghaggar-Hakra river system in the Sind and northwest Rajasthan around 1900 BCE. While satellite pictures have attested to the drying up of the Ghaggar-Hakra river system, it would require further stratigraphic studies in that region and the dating of samples to derive any proximate date for such drying up of those rivers. Lal has also relied on references to plants and river names in the Rigveda to suggest that it was possibly written within the limits of India. He has corrected the perspective by relying on the text of the Rigveda to map out its possible geography as extending from parts of Afghanistan, the Indus Valley (together with its tributaries), to

   Prosenjit Dasgupta

the upper reaches of the Yamuna and Ganga rivers. As against this, it must be kept in mind that *Aryavarta* (or, the place of the Aryas) as commonly understood in India, lies much farther east, in the Yamuna-Ganga Doab, well into eastern Uttar Pradesh, as we now have it.

Unfortunately, textual references in the Rigveda have found no collateral support by way of any inscriptions on stone or clay tablets as have been found in other contemporary civilizations, such as the Hittite in Anatolia, the Sumerian in Mesopotamia, or in pharaonic Egypt. One obvious cause for the lack of such inscribed records may well be that, at least in the Vedic times (be it 2000 BCE or 1500 BCE), no script had been developed to express or record thoughts. It does take a good deal of time to progress from purely symbols to indicate an article or person or event through pictographs resembling that article or person to a phonetic system with more varied symbols to represent the spoken word, e.g., h-a-n-d.

The Indus Valley seals, with their peculiar script dating back to at least 2600 BCE are, in a way, very possibly written in symbolic or proto-pictographic script. It is difficult to visualize that while the IVC had some sort of script (though, as yet undeciphered), a somewhat later historical period and culture, that of the Rigveda, did not apparently possess any script. Or, it could be that the Vedic sages and priests wanted to keep their thoughts to themselves and within their clans, and, therefore, never wrote anything down. Of course, one sees even today in the Sanskrit tols or village schools, in Muslim *madrasas* and in Buddhist monasteries that students memorize the sacred texts – but those sacred texts were written down at some point in time in the past, be it 500 BCE or 700 AD. If the Code of Hamurabbi in Mesopotamia could have been written down in the 18th century BCE, one would have thought that the Rigvedic sages may have also wished to put down at least some of the particulars of the rituals and procedures for the guidance of the householders (and many of the rituals were, in fact, for them), unless there were any overriding reasons for not doing so. It is difficult, if not impossible, at this point in time to be able to make any reasonable conjecture as to why the Rigvedic sages had made this omission. While their thoughts on the creation of the cosmos and life on Earth may have come in the course of their meditation, it is only to be expected that they would have jotted down something, however brief, about their musings. As has been pointed out more than once already, textual references in the Rigveda are "remembered history"; no one wrote them down as thoughts or events occurred or unfolded. Thus, it is not outside the realm of possibility that while the Saraswati River may have dried up around 1600 BCE, this was remembered and written down by the clans or disciples of the sages two or three hundred years later; it does take time for slow geological change to manifest itself. Naturally, issues as to who remembered and how these memories were passed on between generations (memories are notoriously fickle and can be quite selective) can pose problems for later researchers.

Coupled with this problem of an apparent lack of a script with the text and the physical rituals passed on between generations by memory (and the latter is certainly very, very difficult without a codified standard procedure), one of the intriguing aspects of the Rigvedic times is the total lack of any sculptures or sculpted panels that one finds in other ancient sites, be it in Luxor or Abu Simbel in Egypt or Bogazkoye in Anatolia or the many Assyrian sites of similar vintage. As has been earlier noted, stones were to be found in the neighbouring Baluchistan hills or in the Afghan foothills. It would do well to take note here that, of all the cultures that had developed to the northwest of the Indian sub-continent (i.e., in Mesopotamia, or Iran or Anatolia), it is only in the Andronovo and the Bactria-Margiana cultures that came about in the 2nd millennium BCE to the north and west of the Pamirs (and, therefore, north of India), in and around

    Prosenjit Dasgupta

the Oxus or Amu Darya river, that a similar lack of written records by way of inscriptions and tablets is found. It is wholly in the realm of speculation as to whether this lack of a script in these neighbouring regions brushed off on northwest India. Fortunately, there are other specific archaeological remains that tell their story about these cultures. It is also in the Andronovo and Bactria regions that the pre-eminence of the horse in the regional culture is found, just as the horse is also notable in Rigvedic texts. This is not to suggest that the people who wrote the Rigveda had any connection whatsoever with those in Andronovo or the Bactria-Margiana regions; or, they may well have had. In any case, it would do well to bear in mind that these were contemporaneous but separate developments that may have shown some similarities but were not identical.

Further, it is of note that after the Indus Valley seals of the 2nd millennium BCE, the next written records on the Indian sub-continent (as available on date) are that of the Edicts of Emperor Ashoka from about the mid 3rd century BCE; that is, after a gap of more than 2000 years. Interestingly, some of Ashokan edicts found in the Kandahar region of modern Afghanistan are in Greek and Aramaic languages as spoken in the Middle East and the Mediterranean regions; while, of course, many of the edicts are in Brahmi and *Kharosti* scripts. The reason as to why an emperor in the Indian sub-continent should have inscriptions in Greek or Aramaic is a bit of a puzzle, unless his empire had some cultural links with those regions or there were people speaking those languages living near and around Kandahar. Further, Kharosthi was a script that was in use primarily in Gandhara and Bactria, and even up to Samarkand. It has not been found in the rest of India; certainly not in the Indo-Gangetic plains. The Brahmi script was considerably used in the Indian sub-continent right up to large parts of central India, principally to express the *Prakrit* (that is, a colloquial or vernacular form, as opposed to the more formal, "official" or "priestly" Sanskrit) language, presumably because good numbers of common people spoke that form of colloquial Sanskrit. There were, to confuse things, caste distinctions even in Prakrit, in that there was the high-class *Maharashtri Prakrit*, as also *Paisachi*, *Sauraseni*, *Magadhi* and other forms of Prakrit. The complexity of ancient Indian languages and the problems thus thrown up for a study of linguistics would be quite evident from the above.

J.M. Kenoyear, in his essay on the Late Harappan phase of the IVC (in the above-mentioned book) from around 1900 to 1200 BCE, has underlined the paucity of definitive archaeological evidence as to the manner of the decline of the IVC. He has observed that whatever remains, points to a progressive transformation of the IVC rather than any wholesale substitution by another sort of culture as it extended into the Malwa and the Gangetic areas. Scanning the latest findings and reports, Kenoyear suggests that the early IVC phase began around 6500 BCE, going on to the early Harappa phase by 3300 BCE, before developing some regional differentiation by 3000 BCE, then to a mature middle phase by 2600 BCE and to more localized manifestations around 1900 BCE. The late IVC era appears around 1800 BCE, moving on to the "Painted Grey Ware pottery" culture by 1200 BCE. Kenoyear has cautioned against generalizations that are not warranted by the available data but is emphatic that there is no evidence that points to the usage of the horse by Harappan people, be it in 2600 BCE or later, before that civilization faded away. While available evidence does not suggest any notable biological change in population, there were some notable changes in the burial practices and decorative motifs on pottery that suggest some changes in religious beliefs that possibly took place by the time of the late Harappan phase, say around 1400 to 1200 BCE.

J.G. Shaffer and Diana Lichtenstein (also in the above publication) have observed: "The material, tangible, archaeological record is a most vital 'hard data' record for

     Prosenjit Dasgupta

establishing knowledge about the ways of life, and identities, of pre-historic peoples. It is a record that presents the patterns of pre-historic life in both a relative, stratigraphic, chronology, and absolute chronology, through radiometric techniques. It helps inform us of that part of human existence before written records, some 99 percent of human existence."

With this basic foundation to their line of thinking, Shaffer and Lichtenstein have indicated that in Mehrgarh (now in Baluchistan of Pakistan), there is clear indication by about 6500 BCE of farming of wheat and barley together with husbanding of goats, sheep and cattle, while wild sheep, water buffalo and gazelles were hunted and eaten. They have gone on to state that fairly similar but some localized distinctive, cultural patterns had emerged in the Indus Valley by the early part of the third millennium BCE. Contemporaneously, similar cultural patterns also emerged at Kot Diji, Amri and elsewhere in the region that suggested a "mosaic" of cultural practices as evidenced in the archaeological finds. But, apparently, environmental and ecological changes had started taking place by the mid 3rd millennium BCE, leading to the diversion of much of the waters of the Ghaggar-Hakra-Saraswati river system to more eastern river systems. By about 1900/1800 BCE, many (but not all) of the existing sites in the Indus and the Ghaggar-Hakra Valleys had been abandoned and new sites were being populated in Punjab and Gujarat. The decline of the settlements in the Cholistan area was more than matched by the development of new sites in Punjab, north Rajasthan, Gujarat and Haryana. Shaffer and Lichtenstein have, therefore, concluded that there was a notable indigenous cultural continuity over this two millennia period.

Shifting the focus of the evidence from that of archaeology to that of linguistics, the scholarship and the earnestness to seek answers are no less impressive. Particularly impressive is the essay by Hans Heinrich Hock ("Philology and the Historical Interpretation of the Vedic Texts", also in the above publication), in which he has carefully discussed and analysed a number of stanzas of the Rigveda. He is careful to mention that the evidence he would adduce may not be comprehensive and cogent enough to establish either of the hypotheses of an autochthonous origin, or, alternatively, a migrant origin of the India-Aryans; although some readers may find other essays, such as the one by Satya Swarup Mishra (and saying quite opposite) equally interesting! It is pertinent to observe that in the Endnotes to Satya Swarup Mishra's essay, the editors have mentioned that while Mishra had referred to B.B. Lal's views as of 1981 as to whether Indo-Aryans had their origins outside of India, Lal himself has since changed his views as per his essay in Bryant's book. Carl Lamberg-Karlovsky in another essay in the same publication has put it that linguists are not equipped to associate archaeological values to the words they study any more than archaeologists can make their finds to utter words. Only if they could!

Michael Witzel, in another essay, "Indocentrism – Autochthonous visions of Ancient India", in the same publication has discussed at some length the views of S. G. Talageri and S.S. Mishra (who have each in their own way advocated the autochthonous Aryan thesis) and has underlined the absence of any South Asian features in the languages of the Indo-European family west of the Indian sub-continent. Specifically, the archaism in the Old Iranian language has no correspondence to the Vedic language, and this militates against any "out of India" spread of the Indo-Aryan language to the north and west of the Indian sub-continent. Witzel poses the question as to why there should be any "special pleading" in linguistic development for the Indian sub-continent (to derive the autochthonous Aryan thesis) when most other nations are quite content with what the disciplines of linguistics, philology, archaeology, anthropology, etc., have had to say about their past history. More to the point, this insistence on a reading of the Rigveda to establish the indigenous origin of the Indo-

                    Prosenjit Dasgupta

Aryan people, only leads the ancient history of India having to confront contradictions, such as having to establish the existence of horse-drawn chariots in India before any dated remains were found; the use of horses in India before they were domesticated and introduced to the world from Central Asia; or making of iron tools before any first archaeological finds of iron implements that date back to 1200 BCE, and so on. These differences have to be accounted for, one way or the other.

Another interesting input is from M.M. Deshpande in his essay "Aryan Origins" in Bryant and Patton. He underlines the little-known viewpoint that most Brahmins of the Maharashtrian Konkan coast traditionally consider themselves as part of the five regional Dravidian Brahmin groups, while the Gauda Saraswat Brahmins, in and around Goa, consider themselves as immigrants from the north.

While the above essays and comments came very much later, it is of note that the setting up of the Deccan College in Pune in 1860 was seminal in Sanskritic and Indological studies, led from the front by R.G. Bhandarkar and others. But soon, Bhandarkar's students like Bal Gangadhar Tilak and Vishnushastri Chiplunkar were significantly differing with him on the reading of ancient Indian history. This does not seem to have been based on any physical evidence by way of any archaeological remains, or inscriptions but largely on a reading of Vedic texts without sufficient regard for linguistics or philology and the finer points of astronomy (on which Tilak largely relied). The collapse of the distance between the object of study and the scholar, Deshpande has rightly averred, in the heat of rising nationalist sentiments (in the first two decades of the 20th century – parenthesis added) had serious consequences to the subsequent progression of historical scholarship. Deshpande goes on to add that, "The Marathi publications of Chiplunkar, Tilak, and Pavgee, stoking the fires of resurgent nationalist Brahmanical spirit, were instrumental in the development of later Hindu nationalism under Savarkar and others." In the Endnotes to this essay, Deshpande has added that Pavgee had noted, "Tilak never agreed with him on his theory of the Aryavartic home of the Aryans." So, that is yet another angle to be looked at.

It does appear that Indian thinkers and sages at the turn of the 20th century, who had expressed their views on the dating of the Rigveda and had drawn some conclusions about its contents as also about the origins of the Indo-Aryans, were not sufficiently conversant with the progress of the findings of archaeology, anthropology, astronomy, linguistics, philology, etc., by the first two or three decades of the 20th century. These views, while serving the growth of Indian nationalism at the time, cannot be termed as being sufficiently "research-based", as is commonly understood and accepted.

However, as there is as yet no material archaeological evidence (e.g., inscriptions or tablets) relating to the Rigveda, one necessarily has to fall back on linguistic and textual research, and the generally accepted consensus amongst most historians points to the dating of the Rigveda to around 1500 BCE.

As to the origins of the Aryans – or more correctly, the "Indo-Aryans", for the word "Aryan" in the Vedic context means a noble person and has no ethnic connotations – a whole body of knowledge on the *urheimat* or homeland of the Indo-European peoples (from which the Indo-Aryan language is believed to have sprung) has come up over the last sixty or seventy years or so. While this is not the place to discuss this in any detail it should suffice to refer to the pioneering work of Marja Gimbutas with respect to the "*kurgan*" thesis based on extensive archaeological evidence by her and other researchers in southern Russia and Central Asia. Another site of significance is the Bactria-Margiana area just to the west of the Pamir Mountains, where Victor Sarianidi has done much pioneering work. These works are mentioned not because they

     Prosenjit Dasgupta

have, or may have, any direct bearing on the Vedic culture, but merely as a backdrop to the Indo-Aryan cultural features as one finds mention in the Rigveda. Underground burials have been found, though dated somewhat later, in Burzahom in Kashmir and elsewhere. H.D. Sankalia, the noted scholar of ancient Indian history, noting the typical Painted Grey Ware (PGW) style of pottery remains from the Gangetic valley, Sind, and even Baluchistan, has drawn attention to the view of B.B. Lal, a renowned archaeologist, of the possibility of the bearers of this PWG culture being groups of people from Shah Tepe or some such site in Iran, while Sankalia himself has found evidence from Navdatoli near Maheswar on the Narmada river of possibly another lot of people from Iran coming into the Narmada, Chambal and Tapti valleys (page 270 of Sankalia). He goes on to say that, "On the current theory it is held that the bearers of a superior culture came along the principal lines of communications (the coastal areas and along river valleys – parenthesis added) and gradually occupied the fertile river valleys, ousting the hunters and food-gatherers to the central Indian forests and hills" (page 274). There are, of course, many ifs and buts in such a hypothesis, as there is more than one way to interpret archaeological (or, for that matter, linguistic) data.

There are several other historians and archaeologists who argue for the Aryans (i.e., the nobility, as the Rigveda has it, and not an ethnic group as some people believe) as being the original inhabitants of India from ancient times who broke out of India to populate other areas such as Gandhara, Bactria, Iran and elsewhere. When there is a lack of material evidence, such as an inscription or stele (a stone memorial) of Vashistha or Bhrigu or Atri anywhere in India or elsewhere, and one is trying to re-construct a culture or civilization from memorized verses that have seen redaction over the millennia, there is hardly any scope for certitude. One then has to search for approximations that seem to come close to truth. On the face of it, it appears that there is hardly any reason for the Aryans (or the Indo-Aryan language speaking tribes and clans of Bhrigu or Atri or Kanva) to move out of Aryavarta or the land of the Aryans commonly believed to be in the Ganges-Yamuna doab, into the arid plains and hills of Sind, Baluchistan, Bactria, Gandhara and north eastern Iran. One wonders what may have been the reason for them to have left their rice cultivations (domesticated rice, *Oryza indica*, is said to have been produced in India from about 2000 BCE) for an alien diet of barley and wheat, unless there was some compulsion for it. One then would have to look at geological and environmental factors that may have necessitated such a movement; such data would have to be forthcoming. If, however, one takes it that the Indo-Aryan language speaking people were, in any case, basically living in the Sind-Baluchistan-Bactria-West Punjab region for several millennia, then, necessarily, Aryavarta in the Indo-Gangetic plains, as commonly thought of, would have come later as the Indo-Aryans gradually moved eastwards. This had a more equable climate, was greener, and a more seismically stable region. Human geography suggests that people tend—other things being equal—to move to places where living is easier, even if for a short span of time: hence, the long tradition of transhumance in the Himalayan region with shepherds moving to lower altitudes with the onset of winter; so also, with the nomads of central Asia.

Edwin Bryant, in his "The Quest for the Origins of the Vedic Culture" (see Bibliography) has culled out a huge amount of sources and data on the subject for the edification of concerned readers. It is clear from the books "The Indo-Aryan Controversy" and "The Quest for the Origins" that it is when one starts going beyond the plain narrative and descriptive material in the body of the Rigveda to glean more about the Vedic age in terms of the culture of the Vedic people and to inquire about their possible origins (mind you, not about the underlying philosophy or "message" of the Vedas)

     Prosenjit Dasgupta

that the complications start adding up. Then all the nitty-gritty of linguistics takes over. To begin with, if one takes the Indo-Aryan language of the Vedas to have originated within India, then one is hard put to relate it to the very similar Indo-Iranian language (i.e., Old Persian), and to the similarities with the Indo-European group of languages (be it German or Greek), leading back to the Proto-Indo-European language, which a wide cross-section of linguists consider to be the "mother" of all these languages. Then, all the arguments and counterarguments start piling up and "linguistic palaeontology" has a field day, looking at the antiquity or archaic character of individual words, sub-strata of other languages, "loan words", rates of change and diffusion, and all that. There is sufficient evidence in the Rigvedic text of "loan words" or "derived" words from Dravidian and Mundaric (an Austro-Asiatic language) for flora, fauna, agriculture and agricultural implements for this to be ignored. It is, of course, a matter of personal judgement for a linguist or a philologist to consider whether fifty or a hundred or five hundred such words would constitute "sufficient evidence".

Then one comes to the issue of the affinity of the Vedic language with the Old Persian of the Zend Avesta, the Iranian sacred text said to have been compiled by the sage called Zarathustra in early 17th century BCE. Further, the structure of the Avesta and the Rigveda are quite similar, in that both rely on hymns, known as "*Yasnas*" compiled into five books or "*Gathas*" in the Avesta. By way of example, Verse 2 of Yasna 34 is as follows –

> "*At-cha i Toi ma-nang-ha*
> *Mein yeush cha Vang heush vis-pa da-ta*
> *Spen-ta khya cha neresh shyao thana*
> *Ye hya urva A-sha hai chai te,*
> *Pairi gai the Khashma va to*
> *Va mey Mazda ga-ro bish stu-tam.*"

"The pure-minded and righteous man, O Ahura Mazda,
Whose soul is in harmony with truth, thinks of you alone,
And dedicates his good actions to you.
May we approach you, praising you and singing your
songs.

- Zarathustra's message (copied from the
Zoroastrian Fire Temple at Yazd, Iran)

There is mention in the Avesta of "*airiianem vaejo*", or
the sacred land, that has been placed by scholars near the
Hindukush Mountains. Whether this can be taken as the
homeland of the Indo-Aryans and the Indo-Iranians cannot
be stated without further archaeological studies in that area.
There are similar concerns, too, although from the opposites
of a dividing line: the Rigveda extols raiding of cattle from
others to increase one's own herd, while the Avesta frowns
on it. While the RV praises the devas, the Avesta has the
benevolent *Ahura* (which, for the RV, would be "*asura*", who
were considered malevolent).

It is also well-known that there is an inscription at
Bogazkoye in Anatolia (modern-day Turkey), being a treaty
between a Hittite king and his Mittani adversary where words
like "*Indara*" (Indra?), *Mitras* (Mitra?), *Nasatia* (Nastaya?),
and *Uruvanas* (Varuna?) are found to occur. Further east,
in the Kassite records of Babylon, are seen words like *Surias*
(Surya), *Maruttas* (Maruta), etc. For any Indian, the phonetic
similarities and the possible identities of the deities are only
too obvious. While noting these records, Bryant has posed the
question that if Sanskrit being an Indo-Aryan language could
have evolved into Bengali, Punjabi, Braj-bhasha, Gujarati, etc.,
each with its own script and linguistic characteristics, why
the Proto-Indo European language could not have similarly
evolved into Sanskrit, as well as the several languages spoken
on the European continent? Basically, it is a question whether

or not 'the sauce for the goose is also sauce for the gander'. He has gone on to refer to the studies by Johanna Nichols, which places the origins of the Indo-European family of languages around the Syr Darya River, east of the Aral Sea, from which she considers it to have radiated sometime in the mid-3rd millennium BCE towards the north of the Aral Sea and southwards to Iran. Some elements moved north of the Caspian Sea and then farther north to the Black Sea and beyond, and a southern component that went south of the Caspian into the Anatolian region. Nichols has suggested a second wave around the 2nd millennium BCE of Indo-Aryan languages that effectively separated the East European and the Anatolian group of Indo-European languages and the Tocharian language farther to the east, close to northwest China. Still, the basic dichotomy of linguistics lacking credible archaeological evidence and of archaeological finds lacking a language persists.

Bryant has also made a useful review of the studies pertaining to the IVC script in such as those by S.R. Rao suggesting that it is a logo-symbolic type of script, of Asko Parpola, who relates it to a proto-Dravidian language and refers in some detail to the work of Subhas Kak who has adopted a mathematical model relating the IVC script with the later Brahmi script, and coming to the conclusion that the IVC script was some sort of Prakrit.

On another tack, Bryant has emphasized two important characteristics of the so-called Vedic culture, one being the use of the horse, and the other of horse-drawn spoked wheel chariots. Horse-drawn chariots are represented in sculptures and in edicts in India only around the late 3rd century BCE, while actual archaeological remains of chariots are dated to about 350 BCE at Atranjkhera in the upper reaches of the Ganga. Outside of India, the earliest archaeological find testifying to a spoked wheel chariot is from the Sintashta Cemetery of Andronovo, dating back to about 2000 BCE, as also corroborated by inscriptions from Anatolia dating somewhat later. While there are many remains of some equine species in several of the archaeological sites in India, there is considerable controversy as to whether these relate to the true domesticated horse (*Equus caballus*) or to some sort of wild asses, species of which are to be found in extreme western Gujarat and in Ladakh and neighbouring localities. Very large quantities of remains of equine species are found, though from an earlier dating, from sites close to the Andronovo area. There would be need for more DNA studies of these equine remains to come to any definite conclusions.

The issue of the "Indo-Aryan Controversy" then leads to the question of who gains or loses if the Rigveda is dated to 5000 BCE or 1500 BCE; or, if the Indo-Aryan speaking people originated from within India or came as migrants or traders from the west. In the ultimate analysis, one has to examine whether history is expected to serve any sense of victory or dominance for any one or for any community. To be sure, history has been an instrument in arousing and sustaining nationalist feelings in more than one country. But, for notable sections of the political class to be absorbed in a particular reading of history, even quite some time after nationalism has achieved its objective of restoring sovereignty to the people, is more difficult to understand.

As E.H. Carr, the eminent historian in his book of the name, "What is History?", has it that history is more than a mere assemblage of facts, as some historians had tended to do. He considered such a presentation to suffer from the bias of the person who had written that particular account based on his particular selection of events and personalities. This, to Carr's mind, turned "facts of the past" to parade as "historical facts", often successfully concealing the (intended or unintended) bias of the narrator. As to himself, Carr favoured the "middle way"; balancing an objective recording of the facts as far as possible with a subjective interpretation of such facts—in plain

                     Prosenjit Dasgupta

view—by the compiler or the historian. As he saw it, "History is preoccupied with fundamental processes of change. If you are allergic to these processes, you abandon history…The function of the historian is neither to love the past nor to emancipate himself from the past, but to master and understand it as the key to the understanding of the present." Elsewhere, Carr has written, "Great history is written precisely when the historian's view of the past is illuminated by insight into the problems of the present."

It is only when one confronts some issues of the present, be it the emergence of some social practices, such as succession rights in a family, or, observations on the persistent exploitation of a section of the people, that one can be motivated to try and work back into time as to the possible or probable cause(s) of such practice. It is also seen that in much the same vein, Sudipta Kaviraj has observed in his book, "The Unhappy Consciousness", that, "The past was an image created in the interest of the present…It was possible to change the past in the future, simply by making it the past of a different present." These lines underline the tendency among many sections of people to glorify the past in order to bear the travails of the present. Historians, being part and parcel of society, may not be immune or insulated in many instances to similar tendencies. Here, it makes sense to reproduce the maxim that Carr stood for: "Study the historian before you begin to study the facts."

If the study of history is thus reduced to a means for social or economic or political ascendance, that would be a sure prescription for confusion and conflict; for there would surely be others who would contest such a particular version. That, in turn, would militate against a shared sense of a common history, in howsoever general terms, and a deepening sense of shared values that are the very bulwarks of nationhood. D.C. Sircar, the eminent scholar of ancient Indian history, has quoted R.G. Bhandarkar as observing early in 1921 that, "The Indian tendency may be towards rejecting foreign influence on the development of this country's civilization and to claim high antiquity for some of the occurrences in its history" (page 4, "Some Problems of Indian History", see Bibliography). Sircar goes on approvingly to quote Kalhan (the compiler of the "Rajatarangini", a genealogy of local kings, in 1150 CE) that "*Shlayghya sa eva gunanvan raga-clvesa bahiskrita*" (i.e., the man of merit deserves praise when he discards rage and prejudice). Sircar further adds, "The desire to be free from prejudices…What is required for this is the *catholicity of sympathies* in evaluating the evidence should be the keystone of one's approach to historical prejudices" (page 37 – emphasis added).

It is often overlooked that, as early as 1837, James Prinsep emphasized the importance of collecting and collating epigraphic records; or, that Sir Alexander Cunningham, as head of the fledgling Archaeological Survey of India (1871-1885), collected the edicts of Ashoka and the commencement of the "Epigraphica Indica" in 1892 under Burgess. This oversight also includes the pioneering role of H.R. Colebrooke and H.H. Wilson (later, Csoma Koros) in collecting and conserving ancient manuscripts. If some persons subsequently interpreted these records incorrectly at times, that should not obscure the significance of those initial acts of collection and conservation. At the same time, one must place on record the work of Rajendralal Mitra (1824-1891), Dr R.G. Bhandarkar (1837-1925), Hara Prasad Shastri (1853-1931) and many other Indian scholars, who, since the latter half of the 19th century, made major contributions to Indological studies.

Many, if not most Indians, even today, are unlikely to have heard of the Rigveda, much less to have any knowledge about its contents. To those who know something of its contents, the date is not important; the expression of those lofty thoughts on creation of life, *Rik*, or the cosmic order of things and worship of the divinities are the crux of it. It is then much more about a "feel" for the overall landscape, livelihood practices of the

     Prosenjit Dasgupta

Vedic people and others and their common concerns, and less about an over-riding concern about the plants named in the text and whether they occur high on the hills or in the Gangetic plains, implements used in agriculture, etc. These are important markers, no doubt, but involve so much of differences of emphasis and nuances of interpretation that the fundamental significance of the Rigveda as a work of high metaphysical merit tends to get side-lined in any historical discussion. To put it differently, would it really matter if the Rigveda is dated to, say 600 or 500 BCE, and would that invalidate its deep metaphysical insights?

More to the point, the entire narrative of the Indian ancient history, from the time of the stone implements to the rock paintings to the nature and extent of the IVC, the contents of the Rigveda and what it conveys, has to hold together in a rational and reasonable way. If one attempts to pull out one event or fact out of its position in time, one may well find the entire edifice of Indian history going out of joint. As the old nursery rhyme goes, "All the king's horses and all the king's men could not put Humpty Dumpty together again."

It would be far better for the pieces of the jigsaw puzzle to fall naturally into place, than to try and make out a new jigsaw puzzle that would take in a new odd piece. This is not to say that a new narrative of Indian ancient history should not be attempted or a new historical jigsaw puzzle should not be created; but, all of it must then hold together reasonably and rationally with the maximum possible reliance on evidences provided by archaeology, anthropology, epigraphy, linguistics, philology, and so on. If something then does not quite fit in, then it must be examined and re-examined thoroughly so that something sensible may be conclusively made of it.

Chapter 6

The mysterious "forest" knowledge

It is commonly accepted amongst scholars that the *Upanishads*, the second most important of the sacred books of India, in terms of both chronology and metaphysical content, followed the Rigveda after several centuries or so, around 1200 or 1000 BCE. The etymology of the word "Upanishad" indicates a process of passing on of thoughts and views through the medium of discussion or a question and answer session (in the modern parlance) between a scholar and his disciple sitting together. It was as if the thinkers around that time had wearied of the elaborate and expensive rituals and sacrifices prescribed in the later Vedic texts, such as the Yajurveda, and struck out in a completely new direction, where the thoughts were turned inward towards the understanding of the self, and self-realization as revealing the path to self-betterment. Hence, we find that supreme question posed by Maitreyi in the *Brihadaranyaka Upanishad* (later Brh. Up.).

Dr Sarvepalli Radhakrishnan, in the Preface to his work, "The Principal Upanishads", has observed that at the core of all historical religions extant in the world, there are fundamental types of spiritual experiences that have been sought to be passed on to succeeding generations. The Upanishads are very much a part and parcel of that sacred patrimony that humankind possesses, in that unceasing search for the eternal principles of life that in one way or the other, to a lesser or greater degree, characterize all mankind. That is what has drawn man to the temple and church, to the mosque and the monastery, to seclusion in the Himalayan heights or in the expanses of the desert: to find himself, to identify the constant in the midst of unceasing change. It was this message of the Upanishads that led the philosopher Schopenhauer to call it the solace of his life and the solace in his death. Whether others also find in the Upanishads similar mental and spiritual refuge is for each one of us to find out for his or herself.

Dr Radhakrishnan is careful to point out that in this work he has relied mainly on the principal Upanishads that have been commented upon by the great sage Adi Shankara in the 8th century, i.e., the eleven *mukhya* or principal Upanishads, these being the *Brihadaranyaka*, the *Chandogya*, the *Aitareya*, the *Taittiriya*, the *Kena*, the *Isha*, the *Katha*, the *Mundaka*, the *Prashna*, the *Svetashvatara*, and the *Mandukya*. There are others that are also called as Upanishads that appear to relate to more sectional or sectarian thoughts and beliefs and are of a later date. He has also adhered to the texts as commented upon by Shankara as there are other versions and redactions that have appeared over the years gone by. It is of particular note that the Upanishads are not products of logic and research: they are what was "revealed" to, or was "seen" or "experienced" by the sages of that time, such as Uddalaka Aruni, Yajnavalka, Svetashvatara and others, often in the course of their day-to-day life (for they were householders), or in the periods of reflection or meditation in their hermitage by the side of a forest. What was the nature of that revelation or how it came about is difficult to say or explain; but that it was a powerful and moving experience cannot be denied. It was as if the whole being of the seer was being shaken and moved in a manner that was above and beyond all other experiences. This is true of all seers of all ages from times of the sages Uddalaka Aruni and Yajnavalka, to Gautama Buddha, Jesus Christ, the Prophet Mohammad, Adi Shankara, Ramanuja, Madhavacharya, Kabir, Guru Nanak-ji, to Ramakrishna Paramahamsa. It was as if a sudden flash of light, or "knowledge" that is not acquired but experienced and inspired, illuminated the whole of their existence. Thus, the sage Svetashvatara is found to exclaim –

*"Vedahametam Purusham Mahantam
Adityavarnam Tamasah Parastat"*

"That Refulgent Supreme Being
Spoken of in the Vedas,
Shining like the Sun across the Sea of Darkness"

- (Svetasvatara Upanishad, Chapter II, verse 5)

In the Rigveda, many of the verses suggest that man was awe-struck by natural phenomena such as storm and lightning and sought for "light" in the worship of fire, the sun, or dawn. The Gayatri Mantra clearly shows the hankering for enlightenment by reaching an understanding of the reality all around. It is at that stage that man has the first glimmering of the *ekam* or "the One". The Upanishads take this line of thought further ahead. Where man in the Rigveda turned once to Varuna, Mitra, Agni, Surya, or the Maruts or Aditi, the mother of all, they were looking at different manifestations of what was essentially one. The Upanishads are significantly monotheistic, forever turning to *Ekamevadvitiyam*, "the One without any second", or *Tadekam*, or "That is the One". The Upanishads are, therefore, widely considered as part of *Vedanta*, that which concludes and rounds off the fundamental thoughts of the Rigveda and its associated texts, particularly the Brahmanas and the Aranyakas. The Upanishads attempt to go beyond the external observances and rituals as prescribed in the Brahmanas to their inner significance and meaning. As Radhakrishnan has it, it was not to brush aside the concerns and plain beliefs of the common man (as exemplified in the questions put by the students or disciples). The sages of the Upanishads were to lead them on by stages to an understanding of the deeper philosophical meaning behind the beliefs that the Vedas had engendered, such that over time, there emerged the concept of the Supreme Being or the Supreme Reality as the focus and subject of metaphysical and theistic speculation.

                    Prosenjit Dasgupta

More than once, the sages of the Rigveda realized the One behind the many or *"Ekam santam bahuda kalpayanti"* (RV, Book 1, hymn 164, verse 64: "It is the One though it is imagined as many"). So many times, this word *bahuda* occurs in the text of the Rigveda to emphasise this central realisation. The use of the term "realisation" is both deliberate and necessary, because it was not the product of some mathematical formula or any abstruse play of logic: it was the germ of an idea that rose of itself from an interplay of the heart, mind and soul of the thinker immersed in meditating on existential issues. It was by no means a unified and coherent body of thought, but rather ways of looking for the core values or a philosophy of life that emphasized an unceasing search for fundamental verities of life on Earth, and about death, the very thought of which seemed to paralyse the human mind. That was what Maitreyi was seeking in her question: the first glimmering of hope of an "eternal" life beyond the usual *karma kanda* of day-to-day living and rituals.

Each of the principal Upanishads has approached this central question in its own way. The Taittiriya Upanishad tells of the search of a disciple for the Supreme Reality, and after much soul-seeking and search, he comes to the "realisation" and the truth that this Supreme Reality is inherent in—and it "is"—*ananda*, that supreme exhilaration that seizes one on the liberation of the mind and soul upon becoming one with this Reality. This Reality has been ascribed in the Upanishads as *sat* (being), *chit* (awareness or consciousness) and *ananda* (bliss). It has also been seen as *satyam* (truth or verity), *jnanam* (knowledge or understanding) and *anantam* (that which is eternal and infinite). This being and truth is the *atman*, which is normally derived from the root *an*, which is to breathe; although Shankara in his commentaries has derived it from what is all-pervasive. Radhakrishnan has described atman as the breath of life, the very soul, self and essential being of an individual.

Radhakrishnan continues that, in all this, any withdrawal from the world is not considered to be the conclusive end to this spiritual quest; it finds (or "realises") itself in a refusal to take the world as we find it as final and real, and to persist in the quest to find the "satyam, jnanam, anantam". As Shankara has it in one of his commentaries on the Brih. Up.: "If a thing cannot subsist apart from something else, the latter is the essence of that thing." Hence, the importance of that questioning, that search, that "becoming".

All the same, as in the Rigveda, not all of it is high philosophy; there is much in the Upanishads that is quite simple and plain. For instance, a good part of one of the principal Upanishads, the Brh. Up., deals with ceremonies associated with procreation (VI. 4. 1-28), while the Chandogya Upanishad mentions about some of the Vedic sacrifices and then proceeds to ridicule them; the Taittiriya Upanishad covers aspects of pronunciation and the physical mechanism of the tongue and jaws to make such utterances. As Sukumari Bhattacharji (see Bibliography) has observed, Vedic religion has little or nothing on physical mortification or on asceticism. "Liberation was an un-Vedic goal…It is with the Aranyaka and the Upanishads with their philosophical enquiries that the new goal of liberation through knowledge" (page 202 in Bhattacharji) was emphasized. Prof. Bhattacharji goes on to add that the Rigvedic gods were fully and definitively described and could not break out of those limitations and progressively faded from public consciousness and usage. It was only with the intermingling with the cultural needs of different people and the consequent development of fresh ritualistic practices that the later "metamorphosis" occurred. She perceptively observes, "In mythology, as in life, only the fittest survive" (page 203).

However, it goes without saying that the principal Upanishads by elaborate metaphors, by posing questions, and through discussions provide the guideposts to thought, contemplation and action by which man may become

    Prosenjit Dasgupta

something more—more beautiful, more at peace, more complete—than just himself. Man, thus, has options, and is responsible for his acts. He can sleep or work in the field or factory, or study for examinations; he may well do an unkind or improper act to another to satisfy or benefit himself. It is largely his conscious choice; but he also may ask, at least once of himself, whether what he is about to do is the right and proper thing. It is his conscious choice in the act itself, although he may be misled for the time being by ignorance or lack of awareness, whether to confine himself or herself to what provides limited or transitory satisfaction, or to strive to come closer to that sat-chit-ananda. Hence, the prayer that has resounded in a thousand voices in India over the millennia:

"Asato ma sadgamaya,
Tamaso ma jyotirgamaya,
Mrityurmamritam gamaya"

- Brihadaranyaka Upanishad (1.2.28)

"Lead us from untruth to truth;
Lead us from darkness to light;
Lead us from death to life eternal."

The words of the verse themselves sufficiently indicate that there is untruth, there is darkness and there is death all around. It is for each individual to consider whether to remain enshrouded in this untruth and darkness till death should come upon him or her to end it all. It is for each individual to contemplate whether this prayer is just to be mouthed as a matter of course during some religious occasion or ritual, or is something very basic to his or her life, something to be intrinsically believed in; in fact, to be lived.

Another vital thought is encapsulated in our national motto, *"Satyameva jayate"* ("Truth shall triumph"), from the Mundaka Upanishad, used on all Government documents in India. Why these words were chosen and not something akin to "Liberty, Equality, Fraternity" as it is in France, or *E Pluribus Unum* ("The many are made as one") as it was in the USA until 1956, will be found in the debates of the Constituent Assembly. Obviously, the answer lies in a conviction, and a national consensus that truth does triumph in the end, and that this belief has stood the test for two millennia. Whether the time is upon us to question the existing motto and to seek a new one is for the nation to consider and debate. If not, then the answer lies in an unambiguous re-assertion of that ancient conviction that has guided the seers and sages of India over the past millennia.

Chapter 7

Dealing with "pramana" and "anumana"

Closely intertwined with the thoughts and philosophies of the Vedas and the Upanishads are the schools of logic that developed in India over the centuries. In terms of chronology, it would appear that the *Samkhya* evolved the earliest, with some scholars (such as R.N. Dandekar) dating the logic system to pre-Rigvedic days, while others such as A.B. Keith have held that it evolved contemporaneously with the Upanishads, that is about 1000 to 800 BCE.

Samkhya, as the name suggests, concerns itself with the enumeration and consideration of the aspects or principles (there being twenty-five such) that lead to the emancipation of the *purusha* or the soul. It relies on six manners of proof that lead to knowledge and understanding of natural phenomena and of man himself. It is one of the significant schools of epistemology, or the study of the sources of knowledge. It relies basically on *pramana*, or proof or evidence, and is as scientific as any logic system could get. Samkhya considers that knowledge is primarily derived from (a) *pratyaksha*, or what is palpable and self-evident; (b) *anumana*, or what is inferred from observations; (c) *upamana*, or what could be known through comparisons and analogy; (d) *arthapatti*, or a derivation or inference from circumstances; (e) *anupalabdhi*, by analysis and differentiation with the natural cognitive processes; and (f) *sabda*, or the testimony of seers and sages. Two well-known examples that are often cited in discussions on Indian logic are that there is no smoke without a fire, and a rope is often mistaken for a snake at night. These, simply put, illustrate the evidence of pratyakhsa with anumana in the first, and anumana and upamana in the second

Much of the later Indian thought and philosophy has relied on one or more of the sources of knowledge that Samkhya identified and defined. Simplistically put, for instance, the *Charvaka* or the materialist (some have called it a hedonist) school of thought has embraced only the pratyaksha, while Buddhism is considered to have significantly relied on the pratyaksha and the anumana aspects while several Jain schools of thought have drawn on pratyaksha, anumana and sabda. No doubt, Indian schools of logic and philosophy have, over the centuries, gone into finer details, and have divided and sub-divided the primary concepts of pramana, pratyaksha, anumana, etc., into many further extensions and theses. But the fundamental principles of logic and epistemology that Samkhya propounded have stood the test of time.

The second most important school of logic and knowledge in India is *Mimamsa*, which basically refers to reaching a conclusion after careful consideration of an issue. Like that of Samkhya, Mimamsa's primary concern was also what may be reliable means to knowledge, and the nature of such knowledge. It also looked for pramana based on what were pratyaksha, and anumana, and all that. This led Mimamsa into etymology and philology that so marked the intellectual ferment in India in the latter half of the 1st millennium BCE, as exemplified in the work of Yaska and Panini. In the process, although it took into account propositions and contrary propositions, it may be said that Mimamsa remained somewhat doubtful and wary of non-empirical or intuitive knowledge. In this, Mimamsa possibly did not quite accept that *"absence of evidence does not necessarily mean evidence of absence"*. More to the point, it was possibly the case that instead of taking an issue to be "innocent till proven guilty", it was more of "guilty till proven innocent". Things do look somewhat different if stood on their head.

But if Samkhya is more speculative or contemplative, Mimamsa is concerned more with *karmakanda: kriya* and *karma*, that which is to be done, and the act itself is taken

      Prosenjit Dasgupta

to be of great importance. Therefore, it leans more towards prayers, sacrifices, rituals, relative to the spirituality and self-knowledge that the Upanishads stressed on. In this, *Mimamsa* (which was mostly developed by Jaimini) also differs from the Vedanta schools of philosophy that take a more cerebral approach. Further, Mimamsa also developed into several schools of thought, such as that of Prabhakara and Kumarila Bhatta. In the process, it developed into two distinct branches, that of *Purva Mimamsa* that concerns itself more with the rituals prescribed in the Vedas, and the *Uttara Mimasa* that discusses the speculative and philosophical portions of the Vedas. To that extent, Uttara Mimasa maybe said to come somewhat close to the Vedantic schools of thought.

It should suffice to say only so much about the two principal schools of Indian logic, philosophy and epistemology and how they developed in the course of the 1st millennium BCE in India, and came to influence, to a considerable extent, the subsequent developments in Indian philosophy and metaphysics in the millennia that followed. More significantly, they affected considerably how Indians thought about things and debated and dissected such thoughts at every opportunity. It would not be wrong to surmise that this, in turn, developed into an almost instinctive faculty to appreciate a contrary point of view and provided a fluidity and flexibility to the Indian way of life that was able constantly to adjust, to take the rough with the smooth, and emerge with its inner vitality intact, despite so many adversities.

Chapter 8

The Epics – new perspectives

If there is anything that has persistently affected and influenced social and religious beliefs, norms and practices in India over the last two millennia, it is the two epics, the *Mahabharata* and the *Ramayana*. While there are numerous views as to the origins of these two epic narratives, many scholars believe that the Mahabharata emerged around the 7th century BCE and grew and evolved till about the 2nd century CE (i.e., over nearly about one thousand years). The Ramayana is believed to have been composed around the 5th century BCE and went through several additions and alterations till around the 3rd century CE. It must be borne in mind that unlike the Rigveda, which is considered to be a "revealed" document, the two epics were composed by men, not at one go, but were edited and added to, over several generations and centuries, around some core events or narratives.

Tradition has it that the Mahabharata was composed by Vyasadeva; the word *"vyasa"* itself denoting a compiler. Besides an account of the build-up to the Kurukshetra war between the Kurus and the Pandavas, the text also includes the story of Nala-Damayanti that deals with Nala's adherence to dharma except for his weakness for playing dice, and the fidelity of Damayanti, his wife. The all-important *Bhagavad-gita* (popularly known as the "Gita"), or the dialogue between Arjuna, the Pandava prince, and Lord Krishna, at the inception of the Kurukshetra war, on dharma (as "duty" and righteousness), is also part of the Mahabharata, as also a few elements of the story of Ramayana. Thus, the Mahabharata has grown into the largest epic poem in the world with about one hundred thousand verses or shlokas. Based on certain references in the text itself, as also mentioned in the *Ashvalayana Grihyasutra*, it would seem that the epic poem grew around a core of about 24,000 verses, and the names of Vyasa, Vaisampayana and Ugrasrava Sauti have been associated with its three principal redactions. It appears from Panini's *"Ashtadhyayi"* that the core text was known by that time in the 5th century BCE. The extreme difficulty in collating and editing such an ancient text may be seen from the words of Vishnu Sukhthankar who edited the "critical" edition: "It is useless to think of reconstructing a fluid text in a literally original shape, on the basis of an archetype."

In a dispassionate and scholarly Foreword to the book, "Mahabharata – Myth and Reality" (see Bibliography), Dr Nihar Ranjan Ray makes the important point that "myth" is not necessarily *"mithya"* (or, untruth) and considers that myths constitute a highly complex set of beliefs and associated activities, the principal function of which is to suggest certain models of human behaviour in a society, providing context and meaning to day-to-day life of the people. In terms of history, Dr Ray suggests that the epic marked a stage when a process had commenced for the formation of larger states or monarchical systems out of the older tribal oligarchies. The "Introduction" to this book (ably edited by S.P. Gupta and K.S. Ramachandran) provides some "hard data". The Mahabharata comprises three redactions (i.e., versions with various additions and alterations), one with 8,800 verses said to have been composed by Krishna Dvaipayan Vyasa, known as the "Jaya". The second has 24,000 verses by Vaisampayana, which is known as Bharata, while the third is a compilation of 100,000 verses by Sauna elsewhere mentioned as Ugrasrava Sauti, which is taken to be the Mahabharata proper. It mentions that, as per H.D. Sankalia and Sashi Asthana, the epic is centred around the family feuds of the Kurus, and ought to be dated to about 4th century CE (page 8). While some other scholars have controverted this, basing themselves on this or that reference—

there being nothing quite definitive—researchers such as Dr V.B. Mirashi have noted a good deal of interpolations in the text of the Mahabharata. It is also significant that a scholar of ancient Indian history of the eminence of B.B. Lal has, in his contribution in this book, has opined that, "The present text is unlikely to be earlier than 4th century AD…It would be unwise to treat the present Mahabharata text in its entirety as a piece of historical evidence" (page 50 of the above book). M.C. Joshi, in another article in the same book adds, "There is no positive archaeological evidence to suggest the large-scale use of *rathas* with centrally yoked animals prior to the Mauryan times" (page 159) and again, that the necessity of re-interpreting "dharma" was caused by the Iron Age developments around the 5th century BCE. The "Epilogue" of the book mentions that while astronomical calculations favour the 15th century for the initial compositions of the Mahabharata, the archaeological evidence suggests 9th century BCE. It concludes that the epic belongs to the Iron age and, therefore, to about 1100 to 1000 BCE.

Although the narrative aspects of the epic are well-known, it is the emergence of Lord Krishna as a friend and benefactor of the Pandavas that deserves closer attention, more so because the text of the "Song Celestial" (as Sir Edwin Arnold, who translated this into English, put it) or the Bhagavad-gita (as a discourse between Arjuna, the Pandava hero, and Krishna, as his charioteer, on the battlefield of Kurukshetra), is an integral part of the epic. While there may be differences of views as to when the Bhagavad-gita was composed (many scholars date to about the 5th or 4th century BCE), there can be no doubt as to its status as a sacred text that followed soon after the Upanishads. In a way, the Gita also marked a phase leading to the progressive decline of heterodoxies outside the text and thoughts of the Rigveda and the Upanishads, such as that of the "*pancharatras*", the "*apulobdhi*", the "*ajivikas*", Buddhism, etc.; although these were not extinguished entirely.

    Prosenjit Dasgupta

This re-interpretation and re-formulation of the metaphysics of the Rigveda and the Upanishads made *bhakti*, or the path of devotion central in the Bhagavad-gita, without entirely abandoning the *karma* (system of rituals) aspects of the Rigveda or the *jnana* (path of knowledge or self-realisation) theme of the Upanishads.

Once again, much as the Upanishads had done before it, the Bhagavad-gita takes the form of a discourse, or a question and answer session, between Arjuna and Lord Krishna. Here, the latter talks and explains about dharma (what is righteous) for a person, karma or dutiful action without any attachment to the fruits of such action, jnana or training of the mind, and bhakti or selfless devotion to the godhead. Finally, Krishna blesses Arjuna with the *Visvarupa Darshana* or his universal self, encompassing all creatures and actions, brilliant as the thousand suns, emphasizing the temporary and perishable nature of the body and the eternal imperishable soul, and calling upon Arjuna completely and wholly to surrender unto him. Many sages and scholars have delved into the text and philosophies of the Bhagavad-gita, from Adi Shankara in the ancient times to Swami Vivekananda, Shri Aurobindo and Mahatma Gandhi in more modern times. While Shankara relied on it to develop his Vedantist *Advaita* philosophy, the later savants mostly took it that the battlefield of Kurukshetra was an allegory for the soul of man, and the eternal conflict between good and evil within him. The Gita strove to balance the karma (action) and dharma (duty) of the householder, with the search for knowledge by the sages and surrender (by the "bhakta" or devotee in devotion to the Creator and the Supreme Being. In this way, it attempted to lay out for man the path to strive for *moksha*, or liberation from the commonly-accepted cycle of birth and re-birth through self-realization and knowledge of the Supreme Being, which has been a central theme of Indian philosophical thought since the Rigveda, and more so in the Upanishads.

One may refer in this connection to the oft-repeated verses of the Bhagavad-gita, which run as follows -

"...paritranaya sadhunam
vinashaya cha dushkritam
dharma-samsthapanarthaya
sambhavami yuge yuge"

That is, for providing succour to the good and the pious, for annihilation of the wicked, and to re-establish the path of righteousness, Lord Krishna promised to appear and re-appear from time to time.

That this is very close to the idea of the Maitreya Buddha, who is to appear sometime in the future to spread compassion and restore ethical living, or to the Saviour who, Christians believe, will bring salvation to all mankind, or the belief in the Mahdi in Islam, is notable. It also confirms the persistence of an idea of the great significance attached to righteousness that has illuminated Indian philosophical thinking through the millennia.

At the same time, it would do well to recall at this stage that the quiescence that India had enjoyed since the Rigvedic and Upanishadic periods, from about 1500 BCE till about the time of the Buddha around 500 BCE, was broken by the Achaemenid conquest of north-west India that took place around 518 BCE (as per the Behistun inscription of Darius I, in Iran). Political penetrations possibly began even earlier around 580 BCE under Cyrus the Great. Then came the invasion by Alexander the Great in 327 BCE (again into north-west India) and the line of Bactrian or Indo-Greek kings who served in north-western India till up to the 1st century BCE. The Scythian (the *Sakas* in Indian history) invasions followed in the 2nd century BCE, followed closely by the Parthians. That these events considerably affected large tracts of the Indian sub-continent, from Afghanistan to the Indus Valley, into Punjab and western India (and further up to Ujjain and

Mathura, in the case of the Sakas) is a fact that that must be borne in mind. To what extent these invasions affected and influenced lives and thoughts in India is something that only scholars can shed light on; but it would be a fair surmise that they did not leave India unaffected. Some scholars, in fact, consider that this was the same time that the idea of the *Kali Yuga* emerged, as a period of discord, disruptions and strife, which followed the preceding *Satya Yuga, Treta Yuga* and *Dvapara Yuga*, as commonly believed in India. It would not be too presumptuous to believe that such incursions and consequent wars and strife led—by way of reaction—to the identification and consolidation of the so-called "Hindu way of life" that was to gather momentum under the Imperial Guptas from the 5th century CE.

Considering the Bhagavad-gita purely from a philosophical point of view, it brought about at the time a great synthesis between previous beliefs and monotheism (i.e., a belief that there is only one God, or Supreme Reality), put forward in more than one verse of the Rigveda, and a balance between monotheism and monism (i.e., a hankering for oneness with God) that the Upanishads tended towards. Through its predominant devotional or bhakti precepts, the Gita brought together different strands of the prayer and ritual-based life of the ordinary householder, the lofty metaphysics of the Rigveda and the Upanishads, and a devoted and devotional quest for a personal god. The Bhagavad-gita is, therefore, noted for its espousal of *karma yoga* (expression of devotion through action and worshipful activity of the ordinary householder), *jnana yoga* (the constant striving for realization of truth and God, as seen in the life of sages, such as Adi Shankara) and *bhakti yoga* (the unceasing yearning for nearness to a personal god, exemplified by Meera and Ramakrishna Paramahamsa).

If the Bhagavad-gita provided a philosophy of life to India, then the epic *Ramayana* provided a code of conduct. Overlapping in time to some extent with the Mahabharata, the Ramayana, in the views of several scholars, is thought to have been composed around the 4th century BCE to about 3rd century CE. It is not mentioned in Panini's "Astadhayi" of the 5th century BCE and gained prominence in the 8th/9th century *Puranas* (or, ancient histories and genealogies, about which more later). The Ramayana comprises 24,000 verses divided into seven *kandas* or books, and about 500 chapters. It is traditionally ascribed to the great sage, Valmiki, who is considered to have lived in Kosala at the turn of the 4th century BCE. Scholars consider that the epic Ramayana, as it stands today, was progressively built up from the initial 12,000 verses of Valmiki with the later additions of the *"Balakanda"* and the *"Uttarakanda"* (Footnote to pages 32-33 in Whaling – see Bibliography). Questions have also been raised by some as to whether the Ramayana adequately deals with the issues of *rajadharma*, relative to the *Kshatriya* dharma of Lord Rama. It is seldom, if ever, that an epic poem becomes so fundamental to the life and culture of any country as the Ramayana has in all parts of India. It forms a part of later Buddhist tracts through the *"Dasaratha Jataka"*, besides finding reference in Jain holy literature. It has been transcribed into Tamil by Kamban in the 12th century AD, into Telegu in the 14th century, into Bengali by Krittibas in the 15th century, and of course, the immensely popular *"Ramacharitamanasa"* (RCM in short) by Goswami Tulsidas in the 16th century. In fact, Paula Richman (see Bibliography) makes the important point that the original Ramayana by Valmiki being in Sanskrit, did not quite capture the popular imagination in the same way as Tulsidas's RCM did. Through his lilting phrases and cadenced verses in *Braja-bhasha*, Tulsidas brought the Ramayana close to the people, and to enter (as it were) the popular psyche by repeated recitation from one generation to the other. It is interesting to note, though, that Tulsidas omits in the RCM, the episodes of Rama calling into question Sita's conduct while confined in Ravana's palace in Lanka and her later exile from Ayodhya, as

                    Prosenjit Dasgupta

it is found in Valmiki's version. Moreover, while Valmiki and the "*Adhyatma Ramayana*" (part of the *Brahmanda Purana*, said to have been composed by the sage, Ramananda) have relatively small sections on Rama's marriage to Sita, Tulsidas devoted much more space to this, giving full rein to his poetic genius.

As Frank Whaling (see Bibliography) has observed, Tulsidas was faced with growing Muslim power in India, which required a unified response irrespective of caste or creed, in which his hero, Lord Rama, could well represent the Kshatriya caste dharma. Tulsidas also vacillated between holding Sita as the *adi-sakti* of Rama (or the original power, as in RCM I.152.2) while at the same time commenting "*ati daruna dukhada mayarupi nari*" (or, the extreme unhappiness that the guiles of women can bring about, in RCM III.43). If this is taken as poetic licence, then RCM may find it difficult in critical circles to rise above being an epic poem into a sacred text. Richman has mentioned other points that deserve careful attention, such as the shooting of Bali in the back, or of the killing of the Shudra, Sambuka, for his asceticism; these do not detract, however, from the deep veneration that people, in general, have for the Ramayana and the personage of Lord Rama himself. But it needs to be noted that Richman is not singular in pointing some of these discrepancies. Bhavabhuti's "*Uttararamacharita*", the "*Adhyatma Ramayana*", and some Telegu texts have also done so.

Nonetheless, with time, the principal characters in the epic, such as Lord Rama, Sita, Lakshmana, Bharata, the heroic Hanumana, and it may be said, even the demon-king Ravana, have become deeply embedded in the belief systems and popular cultural traditions in India. Indeed, Ramayana, as few other things have, has also become immensely popular in countries like Thailand, Cambodia and Indonesia and has entered intimately into their cultural life.

While the Bhagavad-gita, as elaborated by Lord Krishna,

advised people to accept and to follow his sayings, the Ramayana guided people to act and conduct themselves as per the example and conduct of the *Purushottama* (or, the ideal man), Lord Rama. As Whaling has put it in his book, Rama's life on Earth was a constant sacrifice to bear the burden of grief and unhappiness and still uphold the dharma, variously understood as upholding of the established order, rules of conduct, and eager fulfilment of duties. The first section of people to revere Lord Rama were the Tamil Alvar poets in the 9th century CE. Later, it was taken up by the *Ramanandis* (or the followers of sage Ramananda who lived near Benaras around 1350-1400 CE). As Whaling puts it, if Lord Krishna was a Great Teacher, then Lord Rama was a Great Example to people at large.

Chapter 9

The Eight-fold Path and Onwards

By about the turn of the 6th century BCE, Indian history was slowly emerging from the chrysalis in which it had laid dormant for more than a thousand years, sheltered by the oceans on either side, and the snow-covered mountains to the north. Change was coming and it was gathering pace. No more the dormancy of millennia, but the rigours of multiple centuries.

This was the time of Gautama, the Buddha, and of Mahavira, the great teacher of the Jaina faith. According to the Buddhist sacred texts and most scholars, Gautama was a prince of the Sakya clan of the Kshatriya caste who was born, most possibly, in 563 BCE during the reign of king Bimbisara in Magadha in what is now north-central Bihar. He lived for about 80 years till 443 BCE, during the reign of king Ajatasatru, also of Magadha. Gautama had been much cosseted by his father and lived in royal, but isolated, splendour in the palace. It is said that sometime after his marriage and the birth of his son, Rahula, he happened to see some sick and suffering people on one of his infrequent visits outside the palace and felt disturbed, and started to think about the causes of such suffering and death. By this time, the ascetic and meditative life of the Jain *tirthankaras* (or, those who show the way forward) like Rishabhanatha, Neminatha, and Parshvanatha, who sought true knowledge to overcome human anger, greed, pride, attachment, etc., had come to be appreciated among many people. Mahavira, the twenty-fourth tirthankara in the Jain tradition, had preceded Gautama by a few years and had started preaching. There were other teachers at that time, such as Sanjaya Belatthaputta, Makkali Goshala, Alara Kalama and others who had adopted ascetic ways and were preaching of a simpler, more meditative type of life. It is said that at the age of twenty-nine, Gautama left the palace and his family to embrace the life of a *Sramana* or mendicant. His fierce asceticism and hard meditation left him very much weak until one day, after taking some sweets offered by a young girl, Sujata, in a small village, Gautama became convinced that asceticism was not the way forward. This turned his mind to the "Middle Way" that did not rely either on harsh asceticism or on a life of indulgence, but focussed on moderation in all manners of things. Gautama reached his final realization of "truth" or "enlightenment" at the age of about thirty-five while meditating for a number of days under an *asthvatha* (Ficus religiosa) tree at Bodh Gaya. He came to realize the Four Noble Truths – that life is impermanent, that craving leads to dissatisfaction and suffering, and in turn leads to repeated cycles of re-birth and pain, and that the way to break out of this cycle is to strive for nirvana (or, cessation). To help common people strive towards this nirvana, Gautama, the Buddha (or, the all-knowing), preached the Eight-fold Path that should guide and govern day-to-day life; these being (i) right speech, (ii) right conduct, (iii) right effort, (iv) right way to a livelihood, (v) right view, (vi) right resolve, (vii) right mindfulness and (viii) right meditation. This is exemplified in the "dharma chakra" with its eight spokes in a wheel (of life), commonly used in Buddhist iconography. The Buddha put forward a framework towards practical, compassionate and ethical way of life, away from the previous recurring patterns of rituals and sacrifices, so that an individual could progressively better himself or herself. It is of note that the Buddha provided space (in the 5th century BCE) to women joining the Sangha and the sramanic way of life, if they should so choose. There is enough evidence of the role and position of women in the 2nd century BCE in the inscriptions found at Sanchi, the famous Buddhist *stupa* (or, votive mound) near Bhopal in central India.

                               Prosenjit Dasgupta

By the time Buddha was about eighty years of age, after decades of preaching to his disciples and to commoners in many places up and down the country, he felt his end (or *parinirvana*) was near and advised his close disciples to prepare for it. After a brief illness, the Buddha passed away into *mahaparinirvana*, that is, total cessation of the cycle of birth and re-birth. That Buddha and the Buddhist precepts had a profound influence in India would be an understatement. From Afghanistan to the far north of the sub-continent, along the length and breadth of the country, and into peninsular India, Buddhism held sway for centuries. It affected king and commoner alike, and the best testament to that are the edicts of Emperor Ashoka, of which more later. Even if Buddhism went into relative decline in India since about the 8th century CE onwards, its living presence among the *Dalits* (or, the Untouchables, or lowly castes, in India) in large tracts of central and peninsular India (as well as among the people of Bhutan, Sikkim and many other places in north-east India, as well as in Tibet) testifies to its significance even in modern times. Buddhism also deeply influenced the thought and way of life in many of the neighbouring countries, notably Tibet, medieval China, Thailand, Cambodia, Laos, Japan, etc., and this persists till today.

Bhagavan Mahavira, the twenty-fourth among the Jain tirthankaras preceded Gautama Budhha by a few years but apparently predeceased him. His asceticism and search for knowledge is too well known to bear repetition. It was from him that the concept and practice of *ahimsa* or non-violence has been largely derived, which illuminated the path of Mahatama Gandhi in the struggle for India's independence. Bhagavan Mahavira stood for truth, and *aparigraha* or non-attachment that also culminated in Gandhi's *anasakti* (abandonment of desires) yoga. Mahavira preached *brahmacharya* or chastity, and *anekantavada* (or, the many-sided reality) that may be considered as an extension of the Rigvedic *bahuda vadanti* observation. As given earlier in the text, the Rigveda has several mentions that while there is One Supreme Reality, it is considered by many as being numerous—bahuda—realities. The anekantavada of Mahavira mirrors this One amidst many aspects. In many respects, these tenets are still widely respected and practised in India.

The teachings of the Buddha and of Bhagavan Mahavira have been mostly enshrined in the sacred texts of the Buddhists and the Jains, namely, the *"Tripitaka"*, the *"Dhammapada"* and the *"Agamas"*, which continue to remain popular subjects for study and research.

It is thought that some of these texts had come into use by 6th century BCE (or, perhaps a couple of centuries later); however, those currently available for study are either later copies of some of the earlier texts, or even later commentaries and notes of the 4th or 5th century CE. Thus, one moves progressively from indirect, pre-historic evidence of man in India based on the stone implements, rock paintings, etc., to the Indus valley seals, and then on to written script - and thus to history as commonly understood. One of the outstanding scholars in this field has been Vasudev Saran Agrawala with his researches and notes on *"Manusmriti"* and the *"Ashtadhayayi"* of Panini (see Bibliography). These take us in a trice to the 6th or 7th century BCE and hold up a picture of India as it was then. To begin with, Dr Agrawala mentions that there was more than one redaction of the Manusmriti, the text developed by that ancient lawgiver, Manu, much revered and much-quoted even today. Agrawala, in fact, asserts that it is impossible to state with certainty that Manu lived in this or that period of history. It does seem that parts of Manu's work precede Yaska (6th century BCE), but some parts are also post-Buddhist (i.e., after 4th century BCE). In sum, the Manusmriti was a manual designed for the general masses, culled from pre-existing traditions and customs, beliefs and ceremonies (on Manusmriti - Agrawala, page 7). There are several aspects

　　　　Prosenjit Dasgupta

of Indian history to be learnt from the text of the Manusmriti (as researched by Dr Agrawala) about the state of the polity and the economy in India. What is interesting to note is that there were then various academies ("*charanas*") studying different recessions of the respective Vedas, and *the distinctions between the ritualistic and philosophic elements in the Vedas were well-known* (emphasis added). The caste system was in place and the imparting instructions in the Vedas were confined only to the Brahmans. Towns and cities had come up, with houses built of bricks, stone and timber. There were assembly halls, shops, artisans' dwellings, taverns and theatres. There were inter-caste marriages, leading to *anuloma* and *pratiloma* categories of such marriages, and consequently, the status of such marriages. Food comprised of barley, wheat, rice, milk, curds, honey, meat, fruits and vegetables. Women used collyrium, perfumes, flower garlands and ornaments. Manu prescribed that governments should suppress social parasites such as extortionists, fortune-tellers, palmists, astrologers and corrupt officials (Manu, IX, 258-263). Usury was socially and morally condemned. *Jatis* were caste organisations with the power of legislatures, and *srenis* were guilds of artisans, with rules binding the courts. With regard to religious beliefs, Manu distinguished between *pravritti* and *nivritti*, with the former designed to ensure happiness here on Earth and the latter believed in *moksha* and knowledge without attachment. Manu specifically mentioned "*Ksharanti sarva vaidikyo juhoyajati kriya*" or "All offerings and sacrifices are of perishable results, only Brahma is imperishable" (II.84).

This work on Manu by Dr V.S. Agrawala is surpassed by his other work, "India as Known to Panini" (see Bibliography). Panini, as is well-known, was a notable grammarian of India in the 5th century BCE (others being Patanjali and Katyayana, who followed him), coming somewhat after Yaska, but before the Buddhist period. His work, the "*Ashtadhyayi*", in eights books or parts, comprising 3995 *sutras* or rules for following

Sanskrit grammar of the day, brings together an enormous body of knowledge about India in those distant days. The very fact that Panini's birth is placed at Salature, near the confluence of the Indus and Kabul rivers (Preface to "India as Known to Panini", page 34) tells its own story. Panini gives considerable details of the geography of the country from Kamboja near the Pamir Mountains to Kalinga (modern-day Odisha), besides those of Magadha and Pataliputra that he personally visited. He noted the prevalence of the caste system and refers to a descending order of social ordering from *janapada* (province) to *varna*, to *jati, gotra, sapinda, sanabhi, jnati, samyukta, kula,* to *vamsa,* and finally to *grihapati* or the householder. There was good knowledge about the planets or naskhatra, being named as Krittika, Mrigasirsha, Phalguni, Visakha and so on. Panini has also mentioned the co-existence of both kingdoms and self-governing republics of clans. Apparently, at that time, there were more than 37 cities with populations of more than 5,000 in the area between the upper courses of the Jhelum, the Chandrabhaga and Ravi rivers. Unfortunately, infanticide seems to have been practiced at that time. There was also the practice in that time of Brahmans and other learned men congregating for conferences at one major city or the other to place on record, and to debate their findings on agriculture, medicine, etc. Panini is said to have travelled to Magadha for this same purpose. Panini knew about the epic Mahabharata and also cites texts dealing with the legend of Lord Rama (though more for its significance for the legends about Parashurama and Yayati). He underlined the role of the academies or charanas in analysing, debating and interpreting the different *sakha* (subsidiary or branch) texts, which developed over time into distinctive Brahmanas, Aranyakas, Upanishads, and the *Shrauta Sutra. Vada* or debate and *vivada* or discussions were the order of the day of the charanas. Dr Agrawala then goes on to make the pertinent observation: "With the development of the *Dharma-sutra or legal literature, there set in a process of*

                    Prosenjit Dasgupta

gradual separation between the secular and scientific studies on the one hand and religious and ritualistic studies on the other" (page 301, emphasis added). Again, a little later, Dr Agrawala points out: "Dharma had a 2-fold meaning in the Ashtadhyayi – dharma as *"achara"* or customs and usage (Panini, VI.2.65 – including legal dues) and dharma as religious or moral duties" (Panini, IV.4.41 – page 388). Panini himself mentions several moral virtues valued in that time, such as *prajna* (knowledge), *shraddha* (respect), *tapa* (meditation), *tyaga* (charity), *viveka* (conscience), *dharma* (religious practices), *sama* (balance) and *dama* (restraint). Dr Agrawala also makes the important point that Panini went strictly by the common usage and practice: "Panini invokes the invariable authority of usage, both linguistic and social" (I. 2.53 – page 349). As Dr Agrawala puts it, "This attitude to the realities of life resulted in a secularization of knowledge as patent in the Ashtadhayyi and was not tied to the chariot wheels of Vedic schools" (page 350). Only a glimpse of a small part of the book, "India as Known to Panini" (which runs to well-over 400 printed pages), is provided here, and interested readers would do well to refer to the original text for many other interesting findings. One is led to agree with Dr Agrawala that in Panini one observes a certain scientific detachment in his exposition that gives him a special value in understanding of the history of India at that point of time in the 5th century BCE.

Contributions to Indian history—though, by no means, quite as exhaustive as that of Panini's Ashtadhyayi—include the fragments of notings left by the Greek historians, Megasthenes, Strabo and Arrian (see J.W. McCrindle, in Bibliography), about India around the time of Alexander's conquest of north-western parts of the country in 326 BCE; that is, about a couple of centuries after Panini. The Greeks noted that Aryans were surrounded by indigenous tribes living in what they called as a state of barbarism. They also took note of the caste system. They identified seven castes, including philosophers, husbandmen, shepherds, artisans, warriors, etc., i.e., a system that was more occupational than hereditary. Possibly bearing in mind the tradition in Greece, they observed that: *"People here have no written laws, are ignorant of writing, and in all business of life, trust to memory"* (page 68 in McCrindle, emphases added). Here is, therefore, another bit of corroborative evidence that for some reason, the written script developed somewhat later in India. Another interesting observation is that: "Brachmans (i.e., the Brahmans – parenthesis added) do not communicate their knowledge of philosophy to their wives (lest) they should divulge any of the forbidden mysteries…they say that the Deity who made it (the Earth) and who governs it, is diffused through all its parts (pages 98-103)…They consider that all men are held in bondage by innate enemies like sensual appetite, gluttony, anger, and it is the man who has triumphed over them who goes to God" (page 120). They also noted some observations about the Brachmans (or Brahmans) and *Sarmanes* (or sramanas or mendicants, most probably the Buddhist monks). The former lived in groves near cities in a simple way, sleeping on mats of reeds or on deer skin, eating frugally and listening to serious discourse. The latter lived in woods, usually ate fruits, and wore clothes made from barks of trees. The very fact that Megasthenes was sent as an ambassador by the Greek general Seleucus in 302 BCE to the court of Chandragupta Maurya at Pataliputra testifies to kingdoms, especially that of Magadha, and to a tradition of diplomatic discourse.

While the notes and commentaries in Manusmriti, the Ashtadhyayi and those of Megasthenes and Strabo are general in nature as to the conditions and practices in India, the edicts and inscriptions that follow after the passage of another century in the time of Emperor Ashoka, around the middle of the 3rd century BCE, are more specific to particular rulers and the nature of their rule. What is more, they have remained largely unaltered, except and to the extent they were affected

        Prosenjit Dasgupta

by the elements. These have also not been subjected to any redactions and recessions as were the shrutis and smritis of the preceding centuries. As such, in what may be called historical times, that is, when hard evidence of archaeological remains, inscriptions and edicts, coins, etc., are to be more widely found, there came the great empires commencing from Chandragupta Maurya in the 4th century BCE, through Emperor Ashoka in the 3rd century BCE, to the Imperial Guptas in the 5th/6th century CE. In this, the pride of place goes obviously to the edicts of Emperor Ashoka (reigned 272 to 232 BCE) from about the middle of the 3rd century BCE. These provide a remarkable chronicle of the reign of Ashoka, and some of these are quoted below in full, so that the reader may have an appreciation of his thoughts and concerns, as well as a glimpse of the contemporary history of India.

The 2nd rock edict at Ranighat –*"Everywhere in the empire of the Beloved of the Gods, the king Piyadassi, and even in the lands on its frontiers, those of the Cholas, Pandyas, Satyaputras, Keralaputras, and as far as Ceylon, and of the Greek king named Antiochus and of those kings who are neighbours of that Antiochus, everywhere the two medical services of the Beloved of the Gods, the king Piyadassi, have been provided. These consist of the medical care of man and the care of animals. Medicinal herbs, whether useful to man or to beast, have been brought and planted wherever they did not grow; similarly, roots and fruit have been brought and planted wherever they did not grow. Along the roads, wells have been dug and trees planted for the use of men and beasts."*

The 9th rock edict at Kandahar – *"Thus spake the beloved of the Gods, the king Piyadassi: People practice various ceremonies. In illness, at the marriage of sons and daughters, at the birth of children, when going on a journey – on these, and other similar occasions, people perform many ceremonies. Women especially perform a variety of ceremonies, which are trivial and useless. If such ceremonies must be performed, they have but small results.*

But the one ceremony that is of great value is that of Dhamma. This ceremony includes regard for slaves and servants, respect for teachers, restrained behaviour towards living beings and donations to sramanas and Brahmanas. These, and similar practices, are called the ceremony of Dhamma. So, father, son, brother, master, acquaintance and neighbours should think, 'This is the virtuous ceremony I should practise until my objective is achieved'."

The 13th rock edict at Girnar –"*When he had been consecrated eight years the Beloved of the Gods, the king Piyadassi, conquered Kalinga. A hundred and fifty thousand people were deported, a hundred thousand were killed, and many times that number perished. Afterwards, now that Kalinga was annexed, the Beloved of the Gods very earnestly practised Dhamma, desired Dhamma, and taught Dhamma. On conquering Kalinga, the Beloved of the Gods felt remorse, for, when an independent country is conquered, the slaughter, death, and deportation of the people is extremely grievous to the Beloved of the Gods, and weighs heavily on his mind. What is even more deplorable to the Beloved of the Gods, is that those who dwell there, whether Brahmans, sramanas, or those of other sects, or householders who show obedience to their superiors, obedience to mother and father, obedience to their teachers and behave well and devotedly towards their friends, acquaintances, colleagues, relatives, slaves, and servants - all suffer violence, murder, and separation from their loved ones. Even those who are fortunate to have escaped, and whose love is undiminished [by the brutalizing effect of war], suffer from the misfortunes of their friends, acquaintances, colleagues, and relatives. This participation of all men in suffering, weighs heavily on the mind of the Beloved of the Gods. Except among the Greeks, there is no land where the religious orders of Brahmanas and sramanas are not to be found, and there is no land anywhere where men do not support one sect or another. Today, if a hundredth or a thousandth part of those people who were killed or died or were*

                     Prosenjit Dasgupta

deported when Kalinga was annexed were to suffer similarly, it would weigh heavily on the mind of the Beloved of the Gods.

"The Beloved of the Gods believes that one who does wrong should be forgiven as far as it is possible to forgive him. And the Beloved of the Gods conciliates the forest tribes of his empire, but he warns them that he has power even in his remorse and he asks them to repent, lest they be killed. For the Beloved of the Gods wishes that all beings should be unharmed, self-controlled, calm in mind, and gentle.

"The Beloved of the Gods considers victory by Dhamma to be the foremost victory. And, moreover, the Beloved of the Gods has gained this victory on all his frontiers to a distance of six hundred yojanas [i.e., about 1500 miles], where reigns the Greek king named Antiochus, and beyond the realm of that Antiochus in the lands of the four kings named Ptolemy, Antigonus, Magas, and Alexander; and in the south over the Cholas and Pandyas, as far as Ceylon. Likewise, here in the imperial territories among the Greeks and the Kambojas, Nabhakas and Nabhapanktis, Bhojas and Pitinikas, Andhras and Parindas, everywhere the people follow the Beloved of the Gods' instructions in Dhamma. Even where the envoys of the Beloved of the Gods have not gone, people hear of his conduct according to Dhamma, his precepts and his instruction in Dhamma, and they follow Dhamma and will continue to follow it.

"What is obtained by this is victory everywhere, and everywhere victory is pleasant. This pleasure has been obtained through victory by Dhamma, yet, it is but a slight pleasure, for the Beloved of the Gods only looks upon that as important in its results which pertains to the next world.

"This inscription of Dhamma has been engraved so that any sons or great grandsons that I may have should not think of gaining new conquest, and in whatever victories they may gain should be satisfied with patience and light punishment. They should only consider conquest by Dhamma to be a true *conquest, and delight in Dhamma should be their whole delight, for this is of value in both this world and the next."*

Perhaps the most pertinent for present times are the contents of the major rock edict (No. 12, at Shahbaz Garhi) – *"But Beloved-of-the-Gods, King Piyadasi, does not value gifts and honours, as much as he values this -- that there should be growth in the essentials of all religions. Growth in essentials can be done in different ways, but all of them have as their root restraint in speech, that is, not praising one's own religion, or condemning the religion of others without good cause. And if there is cause for criticism, it should be done in a mild way. But it is better to honour other religions for this reason. By so doing, one's own religion benefits, and so do other religions, while doing otherwise harms one's own religion and the religions of others. Whoever praises his own religion, due to excessive devotion, and condemns others with the thought, "Let me glorify my own religion," only harms his own religion. Therefore, contact (between religions) is good. One should listen to and respect the doctrines professed by others. Beloved-of-the-Gods, King Piyadasi, desires that all should be well-learned in the good doctrines of other religions."*

Straight-off, the foregoing edicts indicate much about the extent of Ashoka's empire. It extended from near Afghanistan and its adjoining areas to Gujarat and beyond. Some of the other edicts show that the empire extended well into modern-day Bihar and peninsular India (i.e., Karnataka). The extent of Ashoka's empire in the 3rd century BCE was about as much what the Mughals were able to achieve in the 17th and 18th centuries CE, and what the British did by the middle of the 19th century. The edicts mention some of the leading ruling clans, such as the Cholas, Pandyas, Kambojas, Kalingas and Andhras. They indicate some of the Indo-Greek kings who ruled in the Gandhara region to the west of Afghanistan. The edicts note Ashoka's observations about women undertaking many rituals. It shows his concern about reconciling the

        Prosenjit Dasgupta

forest tribes. It reports the building of roads and wells for the welfare of travellers and the cultivation of medicinal plants for the care and cure of animals and human beings. Most of all, it underscores his advice to practice restraint in speech, so as not unduly to hurt others. Ashoka died in 232 BCE; but his thoughts and words have lived on for centuries (and are still discussed and appreciated today) and later kings such as Kanishka largely carried on with his principles, and people over generations largely imbibed and inculcated these principles into their day-to-day lives. The basic ethical values and humanism that Ashoka preached, and which informed his administration, endured for long because they incorporated certain basic truths and human values, and may be said to have prevailed to a very considerable extent even into the 20th century.

This was also the time that the well-known *"Artha Sashtra"* is said to have been written by Chanakya (also known as Kautilya), the minister of Chandragupta Maurya. While this tract is often considered to have been written in the 2nd century BCE, the first historical references appear in the Buddhist *"Mahavamsa"* text of Sri Lanka sometime in the 5th century CE. The text of the Artha Sashtra was discovered by chance in 1905 in the Oriental Research Institute in Mysore. It discusses what it considered the basic sources of knowledge, these being the Vedas (from which Dharma, or what is right and moral is understood) besides the further notions of *Nyay* or justice, *anvishaki* (based on Samkhya logic system) and the *Lokayata* (or, existential common-sense practices). The text extols the "sage king" or *"raja rishi"*, who avoids distraction by the senses, and steers clear of flattering advisors. Such a king tries to learn continuously and thinks over what he has learnt. Such a sage king tries at all times to enrich and empower his people, and, thus, gains the loyalty of his subjects. He ought to have a council of learned elders and appoint ministers and officials who should be well trained, being firm in thought and action, and yet well-spoken, enthusiastic about the nature of work assigned to them, of high character, and also possess a kind and philanthropic disposition, free from hate and enmity, and dedicated to justice and righteousness. Thus, it could be said that *Raj Dharma*, that is the course of action that a sagacious king must follow, is always to keep the subjects in mind, and to tend to their welfare. It must be remembered that in drawing up this treatise, Chanakya (whose religious inclinations are not chronicled) may well have been considerably influenced by Jainism (his monarch, Chandragupta Maurya, is said to have embraced Jainism in later life), as well as by Buddhism, which were the more popular religions in India between 6th century BCE and 4th century CE, i.e., for a thousand years. To a considerable extent, this links up with the kingship (especially in the later phase) of Ashoka.

This chapter is entitled as "The Eight-fold Path"; but that is only in the conventional sense of being able to rely on some definite records. History, in a wider sense, began with the finds of stone tools like stone scrapers and stone axes that the pre-historic man used in India, about 25,000 to 30,000 years ago. History is also to be found in the rock art of primitive man in caves dating back to 8,000 to 10,000 years; and it is very much there in the Indus Valley seals of about 2500 BCE discussed in an earlier section. Thus, history is largely, if not entirely, about understanding and interpreting oral, written and material records and evidence, and these stretch back (as mentioned above) from stone implements to ancient archaeological remains, clay or steatite seals, edicts on stone, inscriptions on metal, coins and, of course, manuscripts, mostly on palm leaves. This itself suggests that the use of paper or paper-like material (such as the use of papyrus in Egypt around 2500 BCE), or leather, as in many parts of the Middle East since the beginning of the Christian era, for writing purposes, had not developed in India in those early times.

India has been fortunate to have contemporary records of

                    Prosenjit Dasgupta

events and personalities, since about the 3rd century BCE, on palm-leaf manuscripts, stone edicts and sculptures and inscriptions on both stone and metal. Anyone who has been to Sanchi or to Ajanta and Ellora, or to the Buddhist sites at Karla, Bhoja or Kanheri, or to Udyagiri-Khandagiri in Odisha, would have found themselves confronted with contemporary pictures of the life of the kings and commoners dating back about two millennia, by way of sculptures and frescos. These "speak" to the modern scholar far more directly, clearly and loudly than oral traditions are capable of doing. Some may be representations of narratives (like the "*Jatakas*") or legends, but all pictorialize contemporary life and concerns. It would be no over-statement to say that there is no equal historical documentation in India in stone or in frescos of similar provenance dating back to the 3rd millennium BCE. If something has not been so recorded in seals, edicts, sculptures and paintings, it is just because it was not considered important enough to record it (in the period since the 3rd millennium BCE, or even earlier), or just had not occurred in the same manner as later popular accounts have it, or have been lost to the ravages of time. Notably, while images of the *Varahavatar* of Vishnu, are seen to appear in many places by the 7th and 8th century CE, representations in statuary of Yudhisthira, Arjuna, and Lord Rama, so well known through the epics, are conspicuous by their absence or are hardly to be seen. Why this should be so, is a question to ponder. As compared to this, the earliest authenticated documents in Devanagari script of Sanskrit date back to about the 2nd-4th centuries CE.

Supplementing the rock edicts, sculptures and the like (which are fewer in numbers) are the shorter and more localized inscriptions in stone and metal, said to number nearly one lakh specimens as of now. Interestingly, the largest number of such inscriptions have been discovered in the Telegu-Kannada-Tamil region. Many specialists and scholars have pored over such inscriptions for years, so as to be able to provide valuable inputs that assist in reconstructing genealogies of kings, and about current social, religious and political and administrative thinking and practices. They have immensely helped in the study of the development of languages in India. Many, if not most of the inscriptions, relate to land grants. It would appear that the local kings had usually to purchase the land from peasants to obtain proprietary rights but could not directly confiscate land for this purpose. This was contrary to the British and European practice, where the king was considered the holder of the land and granted land for services rendered by the barons. The land grants were often to learned Brahmans who collected no revenues nor rendered any military service. But, as D.C. Sircar has pointed out, such land grants were also to *shresthis* or merchants, and even to ascetics. Sircar, who has done much work on inscriptions, has pertinently mentioned in his "Indian Epigraphy" (see Bibliography) that those who prepared the inscriptions suffered from a lack of space, as the tablets on which the relevant details were to be given were limited in size, often being just a few inches in length and breadth. Thus, information had to be compressed, or only partially given. Any corrections to be made also mutilated the inscriptions and made parts of it illegible. Details of dates quoted in such inscriptions at times contained mistakes, owing to errors in making calculations from astronomical data, as well as a tendency among ruling families since the early medieval era to fabricate a respectable genealogy. Sircar has also pointed out that while the solar year was taken as comprising 365 days, the lunar year was only 354 days, and further adjustments had to be made for the *mala* (or inauspicious) months. In his book, "Indian Epigraphy", Sircar has referred to the differences in the determination of the commencement of the so-called Kali Yuga, which, based on the Aihole inscription of 634 CE and certain other sources, was taken as 3102 BCE, while the traditions of Varahamihira (a great medieval astronomer) and Kalhan (the compiler of the Kashmir royal genealogies) would place it around 2449 BCE, connected to the birth of Parikshit, the grand-nephew of Yudhisthira, (the Pandava king) who was a major figure in the Mahabharata epic. Some scholars also place Parikshit in the 12th century BCE as per Vedic references.

Sircar observes that several scholars have held that Kali Yuga was not a formal phase in time but was more of a "marker" used by Indian astronomers for calculating time. It will be recalled (from an earlier section) that many scholars also hold that the so-called Kali Yuga was the period of repeated incursions and wars on the western borders, beginning with the Achaemenids of Persia, Alexander of Macedon, and the Scythians, in succession. The dating of inscriptions was also influenced by the use of the *Vikram* era by the astronomers in Ujjain at 58 BCE, while some others based their dating on the *Saka* era commencing from 78 CE. Several later astronomers, such as Kamalakar Bhatta in his "*Siddhantatattvaviveka*", have controverted this, as Sircar notes (page 320 in "Indian Epigraphy").

It is only from a patient and painstaking study of a large number of connected inscriptions that a reconstruction of dynastic genealogies, as also of the social, religious, administrative, economic, educational and geographical conditions of a particular period or reign or region could be undertaken. The initial work of James Prinsep, Alexander Cunningham and J. Burgess in collecting and organising the epigraphic remains was greatly expanded by the work of Indian scholars, such as Rajendralal Mitra, R.G. Bhandarkar, Rakhaldas Banerjee, Haraprasad Shastri and others. Thanks to the tireless efforts of a large number of foreign and Indian scholars during the last one hundred and fifty years or so, the foundations of an authenticated political and dynastic history, both for North India as well as South India have been laid, though there are many gaps yet to be filled by future discoveries. These scholars have also briefly touched on the other topics mentioned above, though the abundance of epigraphical materials now available requires detailed study of these topics for different periods and regions.

            Prosenjit Dasgupta

Chapter 11

New light on Puranas and Other Historical Sources

The Puranas, which are principally concerned with the genealogies of kings and historical annotations, provide significant insights and links into pre-medieval India from about the commencement of the Christian era. One of the seminal works on the Puranas has been undertaken by Rajendrachandra Hazra in his "Studies in the Puranic Resources in Hindu Rites and Customs" (see Bibliography). Going through the various Puranas in their original form and linking up the numerous hints and clues from the authoritative transcriptions and annotations thereon, into a comprehensive study with a high degree of objectivity has no doubt been a monumental task on his part.

Notwithstanding the views expressed in certain quarters about the great antiquity of the Puranas, the checking of cross-references in the various Puranas leads Hazra to date the *Mahapuranas* to about 2nd century CE, and the well-known "*Harivamsa*" to 4th century CE. The Puranas began to go beyond the prescribed features of the *sarga* (preface), *pratisarga* (introduction), and *vamsanucharita* (genealogy) into *achara* (practices), *varnasrmadharma* (the caste norms), *prayaschitta* (atonement), *vrata* (vows), *diksha* (instruction and induction) and *tirhtha* (pilgrimage) by about the 4th century CE (page 6 in Hazra). He refers to the repeated redactions in the text of the different Puranas by the addition of new chapters, replacement of older chapters or sections by newer versions, changing the titles of chapters, etc. (page 7). More importantly, he is of the view (as given in the Footnote on page 7 of his book) that the opinions expressed by the earlier commentators and *Nibandhakarakas* (compilers and editors) show that even at a particular point of time, the contents of a particular Purana were different in different parts of India. Hazra makes the important observation (that is often lost sight of) that the rise of Buddhism and Jainism in the 5th century BCE (and their patronage by great kings and emperors of the time such as Bimbisara, Ajatasatru, Nanda, Chandragupta Maurya, Ashoka, Kharavela, Kanishka and others) led to a notable decline in the number of sacrifices and family rituals that had sustained the Brahmans in the earlier centuries. There was also a greater role for women and the rise of Shudra kings and chieftains (as distinct from the Kshatriya kings of old), and all this meant an overall decline in the influence of the Brahmans in society (pages 244-245). It is only to be expected that this decline in the relative position of the Brahmans and the Kshatriyas by the 1st century BCE would have led to a decline in the historical evidence available about them.

Sukumari Bhattacharji (see Bibliography) has corroborated this dating of the Puranas in her book (page 17) and has gone on to suggest that what she has called "neo-brahminism" came to be largely founded through the Puranas and was further consolidated during the time of the imperial Guptas (page 19). This neo-Brahmanism, that is, an attempt to revert to and resuscitate the Brahmanical role in Vedic style rituals and sacrifices, required the co-option of totems, animist beliefs, and cult heroes into the overall pantheon as facets and manifestations of the fundamental Vedic concept of monotheism. These then manifested themselves either as *avatars*, i.e., human or worldly representations, primarily of Lord Vishnu. That there has not been any corresponding thought among the religious pundits of the day regarding the avatars of Lord Siva or of Brahma is itself food for thought. This, Bhattacharji suggests, was due to the progressive absorption or evolution of the absolute monism or *Advaitabad* of Shankara into the later *Dvaitavad*, and thence into Vaishnavism (page

    Prosenjit Dasgupta

313 in Bhattacharji). Progressively, the household rituals and sacrifices written in the Vedas turned into community temple worship, while pilgrimages assumed prominence and rituals and *vratas* proliferated (page 353).

This was also the time when a number of non-Vedic, or even anti-Vedic, sects came to prominence, such as the *pancha-ratra* or the Vaishnavas, who were quite unfavourable towards the *varnasramadharma*, and whose views were reflected in the Samhitas (or compilations) of the time. Furthermore, Vaishnavism (as Bhagavatism) took in foreigners such as Heliodoros, the Bactrian noble, within its fold, as well as Yavanas and Shudras. The *pashupata* or Shaivas (the worshippers of the god Siva, as the lord of beasts) also came to exercise influence and were looked down upon by the smriti writers (i.e., those who relied on existing texts and commentaries, rather than the revealed truth or shruti of the Rigveda), as may be seen from the "*Smriti Chandrika*" (II. 310 – page 201 in Hazra). The *Ajivikas* under Gosala Mankhaliputta rose to prominence around that time. Further, by about the 2nd century BCE, there came the invasions by the Sakas (Scythians).The Huns invaded in 538 CE but were pushed back after a long-drawn battle. Hazra takes the view— with good reason—that the so-called Kali Yuga (or, what may be called, times of hardship), as the Brahmans came to call it, was due to the rise of the heretical sects and of Shudra kings, and the overall turmoil and tribulations due to the invasions. D.C. Sircar, in "Indian Epigraphy", has also drawn attention to the notable rise around that time in the numbers of Shudra and tribal kings and chieftains in many parts of India. It is but natural for most people to seek elevation in status and position over time, and to seek a noble lineage, and these kings and chieftains were no exception. Who was, in any case, going to verify whether they had, in fact, descended from the sun, or the moon, or from the sacred river Ganga?

The Brahmans were happy to oblige with multifarious

vows, atonements, sacrifices, as well as suitable references in the Puranas that were under compilation about that time and later. Whereas in the Vedic age (i.e. around 1500 to about 1000 BCE) the gifts to Brahmans for performance of sacrifices and other rituals ranged from cows, horses, land, clothes, slave girls, etc., in later times, these grew in quantity and value to gifts of artificial cows made of ghee and sugar, horses, chariots, elephants, gems, small mounds of gold, etc. More events were identified for such rituals and sacrifices, e.g., *Samkranti*, *Chaturdashi*, *Ashtami*, *Dvadashi*, or, for curing bad dreams, and later extended to *Amavasya*, *Ekadashi*, etc., related to the phases of the moon – "the more the people gave, the better" (Hazra, page 249). He has also discussed each Purana in detail and provided cross-references that help in noting the similarities and dissimilarities between one Purana and another. One such example will suffice: Gautama Buddha is not enlisted as an avatar or an incarnation of Vishnu in the Vishnu Purana but is shown as such in the Brahmanda Purana. The respective texts also help in highlighting the position of Magadha, Vaishali, Shravasti, Vidisha, Ujjain and Mathura as major centres of learning and for dissemination of knowledge concerning astronomy, medicine, and so on. Of course, under the Imperial Guptas from the 5th century to the 6th century CE, there was flowering of literature, astronomy, the sciences, arts, sculpture, etc. Furthermore, as followers of Vaishnavism, the Guptas no doubt also helped in promoting the various beliefs and practices in the worship of Vishnu; although Buddhism and Jainism also flourished under their regime.

Glimpses of India in the Gupta and the immediate post-Gupta era, around 400 to 600 CE, may be found in the notes left by the two Chinese pilgrims, Fa-hien and Yuan Chwang (also spelt as Huen Tsang or Xuan-Zang). The latter came to India via Kashmir (631 CE) and after extensive travels and studies in Buddhist scriptures, even as far east as Bengal,

     Prosenjit Dasgupta

went back in 645 CE. Notably, he pointed out that the natives had designations for only their regional states, e.g., Magadha, Kausambi, etc., without a general name under which these regions could be included. In fact, he saw that it was the Turks who lived beyond its territories, who gave the name "Yin-tu", or India, to the great territory (see Thomas Watters, in Bibliography, page132). Yuan Chwang found the Kshatriyas and Brahmans to be clear-headed and unostentatious; the dress and ornaments of the kings extra-ordinary. People in general were seen to be somewhat hasty and irresolute and often feared for retribution from their previous lives. He found temples of Pashupata Shaivites near Jalandhar, and again a number of them near Ahichhatra. He saw at Mathura large mango orchards and the presence of several non-Buddhist sects. From Kanauj, Yuan Chwang travelled to Ayodhya, where he found one hundred Buddhist monasteries and about ten "deva" temples and found that the numbers of non-Buddhists were few. This is indeed notable in the light of later claims and developments at Ayodhya. Farther on, at Prayaga, at the confluence of the Ganga and the Yamuna, he found that the majority of the inhabitants were non-Buddhists and this was also the place where Emperor Harshavardhana offered alms to all and sundry (page 364 in Watters). Again, Yuan Chwang travelled north to Kausambi through the "wild country", where he found many deva temples and many non-Buddhists. He then travelled to Benaras (now known as Varanasi) where he again found numerous deva temples and many adherents of different sects, mainly the Shaivites, some of whom had cut their hair, some who kept their hair in a knot, some went naked and some smeared themselves with ash (Watters, vol. II, page 47). Then, at Magadha, he found Buddhists and numerous other sects (vol. II, page 87), while at Gaya, he found a number of families of Brahmans who were reputed to be the descendants of sage Kashyapa. While these notes are no doubt sketchy, they do convey the overall picture as to the co-existence of Buddhism and other sects (particularly the Pashupata Shaivites that he has remarked on) at that point of time in the 7th century CE. He has noted that the country was well-administered and that the people lived on good terms; Yuan Chwang could hardly have travelled so extensively if it had been otherwise. But one question looms large: how is it that a Chinese scholar should have travelled so extensively in India and left these notes, while nothing quite comparable has so far been unearthed from Indian sources. The Puranas, aside from the genealogies, do not provide any reliable historical notes on social and economic conditions on the lines as Yuan Chwang had outlined in his notes, as mentioned above.

In parallel with the Puranas, a large number of *Dharmashastra* texts pertaining to norms of social behaviour and religious practices came to be composed in the early part of the Christian era, which include the *tika* (commentaries on the earlier dharmasutras and smritis according to the times of the composers) and the *nibandha* (collections with comments and conclusions). Manusmriti (a very important document and often quoted even now) and Yajnavalkyasmriti were two such important smritis, widely commented upon by the early medieval commentators, such as Medhatithi on Manusmriti (in the 9th century CE, followed by Kullaka in the 12th century). Vijyaneshvara's *"Mitakshara"* is one of the best known commentaries on the Yajnavalkyasmriti. Aside from the fact that these commentaries help to date the principal smritis, it would appear that there was an increasing formalization of social laws and practices for the firm regulation of the social life of the populace. As a result, Hindu law (as *vyavahara* or rule or practice) came considerably to extend the scope of dharma (or, matters of faith and belief) and was practically considered as almost synonymous with it, and as such, inseparable.

One may perhaps conclude this section by taking note of the further observations of Sukumari Bhattacharji that commencing with Buddhism, which laid emphasis on karma (or, the consequences of one's actions) and the resultant cycle of birth and re-birth, coupled with other heterodox philosophies and practices of the times (leaving aside, for the time being, the consequences of the invasions since the 6th century BCE), people possibly came to view themselves as victims of some inscrutable power that deeply troubled them and unsettled their settled patterns of life (page 354). In such challenging times, the prescriptive rituals and sacrifices of the Vedas, now left behind about a thousand years ago, possibly needed to be replaced by the comforting hopes and expectations likely to be generated by a new set of prescriptive rituals and practices – as now given in the various smritis and Puranas.

Chapter 12

Resurgence of the Bhakti movement

The next significant phase in the development of Indian philosophical thinking, which underpins much of what large parts of India think and practice today, commences with the life and thoughts of that great sage, Adi Shankara. Here, only an attempt at encapsulating his contributions to India's metaphysical development can be made; for, there are scores of biographies on him and many commentaries. Suffice it to say, he was a scholar extra-ordinaire, born most possibly in Kerala in the early part of the 8th century CE. In the short 30 years of his life, he not only assimilated the knowledge of the Vedas and the Upanishads, but synthesized them into the *Advaita* (or, the non-dual) view of man's existence and life. While the various biographies of Adi Shankara are not unanimous about his birth, early education, travels, etc., it is, by and large, agreed that he studied for some time in the northern areas of central India under a Shaivite scholar named Govinda Bhagavatpada. He further studied about the Indian logic systems, and about heterodox sects and philosophies (i.e., those not conforming to the traditional Vedic and Upanishadic traditions), including the hedonism of Charvaka and Buddhism.

Shankara's capability and capacity for discourse and debate has passed into the stuff of legends and his most significant contribution to Indian thought has been the re-emphasis on meditation and monasticism that had marked the life of the sages in ancient India. He repeatedly emphasized the importance of pramana, or methods of reasoning that lead to reliable knowledge. He considered even the shruti or the revealed knowledge of the Vedas not to be sacrosanct, believing that anubhava or palpable experience should help

 Prosenjit Dasgupta

validate it. References to this may be found in section 1.18.133 of *"Upadeshasahashri"* and section 1.1.4 of *"Brahmasutra-bhasya"* as several scholars have pointed out. He, therefore, did not attach importance to the ritually-oriented Mimamsa school of thought prevalent at the time. He abjured what some have called "cherry-picking" of phrases from the Vedas.

Shankara stressed in his *"Brahmasutra–bhaysa"* that the six stages of reasoning and exposition must include the six characteristics of the text under consideration: (1) the *Upakrama* (introductory statement) and *Upasamhara* (conclusions); (2) *Abhyasa* (the exposition); (3) *Apurvata* (unique, specific proposition); (4) *Yukti* (the logic and reasoning); (5) *Phala* (the conclusion thus derived); and (6) *Arthavada* (the significance of the conclusions so derived).

Shankara consolidated and applied it with his unique exegetical method called *Anvaya-Vyatireka*, which states that for proper understanding, one must "accept only meanings that are compatible with all the characteristics", and in the process, "exclude meanings that are incompatible". He considered the *antaratma* (or, the inner soul) of man and the *nirguna* (or, beyond attributes) Brahman to be one and the same, thus laying the foundations of the Advaita (or, non-dual) or Vedanta school of thought that has deeply influenced Indian thought in many ways over the centuries. By this, he elaborated and extended the philosophy of the Upanishads significantly and, in this, his contribution to the development of knowledge in an individual generally and of self-knowledge in particular is particularly significant. He persistently looked for the Real and the Absolute, beyond what was unreal and transitory. In all this, he went beyond monotheism or the concept of One God into monism, that is, identification with that God, and paved the way for the subsequent flowering of devotionalism or the bhakti movements that marked the later centuries. It should not be surprising, therefore, that Shankara did not favour rituals and offerings and turned more to self-discipline and working for the general good (including the avoidance of anger and violence).

One would not be wrong in believing that Shankara largely attempted to synthesize the thoughts of the Vedas, the Upanishads, the Bhagavad-gita and the Brahma Sutra. Rightly, his work is included in the Vedanta, that is the summation and core of the Vedas. It is notable that in his "*Nirvana satakam*", (Hymn 3, 4) Shankara speaks of –

"Without hate, without infatuation,
without craving, without greed;
Neither arrogance, nor conceit, never jealous I am;
Neither *dharma*, nor *artha*, neither *kama*, nor *moksha* am I;
I am Consciousness, I am Bliss, I am Siva, I am Siva.

Without sins, without merits,
without elation, without sorrow;
Neither mantra, nor rituals, neither pilgrimage, nor Vedas;
Neither the experiencer, nor experienced, nor the experience am I,
I am Consciousness, I am Bliss, I am Siva, I am Siva."

These verses, in a way, summarize Shankara's perceptions and thoughts. He strove for *Jivanmukti* or Moksha or salvation through self-realization, by way of a growing awareness of the oneness of self and the Brahma. His was a reasoned and pragmatic extension of the message of the Upanishads by one of the foremost thinkers of India.

Ramanuja, who came in the 11th century CE, was a Tamilian scholar and theologian who developed the thesis that while the *atma* and the Brahma were differentiated and distinct, there is a universality and unity of all the souls in Brahma. He believed that it is always possible for the individual soul to find union with the *paramatma* or Brahma. Known popularly as *Vishistadvaitavad* (or, particular non-dualism), his thoughts were critical to the subsequent development and spread of devotionalism and bhakti among the masses. In this, he, in terms of both theory and practice, extended the devotionalism of the Alvars of the 9th century Tamil Nadu. His philosophies were, in turn, overtaken by the *Dvaitavada* or dualism of Madhavacharya, the 13th century sage from Karnataka. He, too, was deeply influenced by the teachings of the Vedas, the Upanishads, the Bhagavad-gita and the Brahma-sutras. He believed that the antara-atma or the individual soul and the *parama*-Brahma (the Supreme Being) were distinct realities, but the former was fully capable, by the grace of the Supreme Being, of being united with the latter. In this view of finding ultimate unity with the Supreme, Madhavacharya anticipated the later Bhakti traditions of India to a considerable extent.

The word *"Bhakti"* is best understood from the state of mind of the *"bhakta"* or the devotee. This has ranged from the surrender of Radha and the *gopis* to the flute of Lord Krishna to the selfless devotion of Meera, and to many things in-between. For instance, Kabir, the poet and saint of the 15th century, was deeply influenced by his preceptor, Ramananda (late 14th century), who was noted for his Vaishnavite and Advaita monist sentiments. The latter was the founder of the Ramanandi sect, one of the largest disciplined religious organisations in India, devoted to a life of austerity. Kabir is said to have been brought up in a Muslim family and accepted no caste or creed distinction. He was very critical of any sort of ritualism and religious hypocrisy. More than anything, it is his sayings and poems (from Kabir *Bijak* and *Granthavali*) filled with mysticism that truly reflect his religious and social philosophies, and have captured the popular imagination. A few samples are reproduced below –

"I've burned my own house down; the torch is in my hand. Now I'll burn down the house of anyone who wants to follow me."

"Reading book after book the whole world died,
and none ever became learned!"

"I am neither in temple nor in mosque:
I am neither in Kaaba nor in Kailash:
Neither am I in rites and ceremonies, nor in Yoga and
renunciation.
If thou art a true seeker, thou shalt at once see Me: thou
shalt meet Me in a moment of time."

"O friend! Hope for Him whilst you live, know whilst you
live, understand whilst you live: for in life deliverance
abides.
If your bonds be not broken whilst living, what hope of
deliverance in death?
It is but an empty dream, that the soul shall have union
with Him because it has passed from the body:
If He is found now, He is found then,
If not, we do but go to dwell in the City of Death.
If you have union now, you shall have it hereafter.

I am not a Hindu,
Nor am a Muslim!
I am this body, a play
Of five elements; a drama
Of the spirit dancing
With joy and sorrow.
A drop
Melting into the sea,
Everyone can see.
But the sea
Absorbed
In a drop —

                    Prosenjit Dasgupta

That is rare to understand!"

Kabir's simple message of dispensation with elaborate rituals and stress on devotionalism earned him many followers of the *Kabir Panth* (or Kabir's Way) among the village folk of central India. Even today, his *Bijak* or collection of aphorisms has many admirers.

There were other sages and saints, such as Ravidas, Tukaram and others who helped make bhakti or the devotional path for the realization of the Supreme Being very popular in India. Among them, Guru Nanak Dev-ji, the preceptor of the *Sikh Panth* stands out. Guru Nanak was born in 1469 and died in 1539. During this period, he travelled to many places of pilgrimage and imbibed the simple devotionalism of saints like Kabir. He, then, developed his own philosophy of One God, and a social platform of equality and fraternalism, together with a unique message of humility and service to all. This is what marks out the message of Guru Nanak-Dev-ji. Later, many of his sayings were compiled into what is known as the *Guru Granth Sahib*, the sacred text of the Sikhs, who are the followers of the Guru. The Guru Granth Sahib guides both their faith and daily lives. Some of the sayings of Guru Nanak Dev-ji are as follows -

"There is but one God. True is His Name, creative His personality and immortal His form. He is without fear, without enmity, unborn and self-illumined".

"Realization of Truth is higher than all else. Higher still is truthful living."

"Those who have loved are those that have found God"

"Even Kings and emperors with heaps of wealth and vast dominion cannot compare with an ant filled with the love of God."

"He who has no faith in himself can never have faith in God."
"Your Mercy is what gives me my being".

Predictably, the message of Guru Nanak-ji spread far and wide in India, from Sind and Punjab in the west to far in the east and elsewhere.

Interestingly, another great figure in the Indian bhakti tradition arose almost at the same time as Guru Nanak, and this was Shri Chaitanya Mahaprabhu (1486-1534) in Bengal in eastern India. Shri Chaitanya is believed to have attempted to replicate the Radha-Krishna mode of the *bhakti-marga* or way of devotion. He is said to have revived interest in Vrindavana as the place of Shri Krishna's *leela* or place of activity. He, too, travelled widely in India and spent many years at Jagannath-dham or the place of abode of Shri Jagannatha (the manifestation of Lord Krishna as the world-preserver) at Puri. He enunciated the *"achintya bheda-bhed"* (or, inconceivable differentiation) concept, where the world is both separated from and united with Shri Krishna as the *Supreme Reality*. Even today, after the passage of 600 years, the message of universal love and brotherhood that Shri Chaitanya preached and embodied, and his earnestness in being united with Lord Krishna, has many adherents in India and abroad.

     Prosenjit Dasgupta

Chapter 13

The Muslim and the British – up-side/down-side

If one has honestly to look at the past, even in such a work, replete with numerous references to the Rigveda, the Upanishads, the Bhagavad-gita and Indian sages, it is necessary to dwell—however briefly—on that phase of Indian history when Muslim rulers governed large tracts of the country (at the time of the Mughals, much of it), from about the 10th century CE to the latter part of the 18th century. Similar references ought to be made to the British administration, firstly as part of the East India Company, and later as part of the British imperial administration, from the latter part of the 18th century until India's independence in 1947.

It would have been evident from the text so far that Islam was not the harbinger of monotheism in India. Monotheism had been, millennia ago, considered in the Rigveda, and in a more elaborate fashion in the Upanishads. The nature of monotheism was also the principal concern of Advaita Vedanta. The caste system had also been decried and universal brotherhood promoted by numerous Indian sages, the reference to which has just been made above.

It is equally true that the caste system had not withered away by the 10th or even the 16th century CE. If anything, it had become even more entrenched. Monotheism had also not extended much into the popular psyche. It was this environment that Islam was confronted with, as the faith came into India through the minds and books of the Muslim kings and their courtiers and scholars.

A good glimpse of the nature of Indian thoughts and life in the 11th century CE is provided by the writings of the Muslim scholar, Al-Biruni, who had made his notes following the discussions and some controversies with a fellow litterateur. He dedicated the same to Masud, son and successor (following a bit of skirmishing with his brother) of Mahmud of Ghazni, following the latter's invasions of India at that time. This was quite in keeping with the tradition of the great curiosity that Muslim rulers had about India, such as the Khalifa Mansur of Baghdad, who around 750/760 CE had Brahmagupta's *"Brahmasiddhanta"* and *"Khandakhadyaka"* translated to understand the Indian system of astronomy. This was followed by Khalifa Haroun, who had books on Indian medicine and pharmacology imported into Baghdad.

Al-Biruni was a noted mathematician and astronomer of the Khiva region of Persia that had also been attacked and laid waste by Mahmud, who was more interested in filling his treasuries with gold and valuables, than in any permanent acquisition of territory. Dr Edward Sachau, in his Preface and annotations to his edition of "Alberuni's India" (see Bibliography – published by Kegan Paul and Trubner, London, new edition, 1910), has pointed out that Al-Biruni found that many of the scholars in India were monotheists like himself, and had a sense of universal humanism (if not of brotherhood). However, the persistent desire of many of the people for commemorating the dead and providing consolation in adversities to the living, turned them to image-worship of various deities. Al-Biruni appreciated the Bhagavad-gita and quoted Vyasdeva in some places in his own work. Sachau notes that Al-Biruni often attacked the Arabs in his notes and accused their ancestors for having destroyed the civilization of Iran. Al-Biruni found that Brahmagupta, the famous astronomer of India, had developed two theories of the eclipse of the moon, one that it was Rahu swallowing that planet, and another, the scientific one. He berated him in his notes for having pandered to the clergy, and for having tried to belittle the work of his predecessor, Aryabhata. Al-Biruni had no interest in converting the Hindus and gave little or no support to any religious leaders. His one

    Prosenjit Dasgupta

objective was to provide such material as would assist those interested "to converse with Hindus and discuss with them questions of religion, science or literature on the very basis of their own civilization" (page 246 of this book, as given by Sachau). As part of this, he translated the *"Pulisa-siddhanta"*, a work on astronomy, which he considered had not freed itself of religious and theological traces. At the same time, Al-Biruni noticed and complained in his commentary about the indifferent work done in several cases, by copyists of earlier texts, by obscuring parts of the texts and corrupting proper names. He translated Kapila's *"Samkhya"* and the book of *"Patanjali"* into Arabic. In fact, he has quoted from Patanjali in his work, noting the discussions between a teacher and disciple about whether God is absolute and sublime beyond all existence. It seems from his work that he had some knowledge of the Bhagavad-gita, the Vishnu Purana, Vayu Purana, etc. His notes on Buddhism are meagre; although at the time of Ghazni's invasion, the Pala dynasty was ruling and many of its rulers followed the path of the Buddha. This suggests that Buddhism was considerably on the decline in India at that point of time in the 11th century. Al-Biruni found India was more inclined to Vaishnavism than to Shaivism, despite the fact that some of the Pala kings were worshippers of Siva.

In Chapter II of his book, Al-Biruni goes on to quote from the Bhagavad-gita and notes, in particular, that the text stresses on men should all times strive to become as similar as possible to God. He writes disapprovingly of anthropomorphic doctrines of gods and of the prohibition of discussions on religious topics. His approach is rational; typical of a person given to thought and discussions, and he was no doubt a man of very considerable learning, with a sound knowledge of Arabic and Greek philosophical treatises. But he is bookish in a way, and describes only a little of the day-to-day lives of the people. He does note the rigidity of the caste system, although he speaks of guilds of (Shudra) artisans, such as the shoemaker, the fisherman, the weaver and others. He notes, in particular (page 104 of his text), that according to Vyasa (who, Al-Biruni notes is of Shudra descent), one would have to learn the 25 aspects of knowledge, and then one may adopt whatever religion one wants and still gain salvation. He also notes that Vasudeva in the Bhagavad-gita is of Shudra descent, being neither a Brahman, nor a Kshatriya or Vaishya, but of the Yadava caste.

Neither time nor space will permit a fuller description of this most interesting work of Al-Biruni. It should suffice to say that it is most scholarly in its approach, comparing in places Hindu thoughts and practices with those of the Persians, or the Greeks, and those of Islam in general. No doubt, it would be of much interest to any student of Indian history.

One must take into account that in the period during which Muslim rulers held sway, the system of administration, with particular reference to land revenue, and the administration of justice, was largely decentralized, rationalized and refined. It stood the test of time even into the British colonial administration. Sufism is another notable contribution of Muslim philosophers to the Indian psyche and culture. It had a relatively easy passage owing to its closeness in thought and feeling to the Bhakti cults in India. The one and the other acted and reacted over centuries of close contact till it became a wholly Indian product through expression in local dialects like Avadi and Braja-bhasha (and later in the Urdu language) over a wide swathe of the country. Music was also similarly influenced by new variations and styles, such as *ghazals*, *thumri*, *dadra* and the like (as distinct from the classical *Dhrupad* style). Many Muslim rulers, from the time of the Mughals, patronised music, and numerous singers and players, irrespective of caste or creed, found it possible to flourish. It was the same with literature, with special regard to poetry, where *mushairas* or functions with poets, each presenting their work in person, became the order of the day in many regions of the country.

     Prosenjit Dasgupta

The point also needs to be made that Indian art, which had by itself reached great heights by the 6th century CE, was considerably enriched by the miniature art form introduced in the Mughal period. Prince Dara Shikoh took the initiative to have the Upanishads translated into Persian from whence they reached the world through Germany and France. Another notable contribution from the times of the earliest Muslim rulers was in the field of architecture, with the typical arches, alcoves, domes, sculpted screens, and minarets in practically all parts of the country.

An important insight as to the state of India during the transition from the rule of Emperor Shah Jahan to that of his son, Aurangzeb, is provided in the writings of Francois Bernier (see Bibliography), a French physician and philosopher, who came to India in 1656 and stayed for about ten years. While a good part of the book deals with the intrigues of the Mughal court at the time, especially the tussle for supremacy between the sons of Shah Jahan, there were also some letters that Bernier wrote to his friends and well-wishers in France in which he gave his observations on social practices as well. He notes, for instance, that, "In Delhi, there is no middle state. A man must be of the highest rank or live miserably...No one aspires after any improvement in life wherein he happens to be born. No one marries but in his own trade or profession. And this custom is observed as rigidly by Mahomedans as by the Gentiles (i.e., the Hindus – parenthesis added), to whom it is expressly enjoined by their law." In another place, he writes that: "The brahmins encourage and promote these errors and superstitions to which they are indebted for their wealth and consequence. As persons attached and consecrated to important mysteries, they are held in general veneration and enriched by the alms of the people" (page 305). He refers to the practice of *sati* or the self-immolation by widows, and to *antar-jali yatra*, or the drowning of an aged and ailing person in the waters of a river. This, and his description of an incident where a widow was held down on a funeral pyre by the long poles of the priests, or the shackling of a young widow of about 12 years of age, prior to her being placed on the funeral pyre of her dead husband (pages 313 and 314) make for dismal reading. He also makes the important point: *"How can it be believed that men submit to life of so much misery for the sake of a second state of existence, as short and uncertain as the first and which cannot be expected to yield a much higher degree of happiness"* (page 318 – emphasis added). He poses the question more to himself than the Indians he mingled with. He goes on to quote some Hindu *pundits* (or scholars) in Benaras, as: "Images are admitted in our temples because we conceive that prayers are offered up with more devotion where there is something before the eyes that fixes the mind; but, in fact, we acknowledge that God alone is Absolute, that he is an omnipotent Lord" (page 342). One may not agree with Bernier, or some may even ascribe motives to him in so writing; but it is a viewpoint worth noting, as much as the viewpoint of a naturally prudent and reasonable person is worth noting.

The developments in art, music, literature, etc., under successive Muslim rulers were closely followed by the British penchant for documentation and codification. Starting with the Asiatic Society in Bengal in 1784, the British searched for, translated, documented and commented on almost all aspects of life in India, from the classical literature, the sacred texts, the legal systems and codes, art, architecture, the tribes and castes, the languages and dialects, and what have you. The works of Sir William Jones, H.T. Colebrooke and others was also enriched by scholars such as Rajendralal Mitra, and later by Mahamahopadhyay H.P. Shastri and others. The decipherment of the Brahmi script by James Prinsep must be mentioned here as opening up large parts of Indian history. The setting up of the Fort William College at Kolkata in 1800 by Lord Wellesley led to wider learning of Persian and

Sanskrit and gave patronage to several Indian scholars such as Mrityunjay Tarkalankar.

In line with the Muslim historians and commentators from the time of Al-Biruni, numerous British administrators wrote extensively about India and their experiences and impressions here. One of the more well-known among them was William Sleeman, who came to be better known for his suppression of the *thugee* (or, murderous robbers) menace in central India in the early part of the 19th century. What is perhaps less well-known is his considerate and objective view of some of the Hindu practices in that region, such as female infanticide. He took note of the anxiety of major landholders, especially among the Rajput clans who had settled in many parts of Oudh (or, Avad) and adjoining areas (in what is Uttar Pradesh today), for safeguarding their landed properties. Sleeman travelled for about ninety days, covering about ten miles each day (although he halted at places for a couple of days) either on elephant-back or in a *tonjon* (horse-drawn carriage), meeting and speaking with the landed gentry and local people about the land problems and the state of the administration of the King of Oudh. His "Diaries" on this tour in Avad (then called Oudh), cradled between the Ghagra River on the east and the Ganga passing through Allahabad in the west, and running north up to the Terai at the foot of the Himalayas, between December 1849 and February 1850 (now edited by P.D. Reeves – see Bibliography) make for interesting reading. He records with a good deal of detachment the extreme feudal state of affairs in Oudh where the large distances and the large patches of forest helped obscure the extortion and pillage of one another's properties by a large number of the landed gentry, many of whom were drawn from various Rajput clans settled in that part of the country for several centuries. Reading Sleeman, one is constantly reminded of the typical "thakur-oriented" films of Bollywood, of which "Sholay" may be said to be a popular example. Any semblance of administration, centred in Lucknow in the court of the king, was conspicuous by its absence or was dictated largely by the self-interest and greed of those close to the throne. *Nazrana*, or fees or gratuities payable for an audience with the king and submission of offers or proposals in person to him, was up to 20 or 25 percent of the likely revenue that a *zamindar* or *taluqdar* could expect to raise. A zamindar was an intermediary for purposes of revenue collection, while a taluqdar was an assignee of the land, appointed by the king, for purposes of governance and aid in the event of war. It must be noted that the nazrana hardly reached the coffers of the royal treasury and was mostly siphoned off by one or the other of the courtiers.

The situation at the turn of the 19th century (i.e., about 1780s) in Rajasthan has also been well documented by James Tod, in his "Annals and Antiquities of Rajasthan" (see Bibliography), and is germane to the title of this chapter. Tod has relied on documents on lineages and clans that he was able to obtain from some of the temple repositories (e.g., from *Nadolaye* temple, a scroll over fifty feet long). He also relied upon the "*Raj Roopa Akhyan*" of the Suryavamsi kings and references given in local *charan* or bardic poems and songs. Tod's admiration of many of the traits of the Rajputs, such as their forthrightness and loyalty to the clan, and "the given word", becomes clear in the work. The Mughals were possibly also attracted by these traits; for, in many instances, from the time of Emperor Akbar through the next two generations, there were several marriages between Mughal princes and women of the Rajput nobility. This further tied several of the Rajput families by bonds of loyalty to the Mughals, among whom mention must be made of Raja Man Singh of Jaipur and Raja Jaswant Sigh of Jodhpur, both of whom rendered yeoman service to the Mughal Empire. On the other hand, the defiance of Rana Pratap against the Mughal efforts to annexe his kingdom must be taken note of; although later, Akbar took due care to bring about reconciliation and largely left

     Prosenjit Dasgupta

the Rajput princes to manage their own affairs. But Tod also draws attention to the almost incessant frictions and inter-clan fights, the parricide and fratricide among the royalty in one part of Rajasthan or the other that marked the region from about the 12th century CE to the end of the 18th century. He also points to the inroads at that time into Rajasthan by some of the leading Maratha chieftains and the exaction of tribute by them. Thus, it was found that by the end of the 18th century, several of the clans and nobility were more inclined to subject themselves to the supervision of the British administration and to "Pax Britannica".

The British also delved, for the first time, below the surface of things. Robert Bruce Foote, Alexander Cunningham and others visited caves or excavated the earth to expose buried history to light. The Archaeological Survey of India was followed by the Geological Survey of India, and then the Zoological Survey of India (of which the Anthropological Survey was a part!) and the Botanical Survey. The contribution of such efforts to the knowledge and understanding of Indian history and of the resources of the country needs to be more widely appreciated. This was not enough, and the Census of India, again for the first time, was started in 1882, releasing a huge amount of information about tribes, castes, creeds, livelihoods and numbers that aided the administration of the country well into the 21st century. While no doubt there was very considerable colonial exploitation of India and her resources by the British (as has been documented by several scholars), the growth of literacy and education in 19th century India, the introduction of the postal system and telegraphic communications, increased mobility by way of the railways and the rudiments of self-governance also gave rise to a growing sense of nationhood by the last decades of that century. The acts of omission and commission by the British administration in India since the beginning of the 19th century have been too well-documented elsewhere to bear repetition here. All that

may be observed here is that India could not be said to have
been unaffected by the British administration either at that
point of time, or as she emerged into the light of Independence
in 1947.

Prosenjit Dasgupta

Chapter 14

Later Reformers and Sages of note

India has been both fortunate and unfortunate in the number and stature of sages, saints and teachers who have provided light at some stage or the other over the centuries: fortunate, because it is given to few nations to have had so many persons of such knowledge, insight and wisdom; and unfortunate, because the very numbers have all too often led the followers to miss the wood for the trees, and in being content in going their separate ways.

One of the first visionaries at that point of the turn of the 19th century, to appreciate the one Absolute spoken of in the Rigveda and the Upanishads, was Raja Rammohan Roy (1774-1833). He also acknowledged the concept of universal brotherhood of man pervading all major religions in the world, be it Hinduism, Buddhism, Christianity, Islam or Sikhism. Despite his birth in a conservative Bengali landlord's home, his studies into, and grasp of, Sanskrit sacred texts, the Holy Koran, the Bible, as well as numerous Persian and Arabic texts, at Patna, Benares and Kolkata, were both eclectic and deep. His learning, together with his steadfast adherence to rationalism and reason, led him to discard the many layers of myths, beliefs, and rituals and practices that had accumulated over the preceding centuries in India and to uphold the fundamental truths outlined in the sacred texts of these various religions. He came out strongly against sati or the so-called self-immolation of widows, child marriage, polygamy, and gave all-out support to the spread of education. He had to sever his connections with his father's family for these reasons and strike out on his own. His personal belief in the inherent vision and truth of Vedanta, and the intrinsic truth of all major religions, led him to start a reformist movement in 1821 by way of starting the *Atmiya Samaj* (or, the spiritual brotherhood) that led ultimately to the establishment of the full-fledged institution, *Brahmo Samaj*, in 1831.

This is not the place to give any biographical notes on Raja Rammohan Roy, nor any history of the Brahmo Samaj. It should suffice to say that in one way or the other, the Samaj attracted and/or influenced many leading personages and intellectuals of the time, such as Prince Dwarkanath Tagore, Devendranath Tagore, Ramchandra Vidyavagish, Kaliprasanna Singha, Pandit Ishwarchandra Vidyasagar, Keshavchandra Sen, Ramtanu Lahiri, Akshoykumar Datta, Rajnarayan Bose, and yet later, Narendranath Datta (who later was better known as Swami Vivekananda), Bipinchandra Pal and Shri Aurobindo. It is said that even the great sage Ramakrishna Deva, on one or two occasions, visited the Samaj and on one occasion went into *Samadhi* or divine inertness, listening to the *kirtans* or devotional songs there. The missionaries of the Samaj took their message to the farthest corners of India; the Samaj in Lahore being set up as early as 1861 and, by the 1870s, the Samaj had over 100 branches across India. Besides abjuring any elaborate rituals, shunning casteism, etc., the Samaj gave considerable support to women's education wherever possible. Further, some of its adherents, such as Akshoy Datta, Rajnarayan Bose and others were at the forefront of the Indian nationalist movement in the late 19th century. Even after the lapse of nearly two centuries since Rammohan constituted the Atmiya Sabha, the Brahmo Samaj retains its faith and vitality in spite of many odds.

One of the most notable sages who lighted up 19th century India was Shri Ramakrishna Deva (1836-1886). He was touched by some divine grace from an early age and flowered into a great sage and master during his tenure as a priest at the famous Dakshineshwar temple near Kolkata. He received guidance and instructions at various times from a number of

    Prosenjit Dasgupta

gurus or instructors or mentors. Once again, this is not the place to attempt even brief biographical notes on his life and teachings; there are many books on that, such as those by "Shri M", Swami Saradananda and Christopher Isherwood. But it must be mentioned that Ramakrishna Deva was wholly eclectic in both his learnings and perceptions. He had studied and practised Christianity and Islam besides various forms of Yoga elaborated in Hindu scriptures. Many people were attracted to his simplicity and profound knowledge of Advaita Vedanta that he imbibed in a very short span from his mentor, Tota Puri, around 1865. One of the notable aphorisms ascribed to Shri Ramakrishna, is "*Jata mat, tata path*", i.e., there are as many pathways to salvation as there are doctrines. One of his foremost disciples was Narendranath Datta, who began as a doubter and sceptic but soon became Ramakrishna's closest follower and dedicated proselytizer. Narendranath took the name of Swami Vivekananda upon his assuming a monastic way of life in 1886 and went on to spearhead the great institution of the Ramakrishna Math.

It would be appropriate at this stage to refer to Vivekananda's lectures at the Parliament of Religions at Chicago in September 1893; for they represent a major record of his thoughts on Hinduism and Hindu culture. This relies largely on what is readily obtainable from the website of the Belur Math *(www. belurmath.org - https://belurmath.org/swami-vivekananda-speeches-at-the-parliament-of-religions-chicago-1893/)*, the headquarters of the Ramakrishna Math and Mission near Kolkata. In a remarkable paper that he read out on 15th September 1893 at Chicago, Vivekananda recalled the words of that great Vedic sage who had once proclaimed the glad tidings: "Hear, ye children of immortal bliss! Even ye that reside in higher spheres! I have found the Ancient One who is beyond all darkness and delusion: knowing Him alone you shall be saved from death over again."

Continuing in the same vein, Vivekananda stated: "The

Hindu does not want to live upon words and theories. If there are existences beyond the ordinary sensuous existence, he wants to come face to face with them. If there is a soul in him which is not matter, if there is an all-merciful universal Soul, he will go to Him direct. He must see Him, and that alone can destroy all doubts. So, the best proof a Hindu sage gives about the soul, about God, is: 'I have seen the soul; I have seen God.' And that is the only condition of perfection. *The Hindu religion does not consist in struggles and attempts to believe a certain doctrine or dogma, but in realizing - not in believing, but in being and becoming* (emphasis added). Thus, the whole object of the system is by constant struggle to become perfect, to become divine, to reach God, and see God; and this reaching God, seeing God, becoming perfect, even as the Father in Heaven is perfect, constitutes the religion of the Hindus." He underlines the point, "I am proud to belong to a religion which has taught the world both tolerance and universal acceptance. We believe not only in universal tolerance, but we accept that all religions are true…Unity in variety is the plan of nature, and the Hindu has recognized it."

He concluded: "Upon the banner of every religion will soon be written, in spite of resistance: 'Help and not Fight; Assimilation and not Destruction; Harmony and Peace and not Dissension'."

Vivekananda's most stirring peroration to his countrymen was: "Arise, awake and stop not till the goal is reached." It is a matter of individual judgement as to whether his countrymen have been so aroused and awakened; and if not, why not.

Almost contemporary with Shri Ramakrishna was another "god-man", that is, someone very close to God and touched by His grace, the Sai Baba of Shirdi (mid 1850s to 1918). India is famed for its godmen, owing perhaps to the over-arching philosophies contained in the Rigveda, the Upanishads and the Bhagavad-gita. In Sai Baba's case, his simplicity, his meditative nature and his devotion to the basic teachings of

     Prosenjit Dasgupta

Islam and Hinduism, especially to Sufism and the Bhagavad-gita attracted people to him. He gave his advice to those who approached him in parables and simple terms. The recurring theme in his teachings was devotion and bhakti. He was against orthodoxy and rigidity in any religion. His concern for people, spirit of service to others, and his simple message of a straightforward and ethical life brought him many adherents. His very life was an example to others to live a more meaningful life.

It is no easy task to select only a few of the great teachers and sages in India, even within the restricted period of only the 19th century, for reference here. But the name of Ramana Maharshi, the sage of Arunachala (1879-1950), comes easily to mind. In him was combined that simplicity of life, the depth and directness of thought, and the message of compassion that have marked the great men (and women) of India, from Rigvedic times to the 20th century. His basic message was that of self-enquiry, self-awareness and self-knowledge, which have marked the thoughts of the Upanishads and the Bhagavad-gita. A natural corollary was his focus on the very ancient Indian concept of sat-chit-ananda, that is, what may be simplistically translated as the bliss ("ananda") that comes from a consciousness ("chit") of living in truth ("sat"). His message to mankind was both direct and simple by way of aphorisms and analogies, e.g., "Wanting to reform the world without discovering one's true self is like trying to cover the world with leather to avoid the pain of walking on stones and thorns. It is much simpler to wear shoes." Or, again - "Aim high, aim at the highest, and all lower aims are thereby achieved. It is looking below on the stormy sea of differences that makes you sink. Look up, beyond these, and see the One Glorious Real, and you are saved." Many, indeed, could follow a fuller and more meaningful life by imbibing and following his teachings.

Another great soul of India was Shri Aurobindo (1872-

1950), who evolved from being an aspirant to the Indian Civil Services to a revolutionary, and then to a sage in the ancient mould. Perhaps from his father, who was a medical practitioner, Aurobindo came to believe in the theory of evolution, and as an extension of that, to the idea that man was capable of evolving into something better and fuller. On the one hand, he was deeply influenced by the Upanishads and the Bhagavad-gita and, on the other, he closely studied several western philosophers such as Plato, Nietzsche and Bergson. He expressed his views in several books such as, "The Life Divine", "Essays on the Gita", "The Upanishads" and "The Ideal of Human Unity". Aurobindo was much more of a "modern man" than many of his contemporaries and may be said to have been one of the last to have re-considered Indian's ancient scriptures and re-interpreted them for the 20th century.

It is necessary and proper to conclude this section with some notes about the reforms brought about in the Indian society, especially in north and northwest India, by Swami Dayanand Saraswati (1824-1883) through his Arya Samaj. He was a renowned scholar of the Vedas and travelled for many years across India to bring about fresh thinking on the then current rituals and practices. He achieved this through debates and discussions with other scholars and priests. It has been reported that he spent some months in Kolkata in the 1860s, meeting and discussing with Maharshi Devendranath Tagore, a leader of the Brahmo Samaj, about Vedas and Upanishads, and generally about things spiritual. He then went on to establish the Arya Samaj (i.e., an organisation of noble thinkers) in 1875 to spearhead the reformist movement by challenging idol worship, animal sacrifices (which were rampant around that time), the overweening position of the priestly classes, the caste system, discrimination against women, and the like. He held that such practices were against good sense and the wisdom of the Vedas, and was emphatically

     Prosenjit Dasgupta

against any dogma and symbolism. He started several schools for dissemination of knowledge and explaining the true sense of the Vedas. By the time of the turn of the 20th century, the Arya Samaj was at the forefront of the Hindu reformist movement, and also attracted several nationalist leaders like Lala Lajpat Rai and V.D. Savarkar.

Swami Dayanand's testimony is contained in his well-known work, "*Satyartha Prakash*" (i.e., revelation of true meanings), in which he unambiguously stated that he accepted as *Dharma* only that which was in full conformity with impartiality and truthfulness; whatever was not free of partiality or was unjust or was untruthful was *Adharma*, and was to be abjured. This led him to speak out against astrology, while he emphasized the proper study of arithmetic, algebra, geometry, geology, etc., for a better understanding of the universe and the world at large. Dayanand called him just, who regards the happiness of others as much as he does his own happiness. He studied both Islam and Christianity and was critical of some of their beliefs and practices as being contrary to common sense and reason. Possibly as a reaction to the active proselytization being undertaken in India by Christian missionaries around the middle of the 19th century, Dayanand started the process of *shuddhi* or purification that enabled a convert to Christianity or Islam to re-join the Hindu mainstream.

As a result of Swami Dayanand's teachings, the Arya Samaj came to adopt universal values; that God is omnipresent, omniscient, formless, immanent, eternal and the Being worthy of worship; that one should always accept and adopt truth and reject untruth; that in day-to-day life, one should promote righteousness, truth and justice; that one should strive to bring about the well-being of society while permitting individuals the freedom to pursue their own welfare.

Chapter 15

Emergence of the Present - I

So long the search for the present was largely confined to the largely distant past; but now what specifically constitutes the "present" for the purpose of this work needs to be taken up for consideration. The "present" obviously consists of the current social, economic, political and other aspects of national life; but a discussion of all that would take one far afield. If one takes the "present" in terms of social, political and economic development in India to be the product, to a large or significant extent, of the "past", both the distant and the proximate past need to be considered. The "distant past" has already been discussed at some length in the preceding chapters and it is now time to look at the "proximate past"-- more in decades, or at most a century--of the present-day scenario in some detail.

It is obvious that on the one hand there is the remarkable economic progress that India has made since Independence, and especially so from about the mid-1980s. The GDP and the per capita income have grown so many times over the levels in the 1960s and 70s. There has been unbelievable development in Communications and Information Technology since that time. There was then the unstated belief that this economic upswing and the associated economic and social mobility would lead towards progressive ironing out of the economic, social and political differences and points of friction in the populace. That has not happened; at least not to the extent that many people expected over the last thirty or thirty-five years, considering the experience in several developed and developing countries of the world. Leaving aside the agitations from time to time about the sharing of river waters by neighbouring states, or feuds for smaller states, or farmers' distress, issues of terrorism and left-wing extremism, and reservation of education and jobs for one community or the other, it seems that from about the middle of 1980s, a good part of the nation's time, attention and resources has also been taken up by agitations by one section or the other of the populace actively pursuing their political and social agendas through religious movements. Such a specific development had not been noticed over the first four decades since Independence, when much of the nation's attention and efforts were centred on building the economic infrastructure through the Five-year Plans and other immediate issues, such as agricultural development, the provision of education and health services, extension of irrigation, increasing power generation, and so on. The recent years have also been marked notably by some political parties, such as the Bharatiya Janata Party (or BJP), in one way or the other, in providing space and support to some programmes of Hindu religious leaders. On the other hand, the INC, the ML, or other political parties such as the DMK, the TDP, or the BSP or SP have not taken up any such programme that may be said to have any definite religious hue. Coincidentally or otherwise, this step by the BJP seems to have come at a time, when in 1989, the then government unveiled the Mandal Commission Report on affirmative action in support of "other backward classes". There was also a major opening up of the economy shortly afterwards in 1992 (and the "take-off" into a much higher trajectory of growth) under successive governments. The proximate sources for political programmes of the nature mentioned above, therefore, deserve to be considered in some detail.

Most would possibly agree that practically all the major ancient religions of the world, be it Hinduism, or Judaism, Buddhism, Christianity or Islam, have witnessed changes over the past several centuries in some of their external practices and codes, if not some refinements and sophistication in their core tenets. One may hazard a guess that such changes may have come about over the past many centuries due to the migration of people from one region to another (possibly due to some climatic or geological factors); the intermingling with other ethnic communities; the rise and decline of some ruling groups; and, certainly, the progressive evolution of man from being a primitive creature using stone implements to persons with intellect and knowledge capable of sending satellites into space, as has happened over the last five millennia.

Keeping that broad perspective in mind, one may attempt to sketch out the political developments, and, to a limited extent, the accompanying economic and social changes in India since the turn of the 20th century, till date. It needs to be kept in mind that the British administration, partly in keeping with the political changes then taking place in Great Britain, granted self-governance at the municipality and district board level in the last quarter of the 19th century. But this was based not on universal suffrage but on limited electorates subject to several economic and educational criteria, which, by that very fact, was incapable of leading to truly representative self-governance even at the local levels.

In this study of the "proximate past" of the recent developments in the "Hindu identity" and Hinduism-oriented political programmes (as distinct and different from what may be termed as "civil" or "religion-neutral" or "secular" programmes, such as the extension of health and development of irrigation facilities), as it has influenced the Indian political scenario since the early 1980s, one may leave aside the evolution of the Muslim identity and psyche, since this had largely played itself out by the Partition of India in 1947; the Muslims who chose to stay on in India as her citizens, did so not out of any political compulsion, but out of a personal choice of hearth and home. Furthermore, the nature and role of the Indian National Congress since its inception in 1885 has been written about too widely to need any elaboration here. Thus,

                     Prosenjit Dasgupta

for initiating a consideration of the "proximate past", one may take note of what Kenneth Jones (see Bibliography) mentions as the proliferation of religious and social organisations in the 19th century dedicated to reviving the glory of the "true" past and removing the evils of a "degenerate" present. He goes on to state that with Islam introducing new concepts and practices, e.g. a caste-free brotherhood of men and the Sikhs bringing forth new scriptures that were more openly accessible and professed, the dominant castes of the Brahmans and Kshatriyas considerably lost their previously held status under the "new-fangled" British administration with its emphasis on laws, codes, passing examinations, and a stress on merit rather than who belonged to which family. It was now time for commerce, and with it, the rise of the trading community of the Vaishyas, such as the Khatri, Baniya, Arora, Sud and others. Furthermore, Jones has pointed out that being a "Sarin" Khatri meant more than being just a Khatri: "The 'specific tradition' of an individual *jati* or caste more than the great traditions of his religion, began to dictate social behaviour" (page 5 in Jones). The entry of Christian missionaries and the numbers of Christians in Punjab rising to 163,994 by 1911 also had its implications. Jones' outline of the rapidly unfolding social and cultural changes in Punjab in the latter half of the 19th century is masterly, and deserves wider study. Jones suggests that the individuals of the Hindu administrative class, who had followed the British expansion in the North West Frontier Province, Baluchistan and Sind, found themselves surrounded by Muslim gentry and "reacted with a heightened awareness of their religious identity" and increasingly turned to the Arya Samaj (Page 81). As Jones suggests, "The class interests of a Hindu elite converged with Arya ideology" (page 66), around this point of time. As if this was not enough, it was precisely around this time in the last couple of decades of the 19th century that Britain began the tightening of its imperial grip over India.

As has been mentioned above, one of most notable figures at this time was Swami Dayanand, a person much learned in the Vedas that led to his spearheading the great reformist movement of the Arya Samaj. In his well-known book, *Satyartha Prakash*, about Hindu society in the last quarter of the 19th century, he seems to have relied on some parts of "*Manusmriti*" (Canto 1, verse 23 - said to have been composed in ancient times by the great sage Manu) to emphasize that the Vedas were revealed to the sages of the day. He writes in *Satyartha Prakash*, "Brahma learnt the Vedas from Agni, Vayu, Aditya and Angiras." Unfortunately, this seems conjectural and a piece of circular reasoning (or, "hearsay" evidence) where the authority of one sage is derived from, or dependant on, the testimony of another sage and so on. In any case, Brahma is no palpable person any more than Agni (fire) or Vayu (wind) is; and Angiras is a sage mentioned in the Vedas. Dayanand is found further to state that: "So long as education was not introduced by the people of India (the people of - parenthesis added) Egypt, Greece and Europe were quite ignorant...Nor there (in "Aryavarta" – parenthesis added) were any people here before the Aryas" (quoted in Christoffe Jaffrelot, page 36 – see Bibliography).

Whether the people of Egypt or Greece would quite agree with Dayanand's ideas is not at all sure, and the point about there being no people in India before the Aryas is quite controverted by the findings of archaeology and anthropology as discussed in an earlier chapter. Jaffrelot has quoted another senior Hindu leader of the 19th century, Har Bilas Sarda, who had expressed his ideas on the caste system thus: "It (the caste system – parenthesis added) afforded to every member of the social body opportunity and means to develop fully his powers and capacities...this classification existed in its perfect form on the principle of heredity."

But it is precisely this "principle of heredity" that modern consciousness has questioned and hardly any rational person

     Prosenjit Dasgupta

believes this anymore. That all Arya Samaj leaders did not follow this line of reasoning is evident from the presidential address made in 1925 by Lala Lajpat Rai, when he said that: "They (the Hindus – parenthesis added) will be stultifying themselves if they replace their nationalism by communism (or, should it read "communalism"? – parenthesis added)…We know that the Mohammedans do not want a Muslim Raj…we know that the bulk of the Hindus do not want a Hindu Raj…I beg the Hindu community to remove the untouchability of all because it is wrong to consider any human being as untouchable."

Mahatma Gandhi, in his compilation of notes on "Communal Unity" (see Bibliography), bluntly asks the question: "What is the alternative to Hindu-Muslim unity? A perpetuation of slavery? If we consider one another as natural enemies, is there any escape from foreign domination for either of us?" (in "Young India?, 29.01.1921). Gandhi goes on: "My Hindu instinct tells me that all religions are more or less true…but all are imperfect because they have come down to us through imperfect human instrumentality…The Hindus, if they want unity among different races, must have the courage to trust the minorities" ("Young India", 29.05.1924). Again, Gandhi asserts, "True religion means good thoughts and good conduct…True patriotism also means good thoughts and good conduct" ("Young India", 09.01.1930).

It is not necessary that India of the 21st century must follow Gandhi's thought in totality; but at least those who wish to rely on his views and thoughts should take care not to misquote him. And those who wish to know further about Gandhi's views on this subject would do well to refer to the above-mentioned publication in the original; though it does run into more than 900 pages!

It was in this milieu of social reforms that had commenced from about the first half of the 19th century that the Indian National Congress (later mentioned as INC) was constituted in 1885 to bring about political reforms in the country with a greater degree of self-governance, leading ultimately to national independence. Much has already been written about the INC to bear repetition here. It should suffice to say that from the very beginning it was a very broad platform: a congress of the people of India, cutting across caste, creed, colour, economic or social standing. It is instructive to learn about the types of persons who attended the various annual sessions, and those who presided over them. The INC was all of that and was given direction and leadership by persons of learning (many being lawyers, or scholars, or men of standing), for whom independence of the country was much above the promotion of interests of any particular region, language, caste or creed. The persons and personalities who presided over the INC in the first sixty years of its functioning since 1885 represented most of the major religions and regions and had, remarkably for that period in time, three women presidents, viz. Mrs Annie Besant, Mrs Sarojini Naidu and Mrs Nellie Sengupta.

Chronologically speaking, the Muslim League (later mentioned as ML) came next, having been set up in 1906, and was clearly oriented towards the protection and promotion of Muslim interests. As to why the ML came to be constituted is an open question, with reasons put forward by scholars ranging from machinations by some British officers to set up an alternative to the INC that was pushing for independence, or, as a consequence to a wider education of Muslims since the setting up of the Aligarh Muslim University in the 1870s, or, as a reaction to the active Hindu "proselytization" through the shuddhi process in north-western India since the 1880s. It remained a moot point till 1946 as to whether the ML was really about the Muslim populace in India in general or was mainly concerned with the protection of the interests of Muslim landed gentry and clergy in Punjab and northern India. In any case, the ML came to mean, and more importantly, pressed for--and got from the British--a separate electorate and

     Prosenjit Dasgupta

reserved seats for Muslims. By 1940, it had come to demand a separate "homeland" for the Muslims of India in designated regions; but the upshot was that out of a Muslim population of about 91 million (or about 24% of the total population as per the 1941 Census of India), only 77 million Muslims were found to populate the areas designated as Pakistan in 1947, which meant that possibly about 30 million Muslims (taking also into account those who were in the princely states) stayed behind in independent India. It must be acknowledged that western Punjab, Sind, Baluchistan and East Pakistan, in any case, had pre-existing Muslim populations. As per the 2011 Census, Muslims, at about 172 million, constituted about 14% of the Indian population.

Since the turn of the 20th century, many major events affected the world, starting with the First World War and the consequent break-up of the Ottoman Empire, followed by the partition of Ireland, and the setting up of a homeland for Jews in Palestine. In this period of flux, as well as the provision of a separate electorate for Muslims by the British, as also the successive local municipal and district board elections as part of the Government of India Act of 1919 under the Morley-Minto reforms, there were opportunities for different communities and trades and professions to jockey for power to gain or retain advantages. One notable means was the setting up of schools for Hindus and Muslims separately in Punjab and the United Provinces (now largely Uttar Pradesh). Such tendencies progressively coalesced into the platform of the Hindu Mahasabha (later mentioned as HM), formally established in 1915. The HM was plainly for representation of what it considered to be "Hindu" interests; though it was not clearly spelt out what the "Hindu interests" were, other than as counter-poise to the so-called "Muslim interests" that the ML spoke of, also mostly in general terms. Each of them also spoke largely in terms of what were perceived to be threats—demographic, economic, and otherwise—by the other. But the

HM certainly gathered momentum as a political force since the 1920s with leaders like Lala Lajpat Rai and Pandit Madan Mohan Malaviya of whom any organisation would be proud. But there were others such as Swami Shraddhananda, V.D. Savarkar, Dr B.S. Moonje, Bhai Parmanand and some others who may be said to have more particularly represented "Hindu nationalism" (i.e., an aspect of nationalism specifically of, for and by Hindus) as compared to the "pan-Indian nationalism" that was being attempted at other levels by the INC, if it can be put in that way.

Several scholars have closely studied the growth and evolution of this Hindu nationalism over the past one hundred years or so. One may start with the references and commentaries by Christoffe Jaffrelot in his "Hindu Nationalism – A Reader" (see Bibliography). He has quoted extensively from the leaders of HM in an attempt to understand the philosophy and ideology behind this movement. For instance, Swami Shraddhananda, in his "Hindu Sangathan: Saviour of the Dying Race" (published in 1926), gives his views as: "The first remedy is to make the Bharatiya Hindu Shuddhi Sabha a living body...The second remedy is to revivify the ancient Ashrama Dharma and to place it on a sound basis...The third remedy lies in all the unconsummated child widows who have the desire to remarry...The fourth remedy is the revival of the Varna Dharma of the ancient Aryans...Theoretical Dharma is connected with individual salvation and, therefore, there is room for theists, pantheists, henotheists, and even atheists in the broad lap of the Hindu Samaj. *But the code of practical Dharma has to do with the community and here the plea of individual Dharma should not be allowed to prevail* (emphasis added)...The Catholic Hindu mandir should be devoted to the worship of the three mother spirits: Gau-mata, Saraswati mata and Bhumi mata" (pages 82-84 in Jaffrelot). It is neither necessary nor possible to discuss and debate why Swami Shraddhananda should have thought thus; but, in some

          Prosenjit Dasgupta

respects, he extended the thoughts and words of his mentor, Swami Dayanand.

Jaffrelot has similarly quoted from V.D. Savarkar, another notable leader of the HM, who, in his book, "Hindutva - Who is a Hindu" (1921 – reprinted by Bharatiya Sahitya Sadan in 1989), spells out his views. In this publication, Savarkar writes: "Long before the ancient Egyptians and Babylonians had built their magnificent civilizations, the holy waters of the Indus were daily witnessing columns of scented sacrificial smoke and valleys resounding with chants of Vedic hymns…The great mission which the Sindhus had undertaken of founding a nation and a country reached its geographical limit when the valorous prince of Ayodhya made a triumphal entry into Ceylon and actually brought the whole land from the Himalayas to the seas under one sovereign sway…(After the Third battle of Panipat – parenthesis added) never again had an Afghan dared to penetrate to Delhi while the triumphant Hindu banner that the Marathas had carried to Attock was taken up by our Sikhs and carried across the Indus to the gates of Kabul" (quoted by Jaffrelot, pages 91-93).

Savarkar was, no doubt, inspired by passionate nationalism, which he took to be founded on the three pillars of a geographical unity, a racial unity and a common culture. Thus, he is found again to state in the same publication that: "It was the one issue to defend the honour and independence of Hindustan and to maintain the *cultural unity and civic life of Hindutva and not Hinduism alone*" (emphasis added). Savarkar continues: "The story of their conversion (i.e., of Hindus into Muslims – parenthesis added), forcibly in millions of cases, is too recent to make them forget that they inherit Hindu blood in their veins…Some of our Mohammedan and Christian countrymen who had originally been forced to convert to a non-Hindu religion and who consequently have inherited along with the Hindus a common father-land and the greater part of the wealth of a common culture…are not and cannot be regarded as Hindus…if it (Hindusthan – parenthesis added) is not to them a holy land too." (page 95 in Jaffrelot)

Savarkar's view adopts several strands of reasoning in his own way. On the face of it, the point about unity of race and culture is not a rational and a historically correct approach; for, it is known even to college students of history that there had been many incursions and migrations into India, beginning with peoples speaking some Indo-European languages, then the Persians, followed by the Greeks, Parthians, Scythians, Turks, Mongols, and yet later by Ahoms in the east. Each such migration brought with itself their own baggage of history, ethnicity, culture, cuisine, languages, art and so on. Whether "millions" of conversions were made forcibly is a point of debate; for, the crushing burden of casteism on millions of Indians may well have impelled good numbers of them to seek refuge in the brotherhood preached by Islam, Christianity and Sikhism. Whether a "father-land" should necessarily transform and translate into a "holy land" is also moot; as, sons of a father may well go their different ways. There is little in history to suggest that India is necessarily and invariably to be equated with the Hindu, as Savarkar has done as per the above quotation; there are just too many "ifs" and "buts" for this to have come about. The concept of a nation has not been, and is not, synonymous or coterminous with any particular "race" or "religion". A nation is something much more, much bigger. That many of the local Muslims and Christians did not re-convert into Hindus despite the shuddhi programme of the HM since the turn of the 20th century is evidence enough that many (if not most of them) were quite happy as they were. It is clear that the passage of a couple of thousand years has not been able, even by the turn of the 21st century, to reduce this great concourse of peoples to a standard uniformity in race, culture or language. This has been beautifully described by the renowned poet Rabindranath Tagore, in his well-known poem, "*Bharat-tirtha*":

"Hey mor chitta, punya tirthey jagorey dhirey,
Ei Bharat-er mahamanab-er sagara tirey."

(Awake my soul at this holy place of pilgrimage,
This Bharat that is this ocean of humanity)

- a free translation

Chapter 16

Emergence of the Present - II

The next phase of Hindu nationalism (following the work of Swami Dayanand, Swami Shraddhanand, V.D. Savarkar, and others in the late 19th and early 20th centuries) commenced with the work of Dr K.S. Hedgewar in setting up the Rashtriya Swayamsevak Sangh (later mentioned as RSS) in Nagpur in 1932. If space is taken here to quote from the definitive views of leaders like Hedgewar-ji and Guru Golwalkar, as published in their respective books and articles, it is because there is a compelling need for a wider readership to have access to their thoughts and thus to gain a better appreciation of their thoughts and beliefs.

K.R. Malkani (the editor of the "Organiser", the official journal of the RSS, for long) in his book (see Bibliography) has given a historical round-up of the organisation. Necessarily, he starts with Dr Hedgewar who was born in 1889 and lost his parents at the age of about 14 years. He was considerably influenced by Dr B.S. Munje of the HM (whose role in Hindu "revivalism" has been poorly studied), and was sent by him to Kolkata to study medicine. There, he came in contact with revolutionary parties like the *Anushilan Samiti*; he became a Licentiate in Medical Sciences (LMS) in 1914. Hedgewar envisioned the RSS as a movement to rejuvenate those who adhered to the popular Hindu religion and culture, as they had come to be by the end of the 19th century in large parts of the country. Although Dr Hedgewar was initially with the INC, he seems to have become disillusioned with Mahatma Gandhi's non-violence and non-cooperation movements and started setting up *shakhas* (or branches) at the various *akharas* where the youth traditionally conducted physical exercises. He worked hard to set up the basic structure of the RSS. But he wrote little about his thoughts and ideas as to how this would be taken forward.

This work was taken up in earnest after Dr Hedgewar's demise in 1936 by Guru Mahadev Sadashiv Golwalkar, the first, formal *Sanghsarchalak*, or leader, who led and moulded the organisation until his death in 1974. Malkani mentions an interview with Guru Golwalkar where the latter stated that: "What diversity of race we had in the country to begin with was obliterated by time and circumstances...In Bharat, the word "Arya" is a measure of culture, not of a race" (page 62 in Malkani). This, in turn, gives rise to the question as to why the diversity of cultures that came with the diversity of races over the millennia did not get similarly "obliterated" with time and circumstances, and should have remained an "Aryan" monopoly. Malkani adds that Golwalkar further said that: "The Hindu expects the state to be informed by a certain moral quality; but, for the rest, leaves politics and religion sovereign in their respective fields" (page 70 in Malkani).

Malkani has also provided good source material when he mentions (page 127) that on an appeal by RSS to the District Judge against the order of the Joint Charity Commissioner reversing the order dated 22nd May 1974 of the Deputy Charity Commissioner, Nagpur, in which the JCC had stated that: "The objects of the organisation of the RSS are akin to political objects as distinguished from religious or charitable objects."

The RSS stated in an affidavit at the time that: "The work of the RSS is neither religious nor charitable, but its objects are *cultural and patriotic* as distinguished from religious or charitable. It is *akin to political purpose*, though, at present, the RSS is not a political party" (emphasis added).

One wonders what Sardar Patel would have thought of this, had he been alive in 1974; for he had accepted in good faith that the RSS was a cultural organisation and had lifted the ban on it in 1949. The RSS affidavit makes a fine distinction between the "work" of the organisation, and its "objects"; though one cannot quite make out as how such a dichotomy can exist in the functioning of a registered charitable society. It is also a debatable point if "patriotism" can really be a part of a culture, as it has connotations of a political ideology. Patriotism is a sense that develops under conditions of oppression and exploitation by others, and largely progresses to overthrow such oppression and exploitation. Such patriotism can then manifest itself in songs, literature, art, etc., if Atul Prasad Sen's song "*Uthhaga Bharata Laskhmi.......*", Rabindranath Tagore's novel "*Gharey Bairey*", and Picasso's painting "*Guernica*" are taken as examples. Moreover, the RSS affidavit mentions that it is not a political party "at present", i.e., in May 1974. This leaves open the option that it may become so in future.

Interestingly, Malkani has also recorded (page 128) a statement made on 31.07.1968 in the Rajya Sabha by Shri Y.B. Chavan, the then Home Minister of India, to the effect: "I say we do not treat them (the RSS – parenthesis added) as a political party. But we say that they certainly have a political ideology, a political bias, and, therefore, we say that participation in RSS activities will be tantamount to participation in a political organisation."

Evidently, under the Constitution of India, individuals have freedom to associate as they please. But, if at any time in seeking registration as a society or charity, they have publicly declared that their objects are cultural (as commonly understood and practiced), then it would be incumbent on them to abide by that declaration, if they do not wish to be de-registered. Alternatively, they have publicly to amend the "objects clause" in their constitution or rules and regulations. Just as the INC, with its history of over a hundred years, is already known for its views and programmes on nationalism, political and economic development, the foregoing should, to an extent, put in perspective the importance of issues of

 Prosenjit Dasgupta

patriotism, culture and overall philosophy of the RSS coming into public domain and knowledge.

Much of Golwalkar's thoughts on Hinduism and nationhood are contained in his two principal books, "We or Our Nationhood Defined" (published in 1939) and "Bunch of Thoughts" (published in 1966). In the former, he is found to write that: "The idea contained in the word nation is the compound of five distinct factors – Geographical (country), Racial (race), Religious (religion), Cultural (culture) and Linguistic (language)...a race is by far the most important ingredient of a nation...Race is the body of a nation and that with its fall, the nation ceases to exist...Based as it (religion – parentheses added) is on the unshakeable foundations of a sound philosophy of life, it has become elaborately woven into the life of the Race and forms as it were its very soul... We make war or peace, engage in arts and crafts all in accord with religious injunctions...Our race-spirit is a child of our religion and so with our culture is but a product of our all-comprehensive religion." But it seems that at some stage other ideas press on Golwalkar, and he is thus found to write (in the same book) that: "Religion is that by which by regulating society in all its functions, makes room for all individual idiosyncrasies and provides suitable ways and means for all sorts of mental frames to adapt and evolve...As many minds, so many ways – that is the way of true religion" (quoted in Jaffrelot, page 104). Then again, he writes: "To ban religion altogether from public and political life is but one step forward and a natural one" (Jaffrelot, page 105).

Golwalkar goes on to explain his view of Indian history as: "Living in this country since pre-historic times is this ancient race – the Hindu race, united together by memories of common glory and disaster, by similar historical, political, social and religious experiences, evolving a common culture, a common mother language, common customs, common aspirations"(quoted by Jaffrelot, page 114).

One wonders if every person living in India would necessarily agree with this view of Indian history. For a start, it is open to question whether there is, or has been, any "Hindu race" in the sense of a Caucasian race or a Mongoloid race at all. Also, the existence of Dravidian and Mundaric or the proto-Australoid races in ancient India is evident. It is for the very same reasons that there is no "common culture", a "common mother language" or "common customs" in quite the same sense as Golwalkar possibly meant them; even a "common glory" seems debatable. The course of Indian history, as would have been evident from the earlier chapters, has been marked by currents and cross-currents, eddies and whirlpools, and cannot be placed in a straitjacket of uniformity.

As already mentioned in an earlier section, one must read James Tod's "Annals and Antiquities of Rajasthan" (see Bibliography) to get a glimpse of the constant skirmishing and warfare between various Rajput clans until the early 19th century, the parricide and fratricide that occurred in this period and the exaction of tribute from several Rajput princes by one or the other of the Maratha chieftains. Seen in that light, any assertion about a "common glory" seems somewhat out-of-place. One would be far more inclined to fall in with Golwalkar's view that: "The spirit of broad Catholicism, generosity, tolerance, truth, sacrifice and love for life which characterize the average Hindu mind" (quoted in Jaffrelot, page 115). But he again reverts to his original theme, "Only those movements are truly "National" as aim at re-building, revitalizing and emancipating from its present stupor, the Hindu *rashtra*."

In another publication, "We, or our Nationhood Defined", quoted by Geeta Puri (in her book, pages 55-56, see Bibliography) Golwalkar is found to state: "The non-Hindu people in Hindustan must either adopt the Hindu culture and language, must learn to respect and hold in reverence Hindu

                    Prosenjit Dasgupta

religion, must entertain no idea but the glorification of the Hindu race and culture."

Not all Indians, not necessarily confined only to non-Hindus, are likely to feel comfortable with these rather radical views expressed by Golwalkar, bearing in mind the tendency often found among sections of current political leaders to brush these words under the carpet as being not quite convenient.

Guru Golwalkar goes on in his book, "Bunch of Thoughts", to express some anxiety and reservations about talks with Naga rebels, and the push for statehood in the Khasi Hills and in Jharkhand. But that is all in the past now. Both Meghalaya and Jharkhand are very much parts of the Indian Union today. He further writes that: "The ultimate vision of our work is a perfectly organised state of society wherein each individual has been moulded into a model of ideal Hindu manhood and made into the living limb of the corporate personality of Society" (page 88 in "Bunch of Thoughts"). These words need careful consideration. In fact, it is imperative to do so, because words are an expression of a sequence of thoughts of an individual, and more so especially when they belong to a person of eminence, who is in a position to influence the views and thoughts of many others. To begin with, these are not words that one would expect of a cultural organisation, as the RSS has always made itself out to be. The words, "perfectly organised state of society", suggest that the work of the RSS is more about organisation and much less about culture; for the latter necessarily has multifarious aspects, of language, literature, art, music and so on, and little if anything to do with organization. The references to individuals being "moulded" into a "model" of Hindu manhood gives rise to questions whether any such "moulding" (that has connotations of uniformity and standardization) is what India needs; or, that the effort should be better directed towards creativity and enterprise. A "corporate personality" of the "society" is also difficult to understand on the basis of a commonplace understanding of what "culture" is. Can--or should--culture have a corporate personality? It is certainly open to the RSS to define "culture" in its own way so that misunderstandings are avoided.

In avoiding any specific references or discussions pertaining to art, advancement of language and literature, music, etc., with which a cultural organisation is expected to be primarily concerned, a public disservice is done to a wider and a better understanding of the RSS's objects and motives. It is almost axiomatic that the concept of a state is a political concept, and not part of culture as normally understood. Standardization or uniformity of language, religion, or culture is not a particularly necessary pre-condition for statehood, whereas a common geographical area, shared history and experiences are its very foundations. Golwalkar has gone on to speak about moulding each individual into a model of ideal Hindu manhood, rather than a model citizen of a modern state in a progressive world order, as an "inclusive" and modern state policy would demand.

It is also necessary to take due note of what the late Deen Dayal Upadhyay (in many ways, the mentor and ideologue of the Jan Sangh and later of the Bharatiya Janata Party) had to say in his "Integral Humanism" (published in 1965) as again quoted in Jaffrelot. Upadhyay-ji became a member of RSS in 1937 and was later seconded by Guru Golwalkar to the Bharatiya Jan Sangh, when it was constituted in 1951 under the presidentship of Dr Shyama Prasad Mookerjee. This was shortly after the fortunes of the Hindu Mahasabha (of which Dr Mookerjee was a leading member, but from which he resigned in 1948) declined in 1948 when it became somehow linked in one way or the other with the killing of Mahatma Gandhi in that year. The RSS was also banned at that time by the Government of India, until they made changes in their constitution at the insistence of Sardar Vallabhbhai Patel, and emerged as a "cultural organisation", about which brief references have been made earlier.

In "Integral Humanism", Upadhyay-ji shares his thoughts on society and the individual, stating: "In our view, society is self-born. Like an individual, a society comes into existence in an organic way...Society has its body, mind, intellect and soul...Every society has an innate nature, which is inborn and not the result of historical circumstances...Chiti is fundamental and central to the nation...Chiti is the soul of a nation...An individual is not a single entity, but a plural entity...he can and should behave in a way that does not bring different aspects of his life into conflict, but which is mutually sustaining, complimentary and unifying. If the conflict is fundamental, the body cannot be sustained...There should be a tendency towards mutual accommodation in them...The ideals of a nation constitute 'Chiti'... the laws that help manifest and maintain Chiti of a nation are termed the Dharma of the nation...Worship of God is only part of the Dharma...Dharma Rajya does not mean a theocratic state...there is no need to tie up state and religion...The state has the responsibility to maintain an atmosphere in which every individual can follow the religion of his choice and live in peace...The freedom to follow one's own religion necessarily requires tolerance towards other religions...The truth cannot be decided by the majority" (quoted in pages 143 to 156 in Jaffrelot).

These words provide a gamut of views that seem on the face of it to be inconsistent in places. For instance, it is just not true that a given society is not the result or the product of historical circumstances. Every society, whether it is the USA, Sri Lanka, China, or India (which is not excepted), is largely the product of historical circumstances. History is a huge, almost unimaginably huge, and an inexorable force with multiple dimensions, which affects a body of people, and society is first and foremost a body of people. At the same time, Upadhyay is entirely right when he says that an individual is not a single entity but a plural entity, and that he or she should not act in a fashion that brings his or her life into conflict (be it internal or external). It is when individuals are not able to reconcile the different identities, or facets of their lives, those internal or external conflicts tend to arise and disrupt their lives. Those who know better or are at the helm of affairs need to advise, assist and guide them to develop a tendency for mutual understanding and accommodation; not to exacerbate the differences and conflicts. It is this sense and feeling of mutual accommodation and tolerance that has marked the society in India as an outcome of the historical process for the last 3,000 years or more. It is largely because of this sense of understanding, tolerance and providing space (both literally and metaphorically) to other peoples and views that India has been able to overcome so many adversities and asserted herself time and again over the centuries. While she may not have resisted by obvious force of arms, she has adapted and assimilated through a multitude of inter-personal contacts over the centuries, and thus overcome these adversities.

Three other utterances of Upadhyay-ji deserve special consideration. He says at one point that "there is no need to tie up state and religion" (quoted on page 154 in Jaffrelot). Secondly, he states that "the state has a responsibility to maintain an atmosphere in which every individual can follow the religion of his choice and live in peace". The third and most telling point is that "the truth cannot be decided by the majority" (on page 156, in Jaffrelot). These are most salutary thoughts. In just three sentences, he has summed the major principles of a modern state. If, therefore, there are some sections of political leadership, who, on the one side are taking Upadhyay-ji as their political Guru and on the other are unwilling or unable to live up to his tenets as outlined above, they are doing a disservice, both to his memory and to the nation at large.

It would be useful here to have a look at the resolution on

　　　　　　　　Prosenjit Dasgupta

"Indianization" (of all things) adopted at the Kanpur session of BJS in 1951 under the chairmanship of Dr Shyama Prasad Mookerjee. This stated: "It is essential that the whole of India being one nation and *one culture* be propagated...education must be based on *national culture* and tradition...*Indian history should be so rewritten that it may become the record of the Indian people and not merely of foreign invaders*" (emphasis added). Again, how is this "one culture" to be defined, and who is to define it? On the one hand, the Constituent Assembly of India (of which Dr Mookerjee had been a member) had gone into so many aspects of Indian history, practices, religions, languages and so on for more than three years, and had come out with the Constitution of India, which has been accepted and acted upon by all for more than seventy years; one needs to have a look at some of the neighbouring countries to realize if India had gained or lost in the process. On the other hand, it ill becomes a national party, many of whose leading lights had participated in the Constitution-making process to reopen the issue in 1951 on the issue of "one culture". It is the same with the proposals on education and re-writing of history of India. How is one to erase on the ground and from public memory and common practice, the languages, literature, social practices, religion, art, architecture, music, etc., that have been the result of multitude of effects--ill or well--of foreign invasions stretching back for more than a thousand years? Or, is there any compelling need now to do so? Should one attempt in 1950 to put in the dock the family of an individual who, for whatever personal reasons, had adopted Islam or Christianity or Sikhism or Buddhism in the 19th century? Thinking about all these things in the 21st century, it is anybody's guess as to how the Indian political, economic and social status would have worked out over the last 70 years had India adopted a "unitary" and Hinduism-based theocratic constitution in 1949-50 (assuming that that had been possible and necessary). At times, if one looks from the 'wrong end' of a binocular or telescope, the perspective substantially changes.

In another publication that is of note in trying to understand this "proximate history" of the present Indian political and social scenario, Koenraad Elst (see Bibliography) has dealt extensively with the literature and views underlying the present phase of "Hindu nationalism". He has relied extensively on documents by K.R. Malkani, H.V. Seshadri, Sita Ram Goel and others, as well as on interviews with several RSS leaders. Elst has called the rise of the RSS and the BJP as Hindu "revivalism", although he has not specifically discussed or defined as to what is this Hinduism of the distant past that is sought now to be revived. No doubt, there were great empires in the past, such as that of the Mauryas, the Sungas, the Kushans, the Satavahanas, the Guptas, the Cholas, and the Chalukyas. Each of these kingdoms had their own imperial precept and practice. Such changes in the ruling dynasties, each with different belief and administrative systems and the proliferation of religious texts and teachings, commentaries, faiths and practices makes it extremely difficult (if not impossible) to designate any particular set of sacred text, teachings, beliefs and practices to be specifically and distinctively "Hindu". Can we say with any certainty that the ideas and principles enunciated in the edicts of a Buddhist Ashoka are any less typical of India as she stands today? Or that the elegance of Mughal miniature art has not influenced Pahari miniatures to a certain extent? Why is it that the Indian diaspora in the UK, USA or elsewhere has in numerous cases inter-married into the local population, and has not maintained strict caste exogamy? Why is it acceptable there, but strenuously denied in many cases within the country? Should it really matter if something that is good, decent and beautiful is accepted and incorporated into the life and culture of a people? These questions need to be raised and answered, if India is to pull itself up by its boot-straps into the 21st century.

     Prosenjit Dasgupta

The country has the Rigveda, the principal Upanishads, the Bhagavad-gita, the epics Mahabharata and Ramayana, a large number of Puranas, and yet larger numbers of commentaries and notes by a multitude of scholars and sages. Moreover, there are devotees all over India of Vishnu as Narayana, Jagannatha or as Lord Venkateswara, Shiva as Vishvanatha and as Ardhanariswara and other manifestations, Shri Krishna in his many forms, Shri Rama, Kali in her various manifestations, Lord Ayyappa, Lord Muruga, and many other gods such as Lord Ganesha, Vithoba, Hanumana and folk deities like Manasa, or Sitala, or Ma Santoshi. A search for minor deities in Tamilnadu on Google yielded numerous names. How and who is to select and determine what would be this particular combination of texts, beliefs and practices that should guide each and all Hindus, to the exclusion of all other texts, beliefs, interpretations and practices? It is instructive to recall that it took the Bhandarkar Institute several decades to bring out a standard "critical" edition of the Mahabharata, and that a similar attempt on the Ramayana is still awaited. Elst has further gone on to describe this revitalization as an attempt to "decolonize" the Hindu mind by ridding it of all Western (and perhaps "Orientalist") influences on the various studies of the country's history and culture. This begs the question as to whether the entire Constitution-making process from 1946 to 1949 by a galaxy of people of learning and standing was entirely a fruitless process, by a collection of "non-decolonized" minds and hearts? Is it that small tribal republics and the tradition of the panchayat system over so many centuries make democracy an entirely foreign and unwanted experiment in India? To take this question further, is it then to be taken that the nationalism of Surendranath Banerjee, Lokamanya Tilak, Gopal Krishna Gokhale, Lala Lajpat Rai, Mohandas Karamchand Gandhi, Motilal Nehru, Chittranjan Das, Subhas Chandra Bose, Babasaheb Ambedkar and others of their age were all subject to unrequited Western influences?

Elst has further stated that: "This class of mostly Hindu-born Macaulayites has shaped the institutions of post 1947 India, including its de facto state ideology, secularism" (page 27). As observed above, this view seems to leave out of account the Constitutional debates for over three years, and specifically about secularism for more than three months as part of the deliberations of the Constituent Assembly of India comprising 292 elected delegates from British India, 93 from the princely states, and 28 Muslim members besides Scheduled Castes and Scheduled Tribes representatives. Moreover, there was no obvious reason for "Hindu Macaulayites" to have "secularism" in-built in the provisions of the Constitution as a state policy (in fact, the word "secular" was inserted in the Indian Constitution by the 42nd Amendment in 1975), unless they considered it as suitably reflecting the Indian ethos that had evolved over the centuries. They certainly did not have to do this to placate Macaulay who had been dead and gone since two centuries. It is, therefore, a gross abuse of the intelligence and integrity of the Constitution makers to label them "neo-Macaulayites". As already seen above, Golwalkar and Upadhyay at times also did not favour linking state policy with religion.

But somewhere along the way, there seems to have developed a definite link-up between the Hindu religion as understood and practiced by a cross-section of people, and Indian politics. This is evident in the way Hinduism was emphasized in the constitution of the RSS as it was framed in 1949 shortly after it was banned by the Government of India following the assassination of Mahatma Gandhi in January 1948. It is on record that on 11th September 1948, Sardar Patel wrote to Golwalkar that: "Their (i.e., the RSS – parenthesis added) opposition to Congress and that too of such virulence disregarding all considerations of personality, decency or decorum created a kind of unrest among the people." As Andersen and Damle (see Bibliography) have perceptively pointed out, *"Belief systems develop in response to cultural, social and psychological strains, which develop when existing symbols of authority, responsibility and civic purpose do not adequately explain the social situation.........They reduce the ambiguities created by the structural strains ...... They are cognitive maps.... A recurrent theme in belief systems is the identity of hostile forces"* (pages 71-72, in Andersen and Damle – emphasis added).

Perhaps the earliest historically known example of such social, economic and political strains arose in the prelude to the French Revolution of 1789 when the monarchy, and all that it represented, was identified as a "hostile force". But it did not occur in the same manner and extent in the UK in the 18th century where there was still a monarchy and a feudal system in place, because compromises and adjustments had commenced there as early as the Magna Carta. Other typical examples of such social and economic stresses breaking out into some form of popular protest are the Bolshevik Revolution in Tsarist Russia in 1917 and the rise of Hitler in Germany in the mid-1930s. In India, such cultural and social strains may be taken to have manifested themselves in various ways, following the incursions by Scythians in the 2nd century BCE, or the invasion by Mahmud of Ghazni in the 11th century and, again, following the consolidation of the British administration in the early 19th century. At such times, the then prevailing sense of self-esteem and superiority, and the overweening authority of the Brahmans and the Kshatriyas in religious and administrative matters, respectively, were no doubt shaken by these exogenous factors.

The RSS constitution of 1949 starts with a basic premise that would require some consideration. It refers to the "disintegrated condition" of the country as of 1948-49. While there had no doubt been severe communal riots practically from 1946 up till that time, the princely states had been mostly integrated into the Indian Union and the Constituent

Assembly had taken up its task in right earnest. Preliminary steps towards economic planning had also been taken in hand. Even if, for the sake of an argument, one accepts the point about "disintegrated condition", it is questionable if an organisation calling itself the Rashtriya Swayamsevak Sangh (the literal translation being "National Self-help Organisation") should dedicate itself to service the Hindu segment of society alone. Notably, a similar self-limitation has not been practised by the Bharat Sevashram Sangha of Swami Pranabananda or the Ramakrishna Mission. They have worked in all places and with all sections of people without exception. That apart, the RSS constitution further states its express object is "to eradicate the fissiparous tendencies arising from diversities of sect, faith, caste, creed, ……political, economic, linguistic and provincial differences among Hindus." If nothing else, this phrase does suggest that there were such fissiparous tendencies amongst various sections of the Hindu society, which leads to the question as to how such tendencies may be eradicated? Should this be by way of example, education and persuasion, or by providing only a singular template to mould a uniform, standardized version of Hinduism? The word "political", perhaps inserted by oversight in this part of the constitution, would necessarily require the organisation to reflect on, practice and preach some brand of political ideology that would minimize or entirely eradicate any fissiparous tendencies in political thinking in the Hindu populace. The RSS constitution then adds that it shall endeavour "to make them (the Hindus – parenthesis added) realize the greatness of their past, and to inculcate in them a spirit of sacrifice and a selfless devotion to the Hindu Samaj as a whole." By now it should be clear to any discerning reader that the "Rashtriya" part of the name and title of the organisation is just a manner of speaking. The work of the RSS to all intent and purposes is therefore confined to Hindu society only; and a Hindu society as envisaged by them. If at all the RSS would like really to

            Prosenjit Dasgupta

extend their scope of work to the nation as a whole, it must necessarily--and more meaningfully--identify with, and address the problems and concerns of the other segments of the Indian populace, e.g., the Buddhists, Christians, Muslims, Sikhs, the Scheduled Tribes and Scheduled Castes, Other Backward Castes, and all marginalized persons.

Further, the RSS constitution goes on to say that the Hindu Samaj is to be revitalized on the basis of its Dharma and Sanskriti in order to achieve the all-round development of "Bharatvarsha". In thus transiting from the specific to the general, somehow the revitalization of Hindu Samaj is taken *ipso facto* to be equivalent to the development of "Bharatvarsha"; that may or may not be wholly true. The pledge that each and all RSS members have to take, similarly equates the work of fostering the greatness of Bharatvarsha with the growth of Hindu Dharma and Hindu culture. It is notable that among the functions that the RSS annually holds are the Hindu Samrajya Divotsav (coinciding with the coronation day of Chhatrapati Sivaji), and *Guru Dakshina*, the day the *sakha* members of the RSS give donations in front of the *Bhagwa Dhvaja* or the saffron flag of the organisation. This flag embodies for the RSS members the spirit of the organisation and of the Hindu nation. Whether this, in any way, clashes with or diminishes the significance of the Tricolour (as adopted by the Constituent Assembly of India) for the RSS members as the Indian national flag is not clear. At the same time, it is certainly true that India cannot achieve her true potential greatness if the Hindus (who comprise about 75% of the population) are not guided to rise above their distinctions and divisions of caste, creed and gender and make their due contribution to the economic and social development of the country. It is for consideration by each citizen of India whether this would be better served by understanding, appreciating and adjusting for the extant diversities and dissimilarities rather than by placing each and all in a straitjacket of belief, faith and practice. One is tempted to suggest that this process of adjustment and adaptation is very alike an organic process, almost like osmosis or cell growth. In point of fact, one renowned scholar, Vasudev Saran Agrawala, has referred to the nature of this as "symbiosis". Whether or not this symbiotic process should be allowed normally to take place or should be administered an antidote to kill it would be a decision that the RSS would have to take, with consequences flowing naturally from acting one way or the other.

The Bharatiya Jan Sangh (BJS) that was constituted in 1951 had very similar provisions in its constitution, e.g., references to political, social and economic development of the country on the basis of *"Bharatiya Sanskriti and Maryada"* (i.e., Indian culture and greatness). To this were added provisions for the protection and promotion of the cow and, strange to tell, "changes in the judicial system to suit the genius of India". Whether this meant instituting the tenets of "Manusmriti" wholesale into the judicial process, however, was not made clear. As to why Dr Shyama Prasad Mookerjee, a person of considerable political sagacity, considered the setting up of a political party separate from the HM as a matter of some urgency is not known; but it is possible that with the heavy influx of Hindu refugees from West Pakistan immediately following the Partition of India, it was thought politic to provide them with a clearer political voice. Geeta Puri, in her interesting and useful study of the working of the BJS in the Delhi Region in the 1970s (see Bibliography), has emphasized that the initial focus of the BJS was on the refugee population and, by extension, the party focussed on criticizing Government's policies on Pakistan and on Kashmir, cow protection and increased use of Hindi, rather than the equally pressing issues of land reforms, agricultural development, employment generation, education, health, development of industrial infrastructure, and so on. In so doing, she has observed that each political party has a "philosophical past" and expresses the distinct "cultural needs" of its members, besides fulfilling some of their "psychological

     Prosenjit Dasgupta

aspirations". This is close to what Andersen and Damle had pointed out, as mentioned above. Puri has mentioned that the late Deen Dayal Upadhyay, perhaps the chief ideologue of the party, felt that the Indian Constitution runs counter to the unity and individuality of Bharat. Upadhyay-ji had added that: "Our Constitution should be unitary instead of federal" (in his work, "Integral Humanism", 1965, page 31, as quoted by Puri). He goes on to state that: "Any talk of composite culture is not only untrue but dangerous, for it tends to weaken national unity" (at the BJS Pratinidhi Sabha at Vijaywada, 25th June 1965 – also quoted by Puri).

Getting back to Koenraad Elst, following his researches into the literature of the RSS and BJS, as well as interviews with senior RSS functionaries, he is found to state that: "A perusal of the literature of Hindutva movement will leave the reader with an impression of unusual intellectual poverty" (page 225 in Elst). This is a remark of notable candidness, and Elst goes on to add: "The RSS has contributed its own wilful anti-intellectual prejudice" (page 229). Even while questioning the sweeping nature of this statement, one is inclined to think that there is possibly a modicum of truth in it. Elst quotes Golwalkar from his "Bunch of Thoughts" (page (640/641) that: "Everyone has the right to follow his path according to his persuasion," but also notes that Golwalkar "has not bothered to give a decent factual and conceptual basis to his view on the Hindu-Muslim conflict" (page 346 in Elst). Despite his considerable interest in trying to understand the RSS viewpoint (that, in turn, considerably colours the BJP's political ideology), Elst is found to ask himself the question as to why, if India is the natural homeland for all Hindus, Nepal so consistently maintains its separateness; or, why the Tamils in Sri Lanka are seeking a "Tamil Eelam" as part of that country rather than in India (page 465). One is left wondering if Elst's education and training in Europe, where reason and rationality are in-built into the curriculum, led him to ask whether in RSS logic, (when truth may be approached from different angles and may be considered as different formulations of that one truth), false doctrines and untruths are not possible? More tellingly, Elst finds himself considering the proposition that: "It (the insistence that the Hindu state will be a truly secular state – parenthesis added) fails to tell why a Hindu state will be preferred to its alternatives, such as a Nehruvian state" (page 486). Thus, it does appear that the "decolonization" of the Hindu mind is really to no purpose, as the "Indian" mind with its traditions of logic, debate and discussions is more than capable of pursuing its search for "higher truths".

Another book, this one by Tapan Basu, Sumit Sarkar and others (see Bibliography), provides an academic angle to the issue. In their Introduction to the book, the authors observe that, "The communalism that claims to represent the majority community has the tremendous advantage of being able to masquerade as democracy and national." But they make the important point that in a democracy, no majority can ever be assumed to be permanent and fixed. This, it should be observed, is because with passage of time, people get educated, develop their own independent lines of thinking, or they may migrate to other places in search of livelihood and develop other likings and interests, or they may marry into other communities and so on. Society, itself, is transformed over time, as the demographics change and new technologies and new lifestyles intervene. More particularly, in the case of India, the majority line of thinking about land reforms and of building a socialistic pattern of society that had guided Indian politics for the first two decades after Independence, slowly modified and changed, till by the 1990s, the country had moved to a more liberal economic pattern. The earlier stress on developing institutions of higher learning has been considerably supplemented by the "*Sarva Siksha Abhiyan*", or education for all. Such social change has also found reflection in political change. The changes of regime in Kerala, or in

                    Prosenjit Dasgupta

West Bengal, Assam, and even in Uttar Pradesh, over the last twenty years or so, are witness. The political changes that have come in Chhattisgarh, Madhya Pradesh, Rajasthan and Punjab in more recent months are there for all to see. Without labouring this point too much, one may further draw attention to changes in legal interpretation of constitutional rights over time, e.g., in the recent case of "gay rights".

The above book also makes the point that before the development of transport and communications (railways, telegraph and the circulation of journals and newspapers) by about the middle of the 19th century and the consequent coming nearer (in terms of time and information) of different parts of the country for purposes of social and economic interaction, any sharply-defined identities (and, therefore, any resultant acrimony or animosity) were hardly possible. Social, economic and political life was largely confined to the *mohalla* (the local precinct) or to the village, and inter-personal relationships were generally known and accepted as "given". Things began to change as the local self-government elections to municipalities and district boards since the last decades of the 19th century sharpened the quest for loaves and fishes of office. Further, sections of the trading community of north India seem to have been persuaded that investment of time and money in some forms of religious practices assuaged to an extent any sense of guilt over private profits and provided an anchorage in traditional collectivist moorings that do not threaten class interests (page 35 in Tapan Basu, et al.). They go on to add that the RSS shakhas, or local groupings, provided, at least in suburban areas and in small towns, the only form of regular leisure-time socialization and intellectual activity (page 36). They also quote K.R. Malkani (the long-time editor of the "Organiser", the RSS journal, writing on 8th April 1979) that the RSS does not encourage "Doubting Thomases" (page 38 in Tapan Basu, et al), and that the shakha training produces assertive certitudes in the minds of the participants.

The belief generally came to be adopted that the conquest and dominance by foreigners created the illusion that India was a land of many different but equal cultures. This pluralism is then sought to be made subservient to Hindutva (a term first used by Savarkar and later visualized by the RSS), by a simple process of co-option, without quite spelling out the premises for such appropriation. As the book observes, the RSS-BJP-VHP combine arrogates to itself the unique power of defining what being a Hindu means, and, therefore, the will of this political formulation must prevail. Tapan Basu et al., call this a form of "controlled pluralism" (page 63). As the book suggests, gender issues, caste divisions and class frictions, as well as the overriding issue of exploitation of man by man, remain the "Achilles heel" of the RSS-BJP-VHP combine in the long-run, despite notable successes in the short-run.

One obvious way to exercise control and supervision over the "others" be they Muslims, or Christians, or Dalits, would be to treat them as second-class citizens and to put their rightful place in the mainstream of public life on the backburner. While this would indeed be most unfortunate, the consideration whether this would be desirable or even remotely possible is a matter that does not appear to have been given much thought. It is not easy to alienate up to 30 to 35% of the population of a country at the margins of public life, when so many of them are closely involved with, and participating in every bit of economic activity, be it in agriculture, industry, textiles, transport, construction, health and sanitation, and what-have-you. Further, the repercussions that any move to marginalize such sections of the population are likely to have on our neighbouring countries, such as Malaysia and Indonesia, and farther afield in the USA or Europe, does not require much imagination to envisage.

Bearing in mind the points made above, so many more questions yet call out for answers and clarifications. One, rather obvious one, is why the very things that so many Indians

     Prosenjit Dasgupta

clearly believe in, such as the "*pushpaka rathas*" or the aerial chariots that the great heroes of the epics travelled in, have not yet been found in any of the archaeological explorations conducted so far – even as relicts? Why is it that so many commentaries and notes have been written on the texts of the Vedas and Upanishads, which pose so many varying thoughts and perceptions--from the sublime to the common-place--to the exclusion of any equivalent contemporary studies and commentaries on the rock edicts of Ashoka (very much evident on pillars, rock faces, etc.) since the 3rd century BCE? Why are the Ashokan edicts in Prakrit language and not in proper Sanskrit? Was the emperor not thought good enough to have been instructed in Sanskrit? Why were the Vedas not written as palm leaf manuscripts and copied and re-copied over the centuries (as has been done for Buddhist and Jain and so many other documents) rather than our having to depend on an indirect source of etymological studies by Yaska in the 6th century BCE, long after they are supposed to have been conceived and discussed? Why are there no Sanskrit inscriptions in the Devanagari script before the 3rd century CE, although Panini had written his famous Sanskrit grammar in the 5th century BCE? What was the benefit or the advantage in committing great thoughts and texts to memory rather than as written transcriptions, especially when accurate reproduction of Vedic texts and proper pronunciation of such texts were considered to be of such vital importance? Is it that (in the most extreme case) no commonly accepted Sanskrit script had developed by the middle of the second millennium BCE? Are these questions at all relevant, or are they childish and of no consequence?

Of course, it must be admitted that the fundamental tenets of a faith, be it the message of equality before God, of compassion and moral order, of forgiveness and the grace that God represents, or walking the path to a personal salvation, will and do attract many people. But it is the mystique of the cadenced chants, hymns and the elaborate rituals that holds many of them together as notable components of a coherent community and society. People do perhaps hanker to be part of a community and quite often shy away from developing that degree of "*individuation*", or emerging as an individual with an identity of his or her very own, as distinct from being just a unit in a larger, amorphous community. Perhaps they would not really know what to do with that individuality and would feel quite lost without the comforting cocoon of an all-embracing community.

At the end of it, withholding of knowledge, be it about the nature of man or nature of God, issues of morality, etc., can only lead to perpetuation of ignorance in the general populace. Such ignorance is often the basic malady that afflicts a people and hinders their physical, spiritual and moral development. One is then inclined to believe that Karl Marx's view that religion is an opiate of the people has more than a modicum of truth. The spread of knowledge about the world, about natural phenomena and about ourselves may, therefore, be considered the fundamental panacea for the eradication of ignorance that impedes man from improving himself and making a meaningful contribution to improvement of the community––and indeed, the nation––at large. But this will come at a cost, a cost to the existing edifice of status, privileges, power and authority founded on unquestioning submission to such authority. That is the crux of it, the questions that will literally explode in the human mind, watered and tended by knowledge. It is such questions that no amount of organisation, "democratic centralism", strictures and diktats will be able to answer; for they will be about the fundamentals of the human condition, about why things are as they are and not otherwise, and they would not be satisfied by contrived answers or solutions. It is the questions themselves that will draw forth the answers; suppression of questions and questioning can only lead to that *dhandh* or *golok-dhadhna* or confusion or

    Prosenjit Dasgupta

mental maze that most Indians are not comfortable with.

And that has been the history of India from time immemorial. The Nasadiya Sukta of the Rigveda, "*Na asat asit na u sat asit tadanim*," expressed that question and the ability to live with that lack of certitude so well. The same line of thinking looms in the observations by sage Uddalaka Aruni to the questions put by his son, Swataketu: "*Tat tvam asi, Swataketu*" (or, "Thou art that, Swataketu" pointing to the tiniest particle of a seed). It was the persistent questions by Swataketu to Uddalaka, by Maitreyi to sage Yajnavalka, by Nachiketa to Yama, that led to the emergence of the majesty of Indian metaphysics in the Upanishads. It was this majesty that led to the great German philosopher, Schopenhauer, to exclaim, "It is the most satisfying and elevating reading which is possible in the world; it has been the solace of my life and will be the solace of my death."

Is there an Indian who has not heard those words from the Brihadaranyaka Upanishad in school or at some public function: "*Asatoma sadgamaya, Tamasoma Jyotirgamaya*", or "Lead me from untruth to truth, from darkness to light"? It is this eternal search of man for truth and light that has led to this quest and questioning, which is to be allowed and accepted, and even encouraged. It is, in turn, the Upanishads that have leavened the philosophy of the Bhagavad-gita, that other of great Indian sacred texts, and indeed set off the sage Adi Shankara on his quest for Advaitabad. They also set the stage for the "*Vishistadvaitavad*" of Ramanuja and "*Dvaitavad*" of Madhavacharya. The great Indian tradition of Bhakti Marga or the path of devotion to a personal godhead, found its source in these philosophies, leading further to the teachings of Kabir, Shri Chaitanyadeva, and Guru Nanak-ji. It is the very salt and breath of India. And so, one comes at the end of this quest to that fantastic assertion, "Ayamatma brahma" or 'this inner Self is the Brahman', as given in the Mandukya Upanishad, on the ultimate conviction that there is a reflection of God in each person. As it is said, the *briefest and simplest hypothesis possible is the Truth*. It is the dharma of every Indian; indeed, of every human being, in his or her good time, if he or she should so choose, to embark on that quest.

Going over these various books by Jaffrelot, Elst, Geeta Puri, Tapan Basu and others (as mentioned in the Bibliography), that provide insights into the thinking and organisational approach of Hindutva, one gains much material for the inquisitive and inquiring mind.

If one has carefully followed the story so far, it would seem that in the recent present, that is, in the decades following 1984-85, the RSS on the one hand and the BJP on the other hand, as the principal adversary to the other national party, the INC, have come to define Indian nationhood largely as "Hindu nationhood" to the exclusion (to the extent necessary or possible) of "hostile forces". The hostile force, in the main, is taken as the INC, as the propagator of an alternative narrative of India as a nation and, perhaps, as a "Macauley-fied" set of people that Konraad Elst earlier referred to. Others, believed also to be inimical to the Hindu nationalism, have been from time to time, identified as the Muslims of India, Christians and any "apostate" Hindus, who refuse to be confined in any straitjacket of beliefs and practices, following thereafter. The INC, on the other hand, is fundamentally opposed in principle and in ethos to the concept of a Hindu rashtra with its uniquely defined characteristics. If the INC, in turn, had considered some forces as "hostile", they were primarily some external quasi-imperialistic and hegemonistic forces outside the country, or terrorist elements within. Somehow, that children's story by Hans Christian Andersen on "The Emperor's New Clothes" springs up in the mind and one is left somewhat bemused at the sheer number of Indians happily residing in other countries (about 6 million in the USA alone) and so many students competing to study overseas far away from Bharatavarsha without really being conscious that what

     Prosenjit Dasgupta

they may be doing militates against what they and their parents may have believed in and practised. As someone put it gently, "situational ethics", that is, developing an ethical system to rationalize a situation one is prepared to live with, has come to be quite an accomplished art form in India.

Up to this point, it should thus be evident that there are basically two principal narratives of the emergence of India as a nation and as a state that are playing themselves out. There is one of the INC, dating back to 1885, that spearheaded the national movement for self-governance and independence with a distinctive ethos based on its reading of Indian history and culture. The other is that of the Arya Samaj-Hindu Mahasabha-RSS-BJS-BJP, since the first decade of the 20th century, based on their understanding of the historical process in India over the past many centuries. There would also be claims that the various sections of Communists since the late 1920s and mid-1960s have developed their own theses of historical developments based on Marxist interpretation of the economic, political and social evolution in India. No doubt, other political parties, such as the Bahujan Samaj Party, or the Samajvadi Party and some others may similarly put forward their own interpretations.

Be that as it may, one must on no account overlook that there is yet a third narrative that gets usually crowded out in considering only the "pan Indian" and the "Hindu-oriented" viewpoints of the INC and the BJP, respectively. This is the view of Indian history and of themselves by the Other Backward Classes, the Scheduled Castes and the Scheduled Tribes, constituting the fourth caste, the Shudras, as commonly believed in India's varnashram or caste structure. Only a few historians in the past, such as D.C. Sircar, Dr Suniti Kumar Chatterji, and some others have taken note of the early tribal communities and republics that had once come up in various parts of India over a millennium ago. One tends to presume that since they were not Christians or Muslims, they should be considered as Hindu by way of religious practice and character. Anyone who has travelled extensively in central India or in parts of Andhra Pradesh (now bifurcated also into Telangana), Tamil Nadu, Odisha (previously Orissa) and some other states would have noticed that in many places the religious practices are quite different and even gods have different appearances to what one is usually accustomed to elsewhere in India; the Hidimba temple in Manali in Himachal Pradesh is a case in point. One has to go back to the books by E. Thurston, Verrier Elwin, Sarat Chandra Roy, J.H. Hutton, Prof. Nirmalkumar Bose, Dr D.N. Majumdar and some others to have a glimpse into the lives of these peoples. It is, as if, a separate reality, distinct and different from what one normally takes for granted had existed in our midst, which few, if anyone, had even noticed. It was Jyotiba Phule in the 19th century, and later Dr Bhimrao Ambedkar and E. Ramaswami Naicker, who brought their lives, identities and concerns into public gaze and concern. What it meant to be a Dalit under the shadow of upper caste domination, to be segregated to the outskirts of villages, to be denied water from the village well, de-barred from worshipping in the village temples, prevented from being properly educated, de-barred from inter-dining, to be asked to move away lest their shadow fall on an upper caste person, prevented from sitting on a chair in front of an upper caste, or travelling on a horse or a palanquin through an upper caste neighbourhood, has been progressively revealed in Dalit literature of, by and for the oppressed, the exploited, or the untouchables, since the mid-1950s.

To know more about the personal experiences of the OBCs, though anecdotal, it would be eminently relevant here to refer to the book by Shri Kancha Ilaiah (see Bibliography), which is most informative and instructive about the real position of the Dalits in the 1950s and 60s that the rest of India ought to be made aware of; although the position in Telangana (where Shri Ilaiah was born and spent his childhood) may have been more acute than perhaps in West Bengal and Assam. One is taken aback by the insights that he provides into what being a Dalit meant in the given social, economic and cultural milieu of Andhra Pradesh at that point of time. It is especially notable that he has underlined the "conspiracy of silent violence" that he witnessed in his childhood; though it may be more properly described as "violation" rather than as violence, for the attitude and behaviour of many of the upper castes militated against every civility and decency due to a human being. As Shri Ilaiah puts it, morality or immorality as understood and practised in Dalit society is not based on divine edict but in terms of the promotion of harmony in society; that idea surely deserves careful thought. He considers that the "textbook" morality of the caste Hindus in the community was different from the "living" morality of the Dalits in that they lived and loved in a far more transparent manner. Shri Ilaiah also makes the important point that some among the Shudra "upper castes", such as Reddies, Kammas, Marathas, Patels and Bhumihars, have tended increasingly to emerge as "neo-Kshatriyas", as part and parcel of the overall Hindu caste system (page 35 in Shri Ilaiah). Possibly this is due to the natural inclination of each person and each community to make self-advancement as far as possible, even if it means severing their identity from the omnibus Shudra population. He is, at the same time, hopeful that this conflict between the open, empirical and real-life outlook of the Dalits and the prescriptive, textual, closed mind of the Hindu upper caste system will lead to new hope for a national future in the days to come (page 65). One may not agree with each and everything that Shri Ilaiah has stated; but, overall, his book offers a perspective that is most valuable if conscious attempts are to be made for "real" thorough-going social progress and true equality of the citizens in the eyes of the law.

While sages and saints of India since the medieval times, such as Kabir, Tukaram and Guru Nanak, had pleaded for the brotherhood of man, it would not be wrong to say that later reformers like Raja Rammohan Roy, Ishwar Chandra Vidyasagar and others in the early part of the 19th century, through their advocacy of reforms such as the abolition of widow-burning, avoidance of child marriages, promotion of widow re-marriages and women's education in general, struck at the some of the practices of caste Hindus. But, it was left to one of the Backward Classes, the Untouchables themselves, Mahatma Jyotiba Phule, who highlighted the self-identity of the Dalits through his pioneering work in the "Satyashodhak Samaj" and women's education in the middle of the 19th century. This identification and projection of the Dalits was taken to new heights by Dr B.R. Ambedkar since the 1920s. He crossed swords more than once with Mahatma Gandhi on the need for thorough-going social reforms as a condition-precedent to political reforms. He argued for a separate electorate for the Depressed Classes (i.e., those who were subjected to severe social discrimination) at the Round Table Conference in London in 1932 leading to the "Communal Award" in that year and the fast unto death by Mahatma Gandhi. The moral and political sensibility of Ambedkar must be recognised in that he entered into negotiations with Gandhi that culminated in the Poona Pact of 1932, by which, instead of separate electorates, the Scheduled Castes and Tribes and the Depressed Classes were given reserved constituencies, and Gandhi-ji broke his fast.

Ambedkar used his wide scholarship of both Indian sacred texts and western political philosophers to make his fellow citizens aware of the enormity of the injustice done to the Untouchables. In one place, he quotes Edmund Burke to point out: "A nation is not governed when it is perpetually to be conquered." At another place, he refers to the significance given in the Bhagavad-gita to both the "Karma Kand" of Jaimini in his "Purva Mimamsa" and to the "Jnana Yoga" in Badarayana's "Uttara Mimamsa". He quotes from Prof. J.

                    Prosenjit Dasgupta

Dewey's "Democracy and Education – An Introduction to the Study of Education" that: "An individual can live only in the present. The present is not something that comes after the past, much less something produced by it. It is what life is, in leaving the past behind it" (page 313 in Ambedkar's "Essential Writings" – see Bibliography). As a scholar in economics and public finance, he underlines the point that by not permitting readjustment of occupations and, binding that down to an accident of birth (i.e., in reducing economic mobility) *the caste system adversely affects employability and employment* (page 264 in "Essential Writings", emphasis added). In another article, he refers to the thoughts of Ernest Renan, the French scholar, who in 1882 discussed at length about nationhood and who had observed that, *"Race must not be confounded with nation* …a nation is a living soul…the common possession of a rich heritage of memories …the consent and desire to live together …the past an inheritance of *glory and regrets* to be shared, in the future (the) ideal to be realized and hoped (for) together …*suffering together is a greater bond of union than joy* (emphasis added – quoted on page 459 in "Essential Writings"). Hero-worship of Dr Ambedkar is commonly done, and it is necessary to do so, not just as a "tokenism", but as an act of faith in truth, justice and basic humanism.

J. Michael Mahar in his book (see Bibliography) has rightly pointed out the possible displacement of the "old dharma" of religious and social prejudices of caste Hindus against the Depressed Classes by the "new dharma" of the Constitution of India, especially in Article 15. Subsequently, the Special Marriages Act 1954 allowed for inter-caste and inter-faith marriages and the Untouchability Offences Act of 1955 further elaborated on the provisions of the Constitution. Despite all this, the deep-seated prejudices that have persisted even after 70 years of coming into force of the Constitution, tell their own story. It ought to be recorded here that the Government of India initiated the setting up of the National Commission on

Backward Classes (NCBC) in 1993 following persistent pressure from several political parties espousing the cause of the OBCs. The "Socio-Economic Caste Census" followed in 2011; that is, more than 60 years after the attainment of Independence to gain a better understanding of the social and economic standing of the backward castes and to take measures for their amelioration, however belated or minimal that may be. At least the data is now there in black and white. According to the 2011 Census, about 74% of the rural households subsisted on a family income of Rs.5000 per month; 36% of the 884 million people in rural India are illiterate; about 60% of the 179 million rural households were in a deprived or extremely poor condition in 2011-12; and 56% of the same 179 million rural households did not have any land of their own. As per the report of the NCBC in 2013-14, India had 2416 categories of OBCs in which Maharashtra topped with 261 categories, Odisha had 200, Karnataka had 199, Tamil Nadu 181, Bihar 134 and Andhra (then undivided) 111 categories. Also relevant is the finding of National Sample Surveys conducted in 1999-2000 and again in 2004-05, that shows that about 43% of the population that considered themselves to be Hindus were OBCs, while over 39% of Muslims were similarly found to be OBCs, the corresponding numbers for Christians being 25% and Sikhs over 22%. Obviously, the nation has to formulate specific policies and programmes that would result in more "inclusive" and more effective amelioration of their conditions.

If it be taken that Muslim self-identity in India in modern times started with the work of Sir Syed Ahmed, and that of Hindu identity with Swami Dayanand (it being borne in mind that the work of Raja Rammohan Roy, Ishwar Chandra Vidyasagar and others in the early part of the 19th century was in social reforms, without regard to caste or creed), it should be appreciated that similar self-identity of the Dalits started with the pioneering work of Jyotiba Phule and Narayana Guru in the middle of the 19th century. It was taken to new heights by

     Prosenjit Dasgupta

Dr B.R. Ambedkar, not only during his lifetime but also after his passing away by several of his adherents. The Ambedkar Centenary in 1991 and the availability of his books in regional languages provided a new impetus to the Dalit movement.

Unless one makes a deliberate effort to find out, it will not be known that a search for "Dalit literature" on Google leads to over 12-lakh "finds" while references to Dalit literature in English or English translations number over 2 lakhs. It is a growing body of work, with several anthologies of Dalit literature available, besides biographies and general academic work. These need wider awareness, study and appreciation, at least in the Indian academic community, so that study courses on Hindi or Marathi literature necessarily include elements of Dalit literature in Hindi or Marathi; although, no doubt, the position may now have somewhat improved from the acute position of the 1950s. Attempts to undo the "conspiracy of silent violence" must be undertaken, not by press statements and academic writings in journals, but by example, with all concerned sections standing in with the dispossessed and marginalized, voicing their concerns and working to address them, much as Mahatma Gandhi and other leaders had done in the early part of the 20th century and many of the social reformers who had preceded him in the 19th century.

One must also take into consideration the progressive unfolding of "other narratives" that "higher" OBCs, "lower" OBCs, Dalits, Scheduled Tribes and others who were beyond the pale till about the 1980s, will bring to the table. Much of all this is, therefore, "work in progress" and only time will tell how the situation develops in the future. Even then, there will no finality; for there can be no check on Father Time.

Chapter 17

The Present takes centre-stage

This narrative has been long in telling. One compelling reason for that has been the persistent emphasis in recent years, by at least a notable section of political leadership, on their particular reading of the "past" to explain their view of the "present" and in projecting their concept of the "future". This would have been quite understandable from about the latter half of the 19th century when the Indian identity and the Indian sense of nationhood were in the making. There is some cause for bewilderment, therefore, when this attempt is renewed in the last decades of the 20th century, after the country has been independent for 70 years and has charted out its own course for the future with a broad consensus on the major issues; further, different political parties have tasted power at some time or the other, and have gained a good idea about the immense problems that the administration of a country of the size and diversity of India presents. Under these circumstances, for a meaningful discussion of the current issues in context, one is compelled to make an overview of the past from the time of the Indus Valley Civilization (or even earlier) through the Rigvedic times to the great epics, Puranas and onwards. This should provide perspective to the "particular past" that is sought to be reconstructed, and from which, the present is being interpreted and acted upon.

As mentioned in an earlier section, Geeta Puri has observed that each political party is constructed on a "philosophical past", and represents the distinctive cultural pattern of its members, besides fulfilling some of their "psychological aspirations". Thus, relying on a particular reading of the past by a political party should not be entirely surprising; because

    Prosenjit Dasgupta

each section of the political class would like to consider itself as representative, in fact, overwhelmingly representative, of the populace at large, so as to generate a mandate to rule. The Democrats and the Republicans slog it out in the USA as do the Conservatives and the Labour party representatives in the UK, the Social Democrats and the Christian Democrats in Germany, and so on. Finding and defining one's political space in a country like India with its size and diversity is particularly difficult and, that has been one of the main reasons for the rise of regional parties like the DMK, Shiv Sena, Biju Janata Dal, Asom Gana Parishad, Telegu Desam Party, Telangana Rashtra Sanghatan and so many others focussed mainly on regional issues and sentiments.

In the middle of all this, if there has been any remarkable development and rise of any political party over the last 30 years or so, it has been that of the Bharatiya Janata Party (or BJP) that was constituted on 5th April 1980. One major reason for this could be the relative decline of the INC since 1967, when, for the first time in India, several state governments that had been ruled by the INC since Independence came under coalition governments. The second was the ouster of the INC at the national level in 1977. Possibly, the party that had provided the vanguard for the Independence movement from the 1880s was just growing older and was no longer able to keep a grip on national issues. Only time will tell if it is able to rejuvenate itself and again become a political force to reckon with.

The constitution of the BJP progressively evolved over the years, and as it emerged by the early 1990s, it attempted to avoid mention of either *Hindu Samaj* or *Bharatiya Sanskriti* and *Maryada* that were the hallmarks of the RSS and the erstwhile BJS. Notably, these words and phrases are primarily Sanskritic in origin, and thus their true meaning may be out of reach of much of the illiterate population, besides being clearly differentiated from any non-Sanskritic (including English or

Dravidian) languages. Such terms are also distant from the Urdu spoken by the majority of the Muslims in India. While seeking to bring about a "modern, progressive and enlightened nation", it sought to draw inspiration "from India's ancient culture and values". In that seemingly innocuous turn of phrase is embedded a whole compendium of value systems. It is also not clear as to who should define and interpret this ancient culture and values. At times, it does appear that the BJP would like to take upon itself this onerous task and it certainly seems that they have made considerable progress in this direction (see Tapan Basu, et al, earlier). Moreover, it also paved the way to a possible clash and contradiction between having a modern, progressive and enlightened nation on the one hand and unquestioning reliance on ancient culture, values and practices on the other. Where is one to draw the line between modernity and the ancient is the vital question. Often, one can land up somewhere in the middle and be pulled both ways. That would not be an inaccurate picture of India at present. The worst would possibly be to put on a veneer of modernity on untested ancient beliefs and practices without going into them in some detail on the basis of reason and rationality. It is possible, no doubt, to argue against the application of logic and rationality and to term it as a matter of belief and faith. What is then to be termed as faith and left out of the purview of rationality would then depend largely on the education, upbringing and experience of the individual concerned. Obviously, the choice of beliefs and practices that should be the articles of faith may well vary between one individual and another for no two individuals are likely to be identical; nor are they likely to choose or make identical choices. Without such a pragmatic approach, the possible contradictions between what is modern and what is ancient would persist in the body and psyche of the nation as much as in that of the individual concerned. Further, this would tend to divert the individual from pursuing his or her personal

                    Prosenjit Dasgupta

goals for betterment, as it would distract the people at large from focusing on national tasks, such as social upliftment and economic development. This is, of course, presuming that the concerned political circles are, in fact, interested in such social upliftment and economic development and are not principally committed to ensuring a particular social and cultural pattern, and holding on to power. As observed earlier, a fixed and rigid cultural system may not be conducive to dynamic social and economic growth. It may even turn out to be not "inclusive", but rather more conducive to an exclusive pattern of growth. Rationality, after all, seems to be so detached, so free of individual predilections, that it may appear somewhat fearful to many.

The BJP constitution also speaks of basing its policies on "integral humanism" (propounded by the late Deen Dayal Upadhyay, as mentioned above), "Gandhian socialism" and "positive secularism" (that is, "Sarva Dharma Samabhava", or equal treatment for all religions, as the document has it). On the face of it, these sentiments do seem attractive. However, little or no attempts have been made by the BJP or their affiliates to define and describe these more fully. As discussed above, there could be more than one interpretation of what Upadhyay-ji has written on integral humanism and it would certainly be important to fill out the details of his ideas in a cogent and coherent manner. Gandhi himself did not spell out his vision of what he thought of socialism and what it ought to mean for India. His was more of an overarching concern for humanity and humanism, even outside of India. He also had his own ideas about village industries and a general abhorrence of big industries and sophisticated technologies. As to what "positive secularism" is, BJP ought to spell this out in greater detail so that there is a wider understanding of its meaning and implications.

Currently, there seems to be a propensity among many sections of political circles on being questioned about issues, to start off with "As already said" or "As earlier stated", as if an earlier statement (if at all made or can be recalled at that point of time) gives sanctity to what is being presently said. It is also a convenient device to gain time to formulate a reply that often goes off at a tangent. A previous statement (even if made) does not necessarily become definitive, or even true, at a future time. It is only when a statement of political thinking is put in black-and-white, as a formal resolution adopted at a general meeting or published as a party manifesto, does it become definitive. Otherwise, it can develop into what has been termed as "situational ethics" (as mentioned earlier), that is, tailoring thoughts, words and behaviour to each segment of the target audience at a given point of time. That this may well lead to heights of cynicism is immaterial and is also subsumed to the compulsions of every-day life. Therefore, the absence of any such definitive resolution or statement in a manifesto makes it clear that no such specific view or position was, in fact, taken by the political party concerned. For instance, "corruption" is a general term and it has many faces and modes of operation. Indeed, there are many agencies that deal with different aspects of corruption. But, in the end, it does seem at times that corruption in India is flourishing rather than being checked or extinguished. Generally speaking, the tendency may be to come out with rather general statements about political, economic or social issues but little effort is made to arrive at an overall consensus about such issues. India, with its immense size, huge population and great diversity is a veritable model where "exceptions prove the rule" in practical terms.

Coming back to the realities of the present, while the BJP was thus trying more clearly to define its political agenda over the last three decades, the RSS had already taken the initiative to set up a larger "family" of associated interests to further its "cultural activities" through different channels. First of all, the RSS has grown its branches or shakhas, which, according to some sources, number about 75,000 in recent years. Of these, about 60,000 are said to meet daily. The RSS also presently represents about 20 affiliated or associated organisations. Among the first of such organisations was the *Vishva Hindu Parishad*, set up in the early 1960s to try and bring together all the sects and sections of Hindus under its fold on one religious platform. The second was the *Akhil Bharatiya Sant Parishad* comprising leaders of the various Hindu religious sects. The third was the *Antarjatiya Hindu Mahasabha* (or the international community of Hindus), with major centres in East Africa, United Kingdom, Canada and the USA. For one reason or the other, it appears that most, if not all, of their concerns and activities are organised and centred on two major cultural issues: the Hindu religion and Indian history. It is no matter that while culture includes elements of religion, the converse is not wholly true; that is, religion is not the sum total of any culture. Language, literature, art, architecture, crafts, music and dance are also notable elements of culture. Neither the shakhas nor the bodies associated or affiliated to the RSS in India or abroad seem to be much concerned about systematically studying the vast ocean of Indian literature, be it of Kalidasa, Bhavabhuti or Dandi, or even later authors such as Premchand, Sumitranand Pant and others. They seem least interested in the arts of Ajanta and Ellora, Brihadeeswar, Konarak, Kanchipuram, Modhera, Khajuraho or Bundi for that matter. If, therefore, the RSS leaves aside such important elements of culture, one can only draw the conclusion that their concept and definition of culture is somewhat limited and one-sided. On the other hand, their singular focus on matters religious would lead many to think that is what the RSS is really all about.

So far as the other concern of the RSS is concerned, regarding a reading of Indian history, it is certainly understandable that, as Dr Shyama Parasad Mookerjee put it (quoted earlier), "Indian history should be so rewritten that it may become the record of the Indian people and not merely of foreign invaders." It is for each student of history to judge whether the books by Max Muller, Monier Williams, John Muir and others on the ancient Sanskrit texts were a service or disservice to the study of India history. Similar mention may also be made to great historians like Sir Jadunath Sarkar and Dr H.C. Raychaudhury, scholars like Dr S. Radhakrishnan, Prof. V.S. Agrawalla, Dr Suniti Kumar Chatterji, archaeologists like Rakhaldas Banerjee, H.D. Sankalia, S.P. Gupta and the seminal work on epigraphy by Prof. D.C. Sircar that provided the basic groundings in Indian history which later scholars have further enriched. Here one must also mention the work of D.D. Kosambi that provided a new direction and thrust to the study of ancient Indian history. It is equally interesting that two notable publishing houses, Munshiram Manoharlal and Motilal Banarasidas, have over the past several decades brought out many useful books on Indian history and Indology. These were not books by or on "foreign invaders", but on the history of India in general and on its great course along the length and breadth of the country over the centuries. Even later work, since the 1940s, on "subaltern history" of India has brought forth many interesting and useful aspects of Indian history. But at the end of the day, if one has not read a wide range of books on an equally wide range of historical topics, it is unlikely that one would gain any reasonable grasp of Indian history. The caveat by that eminent scholar of history, E.H. Carr, that before reading a piece of history, ask who has written it, stands true across all views--whether pro or contra--on history.

Prof. Karl Popper in his book, "The Poverty of Historicism" (see Bibliography), has provided another aspect to the study of the social sciences, such as history, sociology, economics, etc. He has opined that an organism learns by experience and a society can do so, too; it will have its history, but is only partly conditioned by its past. He adds that: "We must not assume uniformities of social life to be invariably valid through space

                    Prosenjit Dasgupta

and time since they apply only to a certain cultural or historical period…the only universally valid laws of society must be laws that *link up successive periods of historical development*" (page 37 – emphasis added). In other words, any valid laws or hypotheses or interpretations pertaining to society must take into account succession of historical events or phases over time; to that extent there is no historical destiny to be hankered for. Prof. Popper further observes that, "Social revolutions are not brought about by rational plans but by social forces, for instance, by conflicts of interests…it will always be the resultant of the momentary constellation of contesting forces" (page 42). He considers that any wholesale attempt at social engineering is likely to overlook the fact that it is easy to centralize power but impossible to centralize all the knowledge that is distributed over many individual minds (with their individual interpretations and inclinations). Therefore, Popper finds that such a central authority or planner must then try and simplify this problem by eliminating individual differences. He must control and stereotype interests and beliefs by education and propaganda; but this must ultimately destroy knowledge, and the greater the gain in power, the greater will be the loss of knowledge (pages 82-83). This may not, of course, lead to a loss of livelihood or of income, but it is likely to lead to a diminution of the individual--the individual citizen--by doing away with a part of his being and soul. So, the end result of such a complete overhaul of a society can lead to quite unexpected or even unwelcome consequences.

It would be interesting to introduce here an aspect taken from the field of psychology that can well be read with the thesis of Prof. Popper outlined above. This is the "Dunning–Kruger Effect" that postulates a certain bias in knowledge acquisition and presentation by humans due to which many (if not most) people mistakenly assess their cognitive abilities to be greater than what they are. This was first suggested as a scientific thesis by the social psychologists, David Dunning and Justin Kruger in 1999, in which people were found to have an inability to recognize and allow for their lack of cognitive abilities of the desired degree. It is said to be connected with a cognitive bias resulting in a sense of illusory superiority. Without proper and sufficient self-awareness in the process of developing their self-identity, many people cannot objectively evaluate their competence or incompetence. This is said to result from a "miscalibration" by the relatively incompetent in judging themselves, with a corresponding miscalibration by more competent people from an error in reading others. The Dunning-Kruger effect has had its share of critics, but it seems that the corrections offered are more of degree than of kind. In point of fact, many philosophers and intellectuals have directly or indirectly said much the same thing, perhaps in an intuitive manner, starting from Confucius (who was more or less a contemporary of Gautama Buddha) who considered that: "Real knowledge is to know the extent of one's ignorance." Also, the poet W.B. Yeats wrote that, "The best lack all conviction, while the worst are full of passionate intensity." And, the philosopher Bertrand Russell once said, "One of the painful things about our time is that those who feel certainty are stupid, and those with any imagination and understanding are filled with doubt and indecision."

As the old saying goes, "Ignorance is bliss". Yet, philosophers and scientists have devoted whole lives over the past so many centuries to extend the boundaries of knowledge in all walks of life – and some that were not even dreamt of fifty years ago. And this ever-expanding sphere of knowledge has surely benefited mankind in many ways. It is useful to recall here that Sir Isaac Newton himself is said to have remarked that he was just gathering some pebbles on the shores of the vast ocean of knowledge.

Bearing these thoughts in mind to have a better understanding and appreciation of the "present", it may now be noted that unseen and almost unheard to most political

                    Prosenjit Dasgupta

observers, developments had been taking place in India over the last 40 years that appear in hindsight to have taken most of the non-BJP parties by surprise. The proliferation and growth of the RSS and its subsidiaries, that later came to be known popularly as the Sangh Parivar, does make for an interesting and useful study. Whereas the Hindu Mahasabha had its Gurukul and Dayanand Anglo-Vedic (or, DAV) schools since the turn of the 20th century, the RSS had sent Shri Nanaji Deshmukh in 1952 to set up the first Saraswati Sishu Mandir in Gorakhpur, which later came to be further supported through the Vidya Bharati institution. The latter, by 2003 (as Jaffrelot has it, page 269), accounted for 14,000 schools, 73,000 teachers and 1.7 million pupils. It is further seen that Guru Golwalkar initiated the Vishva Hindu Parishad (VHP) in August 1964 under Shivram Sankar Apte to bring about a unity of purpose in the Hindu ecclesiastical community. As Shri Apte put it, the prime objective was "to organise the Hindu world to save it from the evil of all three" (Christianity, Islam and Communism – parenthesis added). It is a matter of doubt as to whether Christianity, Islam and Communism should have thus been clubbed together as the prime source of evil for the Hindu community. After all, it cannot be said with any certainty that equality of man and man and the idea of one God are wholly alien to Hindu sense and sensibility. Communism is the odd man out and has little, if anything, in common with Christianity or Islam.

As per Walter Andersen and Shridhar Damle (see Bibliography, page 134), the VHP had grown by 1981 to about 3000 units in 437 out of 534 districts (later, more districts were created by state governments for administrative convenience), 150 full-time workers, 442 hostels and vocational schools, 150 medical centres and 10 published journals. By 2008, the VHP claimed that it had over 6 million adherents and had set up over 3000 educational facilities. The VHP, in turn, was instrumental in encouraging the growth of the Bajrang Dal, the activities of which have been notable in many parts of India. The Dal is said to have about 10 million adherents according to some sources and that is a big number. Shri Rajendra Singh, when he was the RSS Sanghsarchalak, set up the Friends of India International in the UK in 1976, and progressively the RSS came to be set up in more than 30 countries with over 5 million registered members, the largest numbers being in the USA, Canada, East Africa, the UK and Europe. Earlier, the labour movement had been placed under Dattopant Thengadi and the student issues were organised under the *Akhil Bharatiya Vidyarthi Parishad*, which, in turn, very significantly backed Jayaprakash Narayan's movement against the then Congress Government of Indira Gandhi, in 1974-75, that culminated in the Emergency. By 1977, the RSS had turned its attention to the tribal people and the untouchables, and the Deendayal Research Institute was set up to steer this programme. By 1983 the *Bharatiya Vanvasi Kalyan Ashram* system (as per Andersen and Damle) was operating 89 student hostels, 136 primary schools, 137 health centres, 26 vocational centres and 33 orphanages. Surely, this would have gone up considerably in more recent years, for which data is presently lacking or is not publicly available. To the extent that these measures supplemented the government's efforts to aid and assist the tribal people and untouchables to make progress and to stand on their own, this programme was certainly laudable. All these developments were, no doubt, to reach out to many different sections of society; although, it is somewhat surprising that little, if anything, was done by most other political parties in a similar manner or scale for the backward classes and the Dalits, many of whom live and work at the very margins of society. It needs to be underlined that these activities and programmes were quite in conformity with the provisions of the Indian Constitution. Any other political party could well have acted similarly; but they did not. They seem not to have perceived how a political philosophy could be furthered in

 Prosenjit Dasgupta

so many other indirect ways. They seem to have completely overlooked that political programmes cannot––must not––be confined to the periodic political manifestos and waking up only at the time of elections; it requires consistent hard work. It can, therefore, be stated with some emphasis that no political organisation like the Congress or the Communists or the Bahujan Samaj Party or any other had attempted anything on this scope and scale, and it ill-becomes them now to bemoan their reduced stature.

The work of the RSS (and by indirect influence and effect, of the BJP) in the field of public communications has been notable. In 1947, the Organiser, the major platform of the RSS was launched, followed by Panchajanya in Hindi, and yet later by other journals and newspapers in at least 12 local languages. Another step forward was taken in 1970 by setting up of the Hindusthan Samachar news-service. A more recent development is the Vishwa Samvad Kendra. An important consequence of this was that there could be a steady stream of news and views, as per the respective editorial policies the year around on social, political and economic issues. Such circulation of news would by their persistence and persuasiveness encourage a particular line of thinking and bent of mind in which influencing public attention and attitudes on a long-term basis becomes possible, rather than reacting only at the time of any specific events or development. To what extent the National Herald projected INC's viewpoint is not clearly evident; but it does seem that in reach and influence, it was a very poor second to the Organiser and Panchajanya. Hardly any of regional parties like the Samajwadi Party, the Bahujan Samaj Party, the National Congress Party, the Telegu Desam party, or the Trinamool Congress seem to have had any such "captive" media sources of comparable reach (e.g., the Shiv Sena with its *Samna*), although some of the newspapers and TV channels may have supported them off and on.

One is tempted to bring in Sun Tzu's "Art of War" (that

well-known Chinese classic) into this discourse, although it may seem distinctly odd. But political rivalry may at times reach high pitch and take on some features of warfare; albeit, without arms, and aimed at capturing the hearts and minds of people. Sun Tzu has said: "All warfare is based on deception. Hence, when we are able to attack, we must seem unable; when using our forces, we must appear inactive; when we are near, we must make the enemy believe we are far away; when far away, we must make him believe we are near."

More to the point about political activity, he has also stated: "Engage people with what they expect; it is what they are able to discern and confirms their projections. It settles them into predictable patterns of response, occupying their minds while you wait for the extraordinary moment – that which they cannot anticipate."

It would be far too much to suggest that the Sangh Parivar at any point of time had read or considered these thoughts of Sun Tzu, and that they, at any stage, wanted to follow his dictums. At best, it may appear as a coincidence. But the manner in which all political calculations at all levels were upset by the elections to the Indian Parliament in 2014 suggests strong central planning, theme and thrust that took the opposing political parties by storm. No doubt, the strong, multi-faceted organisational structure, or the *sangathan* of the Sangh Parivar played a major role in this; to which the opposing political parties just had no answer. Even five years later, in the parliamentary election in 2019, the BJP won hands down, steam-rollering the other political parties out of its way. It must, however, be borne in mind that an organisation by itself, without the infusion of some broader ethical principles and (importantly) human values, may not be able to reach the desired high status in the long-run, unable to evolve into something higher and better. That option should not be foreclosed. As Sun Tzu has observed, "There is no instance of a nation benefitting from prolonged warfare." Popper's words

　Prosenjit Dasgupta

of caution mentioned above may also be borne in mind

The other notable development in political communication in the last four or five years has been the intensive use of social media. Practically gone are the days of processions, street-corner meetings and door-to-door canvassing for votes. All this is perhaps no more effective in terms of cost and time. So, social media, which was primarily developed for sharing of photographs and experiences between school and college friends, and close relatives, suddenly found itself deluged with political messages. Social media, by its very nature, is person-to-person; although, there is nothing in the rules that precludes organisations from communicating their messages with a large number of people at a time. But it did bring about a certain change, in that political programmes, which normally take time to implement and play out, were given the colour of the immediacy of a "selfie" taken at a picnic for a friend. It was unprecedented and was like a deluge and it, in a manner of speaking, helped push the populace towards a particular line of thinking and believing. E-mail addresses and mobile phone numbers, known through existing government channels, were accessible and were reportedly used extensively through a large number of call centres to reach out to individual voters to keep them focussed on some of the government programmes. People, whether in a city flat or a rural tea shop, accustomed to a leisurely reading of the morning newspaper, or switching TV channels for the evening news, were now exposed to an intensive and persistent funnelling of news and information that they had not asked for – or bargained for. It rode on the back of the proliferation of Smartphones, which, according to one estimate, numbered about 350 million units in India alone; that's a lot of spread. Its very volume and intensity left little space or time for developing independent lines of thought and discussion, and, in all probability, it was not at all intended that this should take place. At the same time, it cannot be said that all of this was not quite in conformity with laws; except, and to the extent, it may have been a breach of privacy. But, no doubt, it created the possibility that others would get on to the same bandwagon sooner than later. Thus, politics in India quickly graduated from staid processions and street-corner meetings, wall graffiti and posters, to "politics by social media". One is left wondering if, at the end of it all, deliberations in the Indian Parliament would similarly have to take into account exchanges on the social media, and whether the number of "likes" on social media would tend to influence if a law is passed or not. That is, perhaps, a childish and a nonsensical apprehension. Social media, by its nature, is basically one-to-one (despite its going "viral" on occasions, the "virus" being capable of being "managed"). However, the immediacy and transparency of parliamentary debates (now widely televised) may nonetheless be adversely affected to some extent.

A notable feature of the present is the persistent attempt in some quarters to re-define the issues of nationhood, statehood, secularism, etc. This has necessarily found reflection in newspaper editorials and articles, as well as in TV talk shows. Such definition and re-definition is no doubt useful at periodic intervals but must be accompanied by free and frank debate, not as often happens by heaping ridicule on commonly accepted concepts or in slanging matches. It must be noted here that such re-formulations may well veer away from the spirit of the Constitutional Debates from 1946 to 1949. For instance, "secularism", as earlier implicit in the Indian Constitution (later explicitly provided in the Constitution in 1974) has been labelled as "pseudo-secularism" by some quarters. This may be taken as an interesting and useful label, but there is a need to understand what secularism is, before coming to what is "pseudo-secularism". Considerable light on this issue has been shed by Shefali Jha in her article (see Bibliography). She notes that most members of the Constituent Assembly shared the view that "secularism" meant a "Movement for the separation of religion and the state *that was irrevocably*

　　　　　　　　Prosenjit Dasgupta

part of the process of democratization of the latter" (emphasis added - Const. Assem. Debates, Vol. X, pages 439-453, quoted by Jha). "In other words, the word 'democracy' carried within itself the connotation of secularism; one would not be able to survive without the other". The question was asked: "How could a democratic state represent a religious majority at the expense of the rights and liberties of a minority?" (in B. Siva Rao, "Indian Constitution – Select Documents", Vol. IV, page 573, referred to by Jha). Another position on the separation of religion and the state was held by Shri K.M. Munshi who observed that: "We have a living tradition of religious tolerance – the broad outlook of Hinduism that all religions lead to the same god" ("Indian Constitutional Documents", Bharatiya Vidya Bhavan, 1967, Vol. I, page 309, quoted by Jha). Jayaprakash Narayan, another leading member of the Constituent Assembly, referred to the fine distinction between religious "practice" and religious "worship", and further held that only when religion was used to serve socio-economic and political interests, there was communal violence. He called for a prohibition on the use of religious institutions for political purposes or setting up of political organisations on religious basis (mentioned by B. Siva Rao, "Indian Constitution – A Study", page 266, quoted by Jha). Notably, in providing for Fundamental Rights, the Constitution of India clearly allows for the right to Freedom of Conscience as much as the "Right to Profess and Practice Religion". Thus, one has a choice in considering "secularism" much as Munshi did as *"Sarva-dharmasamabhava"*, or equal respect for all religions in India, or as an inherent and intrinsic part and parcel of a democratic state, and last but not least, as a part of the sovereignty of the individual citizen that the Indian Constitution recognizes. One needs to point out here that Shri Kancha Ilaiah, in his work mentioned earlier, has called "religious democracy" as one of the pillars of a functioning political democracy; one would not stand without the other. It would stand to reason that it would be only when any one of the three concepts of secularism mentioned above is set aside, that "secularism" as thought in the Indian Constitution would be infringed. Dr Suniti Kumar Chatterji (see Bibliography) has suggested an interesting definition of "secularism" as being in the "*nature of a protest against the pretensions of organised religion, which interferes with man's behaviour as a social being and seeks openly or covertly to control him for the furtherance of the ends of an organised hierarchy*" (page 29 – emphasis added). Last but not least, when the sovereignty of the citizen within the meaning of the Constitution is sought to be stifled by repeating and enforcing the pre-conceived belief that concepts or ideas that are contrary to some code prescribed by some external agency, are "unhealthy", or "unconscionable", or plain "unacceptable", would "secularism" (howsoever thought of or defined) receive a mortal blow. In the final analysis, "secularism" would stand or fall whenever and wherever there are deliberate attempts to regulate free thought and expression.

It is also worth a thought that the only other organisations with a wide reach and pan-Indian presence concerned with social and cultural issues are the Ramakrishna Mission (RKM) and the Bharat Sevashram Sangh (BSS). The former was constituted way back in 1897 and presently accounts for about 150 centres in India and 15 in Bangladesh. It operates about 750 educational institutions, including 12 colleges, 22 Higher Secondary schools, 4 polytechnics and 48 vocational training centres. The latter was set up in 1917 and has about 46 centres and 300 sub-centres. Its work has been notable in aiding relief, following earthquakes, floods, drought and famine. It cannot be anybody's case that the monks and volunteers of these two organisations are any less dedicated, and yet their growth over longer periods of time has been considerably less, as compared to the RSS. It would stand to reason that funds, which are always a major factor for any non-governmental agency, must have been a limiting factor accounting for the slower growth

        Prosenjit Dasgupta

of RKM and BSS, and the focused objective of the VHP in achieving "unity of purpose" among Hindus was apparently more attractive to the populace at large than the purely cultural, social and community relief work of the RKM and BSS. There is little one can do about that except to ponder over that *unity of purpose of the nation*" would take harder work and longer time. It becomes so much easier if one could directly equate Hindus and Hinduism with the nation; a lot of bother could then be easily saved. But that higher national purpose would entail much hard work, and a lot of time. Political parties with municipal, state or parliamentary elections every now and then, have to work to tough timetables, and time always comes at a premium.

Another of the most notable features of the "present" is the increasing self-identity and push for "representation" in the social, economic and political fields by the Other Backward Classes. This issue of representation of backward or Scheduled Castes had been on the political agenda from about the beginning of the 20th century. This came to a head after the Round Table Conferences in London in 1931-32 and culminated in the Gandhi-Ambedkar Pact at Pune in 1932 when the Congress Party explicitly agreed to reserve seats for the Scheduled Castes and Scheduled Tribes in elections. This was necessarily carried over into the framing of the Indian Constitution in which specific provisions were made for "reserved constituencies" for the Scheduled Castes and Tribes. This issue found added traction in the Report of the Mandal Commission that had been constituted in January 1979 by the Janata government under the prime ministership of late Morarji Desai. Why exactly the Desai government thought it necessary to constitute this Commission cannot be clearly answered at this point of time, except that several of the constituent political parties pressed for it. Obviously, India still had very large numbers of deprived, oppressed and impoverished people across the board from upper castes to lower castes at that point of time. The question was how to assure them better opportunities and a better prospect of life. Thus, in the Mandal Commission, in addition to the time-worn category of Scheduled Castes, "Other Backward Classes" horizontally covering the entire population, came to be defined. As the successive Census of India had not been able to identify these OBCs with clarity, the Commission formulated several criteria according to social standing, education, employment, income, etc., and came to the conclusion that about 52% of India's total population were Hindu OBCs by the simple arithmetic of deducting the numbers of the known upper castes among Hindus, as also the Scheduled Castes and Scheduled Tribes (themselves numbering about 24% of the total population). It is an open question as to whether this was the right way to have gone about this important issue; but that was the way it was done. In about two years' time, in December 1980, the Mandal Commission Report was finalized and submitted to the government. Implementation of this was held over, till in August 1990, when the then prime minister, Shri V.P. Singh, declared his intention to implement the Mandal Commission recommendation for 27% reservation in the total number of jobs in the central government and in the central government public undertakings as a form of "affirmative action" for OBCs. This was supposed to be over and above the 24% reservation already provided for Scheduled Castes and Tribes. Successive studies have seen the rise in the number of identified OBC from the 3743 as found by the Mandal Commission and even higher as per the National Commission on Backward Classes. Necessarily, the constitution of the Mandal Commission and its subsequent recommendations gave a great fillip to the political movement amongst the OBCs for increased representation in the corridors of power. What was possibly then not understood or appreciated was that even among the OBCs, there was gradation between "haves", "less haves" and "even lesser haves". Under these conditions, there was bound

                    Prosenjit Dasgupta

to be severe competition for garnering of state resources and the resultant squabbles and ill-will.

It is of significance that in the "Shri Shri Chandi", a notable sacred text in India, the invocation to the goddess begins with the words "*Narayani, sarva-bhuteshu, shakti-rupini samsthtita, namastasyai, namastasasyi, namastasyai, namah, namah*". This underlines the point that the goddess is present in all the elements that make up creation. And yet, many people in India still have difficulties in treating the "Untouchables" as equals and in consorting with them. So, effectively, the invocation goes one way and the social behaviour goes in quite a different direction. This is acutely brought out in a recent (September 2019) cartoon and an accompanying poem that was doing the rounds on WhatsApp, which tells of an aged artisan working at a statue of the god, Ganesa, and musing to himself that once the statue is finished and installed in a temple, it will be worshipped with flowers and incense, but no one will remember that he, an artisan from the "Untouchable" class, had fashioned it. That is the paradox--and the contradiction-- that India must constantly confront.

An appropriate way to end this section on the present-day scenario would be to refer to the findings given in the book edited by Asutosh Kumar and Yatindra Singh Sisodia (see Bibliography). In considering and comparing the 2009 and the 2014 parliamentary elections, Rahul Verma and Sanjay Kumar in their article in this publication have opined that in the 2014 parliamentary elections, BJP was able to attract both the upper caste (56%) and the OBC votes (34% - primarily the "first-time voters") in the states of north India and that too, from the urban, young, well-off sections. In this effort, TV and print media became what Verma and Kumar call a "force multiplier" in motivating these "aspirational" sections in voting as they did.

Kumar, in his introductory chapter of the publication, deals with the vital question as to whether "democracy" in

India has come to mean a "minimalist" form of democracy that is characterized by only a multi-party electoral system and periodic elections to state legislatures and the central parliament. At times, one is really tempted to believe that with the spectacle of village-level panchayat elections, the numerous municipal elections, or even elections to students' unions and university councils there is perhaps a "surfeit" of democracy in India. If one turns to more fundamental issues of representation and accountability of "peoples' representatives", a fairly large grey area looms ahead. The Representation of Peoples Act is itself somewhat frugal on the accountability issue, and there is no separate "Prohibition of Misrepresentation of Peoples Act" or any "Accountability of Peoples Representatives Act"; although there are several acts, such as the Prohibition of Corruption Act, etc., that have helped at times. But representative or constitutional democracy does require something more than various acts or statutes. It does require "engagement" on specific issues by individuals and institutions acting as complement and supplement to the elected legislatures. The press and media and the civil society can, and do, help to keep the three principal pillars of a state, being the legislatures, the government and the judiciary, functioning more effectively. Whether India will embark more strongly along this path, only the coming years would reveal.

A very good perspective in this regard is provided by Tom Ginsberg and Aziz Huq in their book, "How to Save Constitutional Democracy" (see Bibliography), which is both thought-provoking and timely. It goes to the heart of the matter by noting that democracies must not only be distinguished by periodic elections to gauge the views and concerns of the people, but must be equally marked by freedom of speech and an over-arching rule of law. As the authors have pointed out with examples from the American South in the 1880s, the Weimar Republic in Germany in the early 1930s, and several other countries (which shall remain unnamed here) in more

Prosenjit Dasgupta

recent times, there may be "illiberal democracies" that attempt to cut down on the political space for dissent and competition for public attention by other political parties. One way to do so is by promoting what the authors have called "moralized anti-pluralism", by the repeated assertions of a singular and morally privileged understanding of history, and of social norms and practices. The tendency, then, is to run political campaigns not based on substantive policy issues but about "belonging" to one part and "excluding" another, leading to questions of loyalty and betrayal.

On many occasions, this is seen to have commenced with overt or covert attacks on bureaucratic autonomy, followed by the centralization of political decision-making and executive action. A curious lowering of regard for the neutrality of data of national significance (e.g., census data, or information about GDP growth, bank credit, etc.) is at times followed by laws, which, while remaining within the four corners of the constitution, nibble away at the fundamental rights of expression and association. As Ginsberg and Huq assert, "Democracy demands from its participants a certain political morality" (page 173) and that is taken to be of no consequence when any anti-pluralistic agenda is followed. To quote Ginsberg and Huq once more, "Pluralism of institutions, of information and ideas is at the heart of a democratic system". (page 235). That the points thrown up in this book are of significant concern to the citizens of India as members of a functioning democracy, goes without saying.

Chapter 18

Some thoughts for the future

This "what now?" poses several problems: there is the issue of "what to do", followed by the key question "why", then "by whom", and finally, "how". To take up the "how" first, to have any thought that a country as large and diverse as India, with a plural culture and ways of thought, it would be plain silly even to think of anything other than through a functioning democracy. The world has moved nearly a 100 years since the 1920s and 30s. It no longer pivots around the imperialistic designs of a few countries. Moreover, this country gave itself a constitutional, parliamentary, representative democracy in 1952 that has been functional for over 70 years. That is possibly time enough for the country to have made up its mind that this format suits the people the best; democracy is slow but sure.

Coming to the "why" of it, one comes up against the counter-question, "Why anything?" The answer to this "why" lies in seeking out and making a meaningful change; a change for the better; changes such that you and I, and all the people can feel, and see that things are better off economically and socially. One hesitates before adding the word "politically" because that word has some connotation of "power" and, most people are more than content to leave that to others so inclined, while they look for a peaceful, fulfilling life with family and friends.

The "by whom" aspect is easily answered because under the Indian Constitution, it is to be by the people of the country acting democratically through their elected representatives. It is often overlooked that it is the people who are sovereign in a constitutional democracy, and not the representatives. It is the responsibility and task of the representatives to act

 Prosenjit Dasgupta

in accordance with the mandate periodically received in elections, by framing suitable programmes and policies.

Since India is a representative parliamentary democracy, political parties have a major role to play in seeking out suitable representatives who basically agree with the party's policies and programmes and help mould the finer details as per their perception of their role as representatives of a particular constituency. It would be, thus, quite possible then for a party "A" in state "B" to have an elected representative "C" who may or may not be wholly in agreement with another representative "D" from the same party but from state "E" about a specific aspect of the programme and the time-schedule in which it is to be carried out. By way of example, it is no thanks to the weather gods that one section of farmers in one part of the country may be facing floods regularly, while another section of farmers is facing drought with equal frequency. Another example would be that some types of soil favour some types of crops and have different irrigation requirements. India has been able in a notable fashion to overcome these difficulties by having a federal system under which the state governments, which are answerable to the local legislatures, have to carry out some specified constitutional duties. It then redounds upon the higher party leadership to iron out these rough edges and to re-work and redefine the particular programme to suit the widest possible cross-section of the people that it presumes to represent. This iterative process and fine-tuning of policies and programmes is, therefore, constantly at work.

As has been discussed above, the very significant economic growth of 7% to 10% per annum in the country since 1992-93 has led to a huge upwelling of aspirations amongst very large sections of the populace, which has profound social and political implications. Few, if any, of the people are prepared any more to carry on as before. They want better clothes, better housing, better medical facilities, better transport, better education and most of all, gainful engagement or employment. No less significant is the sharp growth of urbanization, and researchers have put this at anything between 40 to 50% of the total population (or, even higher); the number would depend on how one defines "urbanization". At the same time, there remain equally large sections in rural areas, bound largely by traditional means of livelihood, who are seeking a way out of the morass of poverty and ignorance. Who will stand by them, and how? Obviously, something special and specific will have to be done for them to reduce the pressure of poverty, the heavy indebtedness, the lack of local employment opportunities, the need for improved health facilities, rural housing, etc. Equally, the surge of aspirations among the urban and semi-urban youth, many of them in north India (it being notable that the per capita income in some of the northern states like Bihar and Uttar Pradesh is actually considerably lower than that in Gujarat, Maharashtra or Tamil Nadu, or for that matter, even West Bengal) has to be addressed. To try and occupy their energies and attention with non-economic issues such as T20 cricket, some sequences in a popular film, or some passages in a book, or the entry of women in certain shrines, etc., can at best be temporary diversions and equally temporary vote-catching devices that are unlikely to lead to any significant betterment of their economic wellbeing. However, a cautionary note has to be struck here that what seems at times just temporary may assume permanent features due to persistent sectional pressures. It is important, therefore, that what is sectional must be seen as sectional, and ought not to be given the colour and garb of anything more than that. Furthermore, most of the aspirations of the people are "secular", in that they involve little or nothing of the religious. Thus, they would require "secular" solutions, such as improved rural and urban infrastructure, improved health facilities, sanitation, skills improvement, housing, etc., that are quite "religion-neutral"; that is, neither the providers nor the recipients of such social

        Prosenjit Dasgupta

and economic services need to be—or, in fact, are—of any particular religious persuasion.

One may here refer the words of Dr Suniti Kumar Chatterji in his "Indianism and the Indian Synthesis" (see Bibliography). First of all, note must be taken of his use of the word "Indianism", possibly the first use of an interesting term to describe the philosophy of life and the ethos of India. He has summed it up from the words of the Taittiriya Upanishad as follows –

"Yato va imani bhutani jayantey, yena jatani jivanti, yat prayantey,

Abhisam visanti, tad vijijnanasva tad Brahma."

(That spirit from which the consecrated beings proceed, through which, having proceeded from it, they live,

Towards which they trend, and in which they are ultimately absorbed, that spirit is the Great One.)

This distilled, so to speak, the recurring theme in all speculations about life and the living phenomena that India has been witness to over the previous millennia. Dr Chatterji goes on to quote approvingly from the work of Shri K.V. Rangaswami Aiyyangar in his "Some Aspects of the Hindu View of Life" (Baroda, 1952) that: "Hinduism has no distinctive creed…Hinduism has no priesthood…all persons who are entitled to sacrifice can themselves officiate as such… Immemorial immunity from external dictation and control over its liturgy and principles has been a feature of the history of Hinduism" (pages 17-18 in Aiyyangar, quoted on page 31 by Dr Chatterji). The learned scholar further defines "Indianism" as being characterized by a conviction about some "Unseen Reality", whether as a force, principle, order, personality or spirit, in turn signified as "sat-chit-ananda" (page 55/56). One may add the persistent views of Prof. Nirmalkumar Bose, the noted Gandhian, scholar, teacher and practitioner of social anthropology, that Hinduism is a "federation" of beliefs and practices.

If this be true, then the persistent inclination among some sections of the political class in pursuing some religious issues, whether it be about chanting of certain hymns in the morning, or about observation of some daily rituals, or renovation of a place of worship, is difficult to understand. This may be an important part of the agenda of some sections of religious leaders, but to assume or co-opt this as part of a national political programme seems uncalled for. As Swami Vivekananda perceptively noted over a century ago, religion will not fill the stomachs of people. It is, as if, that one section of the people are reading from one sacred text and another section from quite another text with hardly any sensation of there being a meeting point. One can hardly bring in a binary system or Boolean logic on an either/or, or true/false basis, into the sphere of governance of a country. There are far too many variables and so many nuances to a situation that have to be taken into account. As has been discussed in a section above, the experiences and views of the Dalits must be taken on board if any meaningful long-term gains are to be made.

Politics, at its very basic, is about influencing and persuading as many of the people towards a certain given political programme as possible; it could hardly be about expressly excluding any particular section from say, the benefits of housing, health or rural roads. Nor should politics be coloured by religious considerations because the two pertain to two different spheres of human activity: politics at the level of the state and its policies and programmes, and religion at the level of the individual and his or her spiritual well-being. While religious rituals and practices can certainly be at the level of a group of people or a community, or, put in another way, common practices being followed by a large number of individuals, matters of religious belief and faith may not be so easily reduced to an algebraic sum of individual beliefs; there would be "n" number of variants in matters of such belief and faith.

    Prosenjit Dasgupta

Seen in this light, the elements that comprise what may be termed the Hindu-oriented components in the agenda of BJP have notable implications for gaining political advantage; for, Hindus across the board and of all persuasions, comprise about 75% of the populace, and democracy at some stage or the other does mean "numbers". But as the NCBC Report for 2013-14 has it, over 70% of the Hindus are not "caste Hindus" (i.e., Brahmans, Kshatriyas and Vaishyas), but comprise Scheduled Castes, Other Backward Classes, and Dalits who have different ways of looking at things that we may be taking for granted, and they certainly want to be heard and counted. Moreover, as has been noticed over the last three or four decades, there is some element of stratification even among the Dalits, such that those who have made some headway, are more inclined to align with higher castes and to leave their brethren to find their own way out. Democracy, as has been repeatedly said, means at its very basic, "rule by the people", where the sovereignty rests with the people. It has taken democracy many centuries to assume its present form from the unalloyed autocracy of the ancient monarchs. In the last few centuries, it has taken many forms, such as the oligarchy of nobles, councils of ministers and so on, till it began to take some semblance of its present form in the 17th and 18th centuries in the U.K., Europe and North America. The form which the democracy has presently taken is that of "constitutional-cum-representative" democracy, which is what we have in India. This means the people here rule themselves through elected representatives under the overall rule of law as enshrined in the Constitution of India. At the cost of repetition, one must recall that the Indian Constitution takes cognizance of some basic "human values" of liberty, equality and justice (that have moral and ethical connotations for human conduct as distinct and different from the religious) that inform and instruct governance in India. Equality is equality before the law and equality of opportunity irrespective of caste, creed, or gender. Liberty is enshrined in the fundamental rights of thought, expression, freedom of association, and to one's beliefs and mode of worship. Justice means not only justice in a court of law, but also social and economic justice irrespective of status and birth. Any attempt, wilfully or otherwise, to limit or truncate these principles, would be undermining the constitutional provisions, and ultimately, the will of the people of India. If the process of undermining—overtly or covertly—goes too deep or goes on for too long (as Ginsberg and Huq have shown in their book), the constitutional edifice would be in the danger of falling down. And then you and I and all of us will fall down. And, like "Humpty Dumpty", it may not then be possible to put things together again. Perhaps that's why, in a country as large and diverse as India, still steeped in ignorance and in old customs and practices, it makes sense to make haste slowly with the engineering of desired social and economic changes. It may not do to try and change things by executive fiat or diktat. So, the need of the hour is more of democracy, more openness, and more engagement; not less.

But an important feature of democracy, which is often overlooked, is that certitude is anathema to both the concept and functioning of a democracy; for, as argued earlier, what may be a majority at a point of time in thought or views or aspirations is likely to mutate with time and circumstances. As Prof. Nirmalkumar Bose has asserted time and again, social practices and culture mutate over time due to endogenous and exogenous factors. Assertions made at one point of time or the other may seem to lose relevance and may be overtaken by events. If the person making such assertions is not duly mindful of the on-going shifts and changes, he or she may well find themselves dumped in the detritus of time. One may do well to recall what Shakespeare wrote in "Julius Caesar": "The evil that men do lives after them; the good is oft interred with their bones." One must be aware of being overeager to jump into the pages of history; for, history is a hard taskmaster.

     Prosenjit Dasgupta

If democracy, as suggested above, is likely to be confronted with ever-changing social, economic and political scenarios, each and all can, and should, partake of the changes and on-going improvements, if any. If in the middle of this, any one section should attempt to hold on to some benefits and advantages that they may have enjoyed for a good length of time (and, many, in fact, would have), what should be role of the political powers that be? If these benefits or advantages are cornered only by some, to the cost and inconvenience of many others, it would stand to reason that political leaders would have to justify the relative costs and benefits to the populace and society at large and develop a political programme accordingly; and, if need be, progressively to dismantle this system of sectional benefits and advantage. This is not new, and has happened since the middle of the 19th century in many parts of the country with respect to the ownership and distribution of land, in the suppression of usurious practices, in patterns of municipal taxes and duties, removal of caste disabilities, prevention of cruelty to animals, and even in the case of the administration of some places of religious worship. Naturally, this pace of change has accelerated after the coming of Independence. Therefore, the persistence of some such benefits, advantages and privileges into recent times gives rise to questions as to how this could have happened, who directly benefits from such persistence, what is the value-added to society at large, and who pays and why?

One may then ask oneself an unusual (or even silly) question: Can a community have a strategy as part and parcel of survival, primarily to hold on to some privileges? Or, does it need to? Even if it is felt for any reason that it needs to, a community is usually considered to be too large and too amorphous to be capable of developing any such definite strategy. But, if one looks at some aspects of religion (or, more correctly, religious practices and observances), ethnicity, language, caste codes, gender practices, etc., then it would not be over-imaginative to think that developing such a strategy would be very much desirable for a section of the community to insure its power and privileges. After all, it would be for the protection of such rights and privileges of a section of people (be it a matter of caste, or gender) that seems to have been under considerable threat from changing times, changing circumstances and changing values. Obviously, such a strategy is not consciously formulated or decided at a board meeting or even in the panchayat of such a community. It evolves over decades or even centuries, from a perceived impulse or need to preserve such ethnicity, religious practices, language, power, privileges, or authority. Any variation in that equilibrium of status, ethnicity, language, ritual practices and other such factors is perceived as a challenge or threat, to be resisted or beaten back. If that is not directly possible, then it could be indirectly by suggestion and innuendo. It may be as well by denial of information or knowledge to others; or, even by providing misleading information.

It would do well to recall here that in the Vedic ages, there were primarily four categories of priests associated with Rigvedic sacrifices: the *Hotri*, the *Udgatri*, the *Adhvaryu* and the *Brahman*. The last, the Brahman, supervised the arrangements and saw to it that each did his assigned task and chanted the verses properly. He could also take remedial action by chanting from the Atharvaveda, to tide over any wrong move or incorrect use of a chant. And who is to say that the Brahman in Kashmir would be capable of the self-same intonations and inflexions, the same cadence (or, has a lisp, or may be suffering from a sore throat at that point of time), as the Brahman in the Konkan or Odisha, to make such corrections, and that too entirely from memory? In spite of rigorous care in training of Brahmans in most places, it is an open question if one-hundred percent accuracy would have been achieved in all cases. That it was not, is evident from the fact that Brahmans were expected to take corrective action in case of any slip-up

    Prosenjit Dasgupta

by the Hotri or the Udgatri in their utterances and sacrificial procedures. This, in itself, should have underscored the need for a written text even in those early times to act as a standard reference in such matters. Such a text, ready at hand, could, at least, have been widely circulated and used for reference. But, as discussed in an earlier section, written script (with particular regard to Sanskrit) seems to have developed in India at a date considerably later than that in other cultures of comparable antiquity, such as the Egyptians, Sumerians and the Chinese.

In the days long, long ago, much before manuscripts or books were written, relying entirely on memorized verses and hymns would have been a convenient mode of denial of such knowledge to others; or again, by providing knowledge in a particular way that serves a different purpose for a section of the populace. At best, such memorized knowledge would have circulated within a small segment of the community. Moreover, the very act of denial, leaving aside for the time being as to what was precisely being denied, would have imparted a good bit of fascination and mystique to what was denied, and in the bargain, considerable importance and privilege would have been attached to those who participated in the acts of denial, that is, the "chosen few". It would not be too much to consider this as a specifically formulated "conspiracy of silence" (see Shri Ilaiah's views as mentioned above). Any alternative considerations or formulations for the denial of knowledge related to the purpose and procedure of various sacrifices to non-caste Hindus or keeping them in permanent bondage of ignorance do not present themselves readily or logically.

To take this point further, as more than one scholar has pointed out, written script and text have had a profound influence on human civilization. One obvious contribution has been in the expression and communication of complex thoughts; one can only do so much through oral transmission. The other has been in the sphere of political, economic and social ordering and administration; codes and laws make this so much easier. While block printing of fabrics and calligraphic models using wooden blocks was known since the 4th century CE, block printing of text took a little more time, into the 8th and 9th century CE, much of it beginning with the spread of Buddhism into Central Asia. But in 1450, major innovations using movable metal types, a more durable oil-based printing ink and printing presses were made by Johannes Gutenberg in Europe. It is little wonder that the Age of Enlightenment with huge spread of sciences as well as philosophies started in Europe shortly thereafter in the sixteenth century. In a sense, it considerably aided the Reformation of the Church by Martin Luther in 1517, because his thoughts could reach a much wider audience who could now read what was written and decide, each for himself or herself. It has been truly said that with the growth of the printing press, the spread of education began and, with it came a change in how man perceived the world around him.

In India, where hand-copying of palm leaf manuscripts had long been known, there were obvious limits to the number of copies that could be made. The printing press made its appearance in India only in the late 16th century through the Christian missionaries, firstly in Goa, and reached a much wider audience elsewhere, mainly to provide the Bible in native languages, and with it, to have bi-lingual dictionaries. James Hicky, across the sub-continent in Calcutta, started his newspaper (the first in India in any language), the "Bengal Gazette", in 1780. William Carey, during his mission at Serampore near Calcutta, also established a printing press, but somewhat later, possibly in the year 1800 or 1801. Several local newspapers followed in the 1830s and thereafter, so much so that the British government had to pass a law, the "Vernacular Press Act", in 1878, to regulate the development and the contents. Interestingly enough, the print media, as textbooks or as commentaries on notes, largely by-passed the sacred texts of India, and it has been left, even into the 21st century,

   Prosenjit Dasgupta

largely to exposition by the priestly classes to people at large. And, without any "hard evidence" of contemporaneously written texts, edicts, inscriptions, coins, or any other forms of archaeological remains, it may be said that the creation of narratives or myths around a personality or an event from the past becomes so much easier, as compared to that of a living, contemporary person. This is further reinforced when the prevailing political and social set-up is largely feudalistic-- or at least, has strong under-currents of something close to feudalism--and, certainly not given to self-questioning; or, for that matter, hardly any questioning, debate or discussion at all.

It should not be too difficult to appreciate that differentiation and segmentation is at the very heart of any survival strategy for the "chosen" vis-à-vis the "others". Then starts the mystique (also very significant in accentuating differentiation) of special clothing, accoutrements like staves, flags, decorations, etc., special austerities or rituals, special ways of gesturing, and, in some cases, typical hairstyles or special marks on the forehead or arms. Naturally, this is then followed by the "pricing", the ways in which "premia" or "discounts" are extended to a client. Even that is differentiated to suit the market, such as, if you do this, this and this, then the cost would be this; otherwise, it would be more. There is a *mulya* or value attached to everything with regard to many religious rituals in India. This is still very much a fact of life in many major places of pilgrimage in India. However, due to the long-standing practice, people hardly think twice about whether it is right or wrong. If a householder is unable or fails to observe the full range of rituals, he just pays a suitable mulya to the officiating priest who uses his personal discretion to formulate the dispensation, and that closes the chapter.

It must be unambiguously recorded, and emphasized, that such prescriptions on observances and practices are not confined to Hinduism in India. Many such practices and observances are to be seen in practically all the branches of Christianity, wherever it is practised, be it in Italy, Greece, the USA or India. It is also to be found to some degree in Judaism, Buddhism, Jainism and Islam. If one thinks dispassionately, the clergy (whether in Islam or Christianity) also largely deal with the exposition and interpretation of the sacred texts, the "Quran" and the "Bible", much like what is practiced by the priestly classes in Hinduism.

There is one major difference in Islam and Christianity: the lay populace is encouraged to read and learn the Quran and the Bible, respectively. Similar encouragement to read and learn about the basic sacred texts in India, such as the Rigveda, the Upanishads and the Bhagavad-gita, by the population at large is considerably limited, and whatever has taken place has been in more recent times, since about the mid-19th century. Before that, such learning was strictly confined to the chosen few. Studies of the great epics, the Ramayana and the Mahabharata, are, however, more widely done; though less from a literary point of view, and more as a source and justification to reinforce certain beliefs and practices. There is little or no discussion on who Valmiki and Vyasdeva were and what their role in compiling the epics was. Of course, it must, at the same time, be admitted that laypersons, often with the pressure of household duties, pursuit of professions, education of their children, etc., lack the time to follow up such studies, and are quite content to leave it to the weekly discourses by the clergy or the daily rituals at home. Whether or not this materially improves their state of mind and spirit--and, for any significant duration--would be for that individual to answer. Possibly it does, as otherwise why should so many people do it for so long, practically throughout their lives? It should, however, be obvious to any logical and rational person that to have done away with any or all of these external features and observances would have in no way affected the basic significance of the beliefs or the fundamental tenets of

     Prosenjit Dasgupta

the faith. But, it would have certainly diminished the mystery and mystique of it – which is the "unique selling proposition" to people at large and leads to the avoidance of the quest and questioning that helps in building personal, as opposed to community-based, faith.

If this discussion of the current issues and problems stands up to serious scrutiny, then their resolution should not be particularly hard to find; in fact, they almost suggest themselves. First and foremost, it should have been appreciated after the earlier discussions that nationhood does not rest on commonality of religion or race or ethnicity, but on shared human experiences of living together over considerable spans of time in a given geographical region, the diffusion and intermingling of languages and cultures, and thus, the progressive evolution of a common ethos about what we are and what we want to be in future. All this certainly does not happen in a snap of the fingers. Secondly, patriotism is not the monopoly of any one person or of any one section of persons. Patriotism is not something to be worn on one's sleeve; it is something far deeper, far more abiding. It has nothing to do with religion, race or language. In a sense, it defines a person; how he thinks and how he acts and behaves in society. These concepts may well be beyond the usual thinking and understanding of the common people; though one must not jump to such conclusions, for common people are often found to have the sense and sensibility that more learned or sophisticated people may lack. But these principles do definitely need to engage the thoughts and become a part of the belief-system of those who wish to provide political leadership of any significance.

A further point is about democracy and representation. India has already chosen a constitutional, representative parliamentary democracy for itself. The question asks itself: Representation of whom and for what? The "whom" part is more easily answered because of specified parliamentary and assembly constituencies comprising certain numbers of people residing there. "For what", is a little more difficult, because it must not only address the current problems of food, shelter, roads, sanitation, health, education, occupation--and they are big issues--but also to concern itself with wider issues of equality before the law, equality of opportunity, and freedom of expression that the Indian Constitution provides, which is where the problem starts.

How often really does a politician hold forth on equality of opportunity or about freedom of expression? He or she takes it as a given, not something that is still in the making and must be striven for to become a reality. As it is often remarked, knowledge is a major strength in modern times, and this is particularly true of a democracy. How is the electorate to make informed choices, if it is denied knowledge and information? It is here that the relevance of the Right to Information Act lies as an enabling and empowering device, as lack of information (and hence, of knowledge) is a definite disability at any time. It would follow that political leadership must possess the requisite information, knowledge and experience and be willing and prepared to share and impart this to his or her constituency and to guide it into the future. On the contrary, this is often compounded by denial of knowledge of all sorts to the population at large, by the "ones in the know"; or worse, by suggestion of falsehoods. This last can only mislead the people and turn them away from social, economic and political emancipation. Sometimes, it is confusing as to whether such social, economic and political emancipation is to be placed at a significant discount relative to spiritual or religious emancipation. It is a matter of fact that this denial or suppression of knowledge remains a major problem in India and must be eradicated forthwith, together with the *mai-baaap* (i.e., the government is the father and mother of all) syndrome. It is the people who are the mai-baap, and each politician worth his or her salt is to seek a mandate from the people to execute

          Prosenjit Dasgupta

the plans and programmes that their party has formulated, and not just thrust them down the throats of their electorate. One would be doing a great disservice to the people and the nation to believe that the people of India are not fit or ready for knowledge. This knowledge would necessarily be of all kinds and of all hues, be it about economic and social programmes and the need for them, about agricultural development, health and sanitation, irrigation for crops, history, literature, astronomy, environment and climate change, and what not. It is this sharing and spread of knowledge on the widest possible basis that can lead to a true "knowledge revolution", and lead on to a self-reliant, self-confident nation. Whether the dominant sections of political leadership in India will provide the lead in this, remains to be seen.

To be sure, the growth of the Internet over the last 20 years or so has opened up a great vista of information. But this information needs to be internalized and assimilated, and tested, before it is turned into knowledge. So, it is not enough that India can boast of 400 million Internet users. There would have to be 1000 million knowledgeable citizens, knowledgeable about their rights and responsibilities to take the country forward. If their time and attention is being constantly distracted and diverted from the core issues of social and economic development, much valuable time will be frittered away, and the whole process of growth will become entangled with extraneous issues and will be bound to take far more time than otherwise. That is why questions are being frequently asked as to why in spite of 70 years having passed since Independence, India has not made the expected progress. The plain answer is that information and knowledge have not spread far and deep enough in the populace. So, the second point in "What now?" is an "open door" policy for information and knowledge.

But imparting or acquiring knowledge requires a base, which is education. This is also a fundamental requirement for a functioning democracy. Education must be not only in the "3Rs" but also about ethics, civic sense and the ability to think for oneself, to be able to become self-reliant. This education is derived as much from the home environment and experience, as with formal instructions in a school. Unfortunately––and this word is used deliberately––to be able to think for oneself and to progress on the path of education in the true sense requires the vital scope to question: why this, and why not that? If, therefore, there is a definite allergy to questioning in some section or the other of society or the political leadership, they would be doing a serious disservice to the people in being able to think for themselves and to stand on their own. It would demonstrate a two-fold weakness: first, a lack of faith in the people in deciding for themselves, and secondly, in attempting overtly or covertly to maintain a decisive hold over them. This is the very negation of patriotism, which, as seen above, has the fundamental tenet of faith in the people, and in the nation. If significant elements of political leadership cannot rise above themselves in thought, word and deed, how would they be able to help and guide others to do so? Political leadership is not in being just a mirror image of the constituency (i.e., a Rajput for Rajputs or a Nishad for Nishads) but something more. Otherwise, how can one claim to be a political leader; they might as well call themselves political camp-followers. It is about having that extra knowledge, extra experience and that extra desire to help and assist people to a brighter tomorrow. If one does not have that modicum of faith in oneself, how would one be able to pass on that faith to others to believe in a better future, and motivate them to work for it? So, education in the widest possible sense of not just formal imparting of knowledge, but debates and discussions, inculcation of a sense of civic responsibilities, extra-curricular activities, service in the locality, etc., would be the third important component.

If education is taken as a significant requisite for a functioning democracy, rationality is another major (and necessary) element in its make-up. It is a desirable adjunct to the function of questioning concepts and things, and it both precedes and follows the process of questioning. It is only when things do not seem to fit or to fall in place or appear irrational, that rationality leads to the questioning of such a phenomenon. And the answers to the questions must also logically and reasonably fall in place, or else the quest must go on. Answers are relatively easy to find empirically in Physics or Chemistry, Geology or Geography, and such other physical sciences. Answers are, however, much more difficult to find in the social sciences, which often have multiple variables working at the same time, hand-in-hand with the human psyche that can have its own share of biases and quirks. It also takes far more time. Nonetheless, it is possible even in the social sciences, with researches carried out rationally and methodically, to obtain answers at different levels of significance. It needs to be clearly borne in mind that the absence of rationality means irrationality, not half-and-half of rationality and irrationality that again militates against plain common sense. Without a foundation in rationality, education, and gathering of information and knowledge, all fall apart.

This process of learning, understanding and knowing is complex. These ideas and concepts have engaged many philosophers over the centuries. Among them, Konrad Lorenz is not a name that many historians would be aware of. Lorenz was not a historian; at least not in the conventional sense. But if one stretches the point and considers that the study of behaviour-- both instinctive and learned--of animals and humans (and hence, also of culture) occupied his whole life, one could accept Lorenz to be a historian of sorts: a historian of behaviour.

In his various books, he has dwelt on the instinctive as well as acquired knowledge that most animal species (that includes human beings) display in their behaviour. In his book, "Behind the Mirror (a search for the natural history of human knowledge)" (see Bibliography), Lorenz has observed that, "Few people understand the extent to which our culturally conditioned world view apparatus and hence *everything that we consider true, certain, real and right* is determined by the social influence of the culture in which we grew up" (emphasis added, page 175). He goes on to add that the traditional features of behaviour tend to become status symbols; "The emotional quality that comes to be attached in this way to the rituals of one's group, strengthens the cohesion within the group" (page 194). Lorenz points out that the deep sense of anxiety, which overcomes a creature whenever it deviates (or, is forced to deviate) from its habitual patterns of behaviour, is a primitive impulse that was already powerful in pre-historic times and, therefore, provides a comforting sense of security that goes well beyond the elimination of fear (page 200). These comments serve to cast considerable light on individual motivation and group behaviour in human society that, at times, gives rise to concern. But, as Lorenz has himself underlined more than once, there is also inherent in the phylogenetic make-up of humans something he has called "Fulguratio", a sort of a "creative flash", in which two pre-existing and independent systems may give rise to something else with entirely new and unforeseeable characteristics (page 167). Thus, one may well imagine that if suitable conditions are created where such a "creative flash" can be nurtured, it could well lead on to a "creative society" that most nations are striving to become.

The other interesting book by Lorenz is "Study in Animal and Human Behaviour" (see Bibliography) in which he emphasizes the point that forming "constancies" is an important function of perception. Forming "constancies" refers to abstracting properties that are essential, constant and inherent in the object or environment under observation. This leads Lorenz to underline the long-term survivability of what he has called as "specialist in non-specialization", that is someone or something not tied down to a narrow niche

                    Prosenjit Dasgupta

of existence but capable of varied patterns of response to the outside environment. This "learning through curiosity" enables that animal or being to acquire "rich" knowledge of its surrounding environment, which in turn equips the animal or being to determine the biological relevant phenomena that can be exploited for its survival. (page 176). Thus, using an ornithological term, Lorenz suggests that human beings over time undergo "moulting" (that is, growing new feathers to replace the old and tattered ones) over time by shedding some old ideas and practices and replacing them with new ones. That such a proposition has validity at various stages of human history can be tested at different points of time and space, from the stage of the hominids to the pre-historic man, down to the present age. Humans have grown rice, wheat and corn from grass of different sorts, graduated from stone implements to weapons of steel and subsequently to intercontinental ballistic missiles, mastered air travel from horse-drawn carriages – one could go on and on about the progress of man. But take away that "learning through curiosity" and you take away man's capacity to grow and better himself. That is the paradox that man will have himself to resolve.

It truly mystifies one to ponder that, a country that had given birth to some of the greatest systems of logic, Sankhya and Mimamsa, millennia ago, should have turned its face so completely against that basic search for pramana (or, evidence) or to look for the pratyaksha (that what is palpable and self-evident), or take a plunge into anumana (what may be inferred from observations), and consider a topic by way of upamana, through comparisons and analogy, and the yet finer *anupalabdhi*, that goes into differentiation through natural cognitive processes. This takes one to great heights of epistemology, and perhaps even the much more modern thoughts on phenomenology or a consideration of conscious human thought processes. If the great sages and thinkers like Gautama Buddha and Adi Shankaracharya could have relied on such or similar logic systems to arrive at their messages that have moved millions of people, why is there reluctance in some sections of the national leadership to rely on pramana or evidence and what is pratyaksha or the palpable in the present times? Shankara used to rely widely to the methods of "compare and contrast" and often turned into the devil's advocate to establish his point of view. Why is there now a distinct reluctance in some sections of the national leadership to adopt similar methods to carry conviction and credibility to the people at large?

It is a notable historical fact that India enjoyed no specific Age of Enlightenment, as Europe did in the 17th and 18th centuries, when there was immense flowering of the sciences and philosophical discourse. It was marked by the emergence of Descartes, Newton, Immanuel Kant, Hegel, Bentham, Burke, John Stuart Mill, and other great thinkers. It was also then that the discovery of the power of steam by James Watt led to the Industrial Revolution, which, in turn, spurred the extension of the colonial rule by many of the European countries.

In India, this Age of Enlightenment was more prolonged and diffused; starting from the time the Rigveda and the Upanishads gave insights into the human condition and the natural phenomena all around to distinctive developments in logic, astronomy, mathematics, medicine, etc., to name a few. The contributions of Sushruta to medicine and surgery, of Varahamihira to mathematics, Aryabhata and Bhaskara to astronomy are internationally known and accepted. The heights that Indian art, sculpture and architecture achieved from about 200 BCE to the 8th century CE (i.e., for about a thousand years) are more than well-known from Ajanta, Ellora, Barhut, Sanchi, Kanheri Caves, the monolithic temples at Mahabalipuram and elsewhere. These skills and traditions were carried well into the 10th-12th centuries CE, and are reflected in the Martand Sun Temple in Kashmir, the Khajuraho group of temples in Madhya Pradesh, the great temple of Brihadeeswara in Thanjavur, the Sun Temple in Konarak, and at Modhera in Gujarat and elsewhere (one could go on and on). Further, Jai Singh, Maharaja of Jaipur, in the early part of the 18th century, constructed three or four Jantar Mantars for astronomical observations at Delhi, Jaipur and elsewhere, that are still a wonder to behold. The level of empirical knowledge available in India on metallurgy is also exemplified in the great Iron Pillar near Kutb Minar in Delhi and the great canon, the Mendha tope, in Daulatabad. But, by the time the era of the Imperial Guptas was over in the 7th century CE, much of this flowering of thoughts, skills and sciences had by and large notably diminished, and much of it just disappeared from public view. This was possibly the consequence of the repeated incursions and invasions by several groups into India since the beginning of the Christian era, culminating in the rise of the Mughal power, and later, of the British. However, there is hardly any evidence that these powers did anything specifically to destroy or eradicate the great edifice of Indian knowledge of the sciences or metaphysics. On the contrary, there was great curiosity among the Muslim rulers and the British administrators to learn about Indian philosophy and discoveries in astronomy, medicine, etc. Many of their findings and notings have already been mentioned earlier in the text.

Nonetheless, the sort of enlightenment that led Europe to the great flowering of science and technology appears to have petered down in India despite the heights that sciences had reached several centuries earlier. The empirical knowledge and skills that were embedded in the working people, like the potters or weavers, were not allowed to develop into the science of ceramics or into textile technology until much, much later under the British administration. It is of note that many, if not practically all of the major guides and mentors of science and technology in India, be it S.S. Bhatnagar, Homi Bhaba, Vikram Sarabhai, or Satish Dhawan, received a good part of their education and training abroad. Just to be able to announce that Varahamihira found this in astronomy or that Sushruta did that for the treatment of illnesses many centuries ago is no solace to a mother facing malnutrition or dehydration of her child, or a son searching for treatment of prostate cancer for his father; and these are issues of here and now.

It is noted that from about the 8th century CE to practically the mid 19th century, it seems as if India had turned her back on further advances in medicine, astronomy, mathematics and other sciences. Observations on natural phenomena no linger engaged her attention and that naturally affected any progress in the sciences. Coincidentally or otherwise, renewed interest and work on the sciences, technology and engineering commenced only in the middle of the 19th century with the progress of Western education in India.

But what had caused this recoiling, this withdrawal from external influences, and a want of internal regeneration in the sciences in the past centuries? There seems to have been a notable lack of engagement with Islamic and European knowledge, to take the best from them and build up a store of both indigenous and acquired knowledge that could lead to the rejuvenation of the country. One must put on record that there has been no such reluctance since the 1950s on the part of Indian industries seeking technical collaboration with overseas companies or with Indian students going abroad for higher studies in management, science or technology. This shows the hollowness of many of the claims to historical superiority of Indian sciences that some people seem to be intent on propagating. This turning away from the varied sources of knowledge and increasing preoccupation with numerous social and familial practices and rituals prescribed in some texts dated some five or six centuries earlier is difficult to explain. It could perhaps be described as a "displacement activity" by a community at large, owing to some enormous stress placed on them ("displacement activity" being a sort

     Prosenjit Dasgupta

of diversionary activity to take the mind off some immediate stress, e.g., scratching one's head, picking the nose, or dangling a foot). Whether this stress arose out of something internal in the Indian society, such as a growing challenge to the dominance of upper castes, or a contradiction between the noble thoughts of the earlier ages and the present social and economic predicament, or due to external factors like increasing Islamic influences, or even owing to the great famines that ravaged the country in the 18th and 19th centuries, is extremely difficult to say. It would not, however, be wrong to suggest that even at this point of time in the 21st century, one sees new prescriptions, newly discovered devotion to some lesser-known gods, or to new gurus, that had not been seen a few decades ago. Some great anxiety seems to have seized considerable sections of people about money, success, health, education of children, marriage of daughters, travel to distant places, and so on, that leads them to devote a good deal of their time and money to this new-found devotion. Is it through these rituals and acts of devotion that they want to allay a sense of unease at what may be called *unmerited gains* through wind-fall profits or by opportunistic exploitation of others, and not through personal merit and effort? If they truly derive some mental and spiritual solace from such devotion, then there is little one can object to this; except that all this seems to have progressed into an ever-growing spiral. It has gone well beyond the domain of logic and rationality into the wider world of anxieties, imagination, or as a "demonstration effect" (i.e., to copy others without thinking), with the consequent need for constant psychological props.

This leads one to a consideration of faith, which plays a major role in most religions practiced in India and in many other countries as well. It is here that one has to pause and consider, how and where to apply education and rationality to issues of faith. It is of note that even in some higher judicial circles in India there is a definite view that rationality cannot be applied to issues of faith. On that basis, faith "is", that is, it stands by itself. But is it also immutable – to be left for all time to come untested by observable facts, mental speculation or spiritual and human considerations? Is it possible or desirable to think of core faith as distinct and different from external observances that may or may not have any link with such core faith? Is faith enfeebled or is it deepened by questioning or testing of it?

It is our good fortune that we have an ancient and wonderful tradition in India of openly discussing issues of faith, as considered in the earlier sections on the Rigveda, the Upanishads and the Bhagavad-Gita. That has given resilience to the fundamental tenets of our faith to be carried into the 21st century. Here, one can do little better than to quote Dr Sarvepalli Radhakrishnan in his "The Hindu View of Life" (see Bibliography): "It is the insight into the nature of reality ("*darshana*") or experience of reality (*anubhava*)…It carries its own credentials…Blind belief in dogma is not the faith that saves…We call it faith simply because spiritual perception like other kinds of perception is liable to error and requires the testing processes of logical thought…only those parts of the tradition that are logically coherent are to be accepted…Every tradition which helps man to lift his soul to God is held up as worthy of adherence…The dialectic of religious advance through tradition, logic and life helps the conservation of Hinduism by providing scope for change."

He perceptively points out: "The Divine reveals itself to men within the framework of their intimate prejudices…Each religious man spells out the mystery of God according to his own endowments (that are) personal, racial and historical."

He goes on to add that the Law of Karma, which is central to Hindu thought, encourages the sinner (i.e., who has thought or acted against himself or society) that it is never too late to make amends, and thus, it is certainly not a philosophy of despair. He states without equivocation that Hinduism is a

     Prosenjit Dasgupta

way of life than a form of thought. Hinduism is a movement, not a fixed position; it is a process, not a result.

One may agree or disagree with Dr Radhakrishnan according to one's own predilections. While that may be true; it is equally true that one must then to put up with people who may be wholly in agreement with Dr Radhakrishnan. In fact, over the ages, great seers and sages have drawn attention to the basic search for truth as is written of in the Rigveda, the Upanishads and the Bhagavad-gita. The pernicious illness of the caste system that still permeates the body politic has to be progressively eradicated, and human beings have to be dealt with as human beings, with compassion. This is what the great teachers like Gautama Buddha had preached and what is to be found in the later teachings of Kabir, Guru Nanakdev-ji and others. In more recent times, Mahatma Gandhi emerged with his message of non-violence and his experiments in search of truth. It is precisely for that search for core values of human life that India still remembers the Gayatri Mantra and its prayer for enlightenment. This enlightenment is for all, and not just for a chosen few. This enlightenment is not just about the great metaphysical speculations, but also about the realities of the physical world, about health, medicine, agriculture, industry, astronomy and the cosmos. It is also about caste oppression, gender oppression, and economic oppression. Put together, that is a good deal of enlightenment that the country presently needs, which will lead on to India and her people achieving their rightful position in the comity of nations.

No doubt the allure of political advantage holds out promise for social and economic advantage, or even superiority. And who, in his senses, would willingly give up the opportunity for a bit of superiority over others? After all, not all can be sadhus or sages. But India has been fortunate that it has had great sages and seers like Yajnavalka and Shvetashvatara, guides to humankind like Gautama Buddha and Bhagwan Mahavira, and yet later, philosopher-kings like Emperor Ashoka, and seers like Adi Shankara, Shri Chaitanya Deva, Ramakrishna Paramahamsa, Ramana Maharshi and others who have helped to light up the path for many. Are we to turn our back on them and forget about our glorious patrimony?

And all this is there just for the asking, literally. One has just to ask: What is the Nasadiya Sukta of the Rigveda? Who was Yajnavalka? Why did Maitreyi ask the question as she did? What were the advances that Aryabhata made in astronomy? Can we know what procedures Shushruta followed in orthopaedic surgery? What are the active elements in *tulsi* or *vasaka* that can cure coughs? What really is pramana and pratyaksha in Samkhya and does it have relevance in day-to-day life? Who are the Dalits and why are they so considered? What is democracy? Who were Munshi Premchand and Ismat Chughtai? What is the difference between *dhrupad* and *khayal* and any of the other thousand things that cross your mind?

Without questions, there truly can be no answers.

Bibliography

1. Agrawal, D. P., and A. Ghosh, editors. *Radiocarbon and Indian Archaeology.* Tata Institute of Fundamental Research, 1973.

2. Agrawal, D. P., and D. K. Chakrabarti, editors. *Essays in Indian Protohistory.* B.R. Publishing Corporation, 1979.

3. Agrawala, V. S. *Ancient Indian Folk Cults.* Prithivi Prakashan, 1970.

4. Agrawala, V. S. *India as Known to Pāṇini.* University of Lucknow, 1953. Internet Archive. https://archive.org/details/in.gov.ignca.4695.

5. Agrawala, V. S. *India as Described by Manu.* Prithivi Prakashan, 1970.

6. Allchin, B., and F.R. Allchin. *The Birth of Indian Civilization: India and Pakistan Before 500 B.C. Harmondsworth.* Penguin Books, 1968.

7. Andersen, Walter, and Shridhar D. Damle. *The Brotherhood in Saffron: The Rashtriya Swayamsevak Sangh and Hindu Revivalism.* Vistaar Publications, 1987.

8. Banerji, Rakhal Das. *Prehistoric, Ancient and Hindu India; a Student's History of India.* Blackie, 1950.

9. Basu, Tapan, et al. *Khaki Shorts and Saffron Flags: a Critique of the Hindu Right.* Orient Longman, 1993.

10. Bernier, François. *Travels in the Mogul Empire Ad 1656 - 1668.* 2nd ed., S. Chand & Co., 1968.

11. Bhattacharji, Sukumari. *In Those Days: Essays Vedic, Epic, and Classical.* CAMP, 2001.

12. Bhattacharji, Sukumari. *The Indian Theogony: A*

Comparative Study of Indian Mythology from the "Vedas" to the "Puranas". Cambridge University Press, 1970.

13. Bhattacharya, Bishnupada. *Yaska's Nirukta and the Science of Etymology: an Historical and Critical Survey.* Firma K.L. Mukhopadhyay, 1958.

14. Bhattacharyya, N. N. *Indian Religious Historiography.* Munshiram Manoharlal Publishers, 1996.

15. Bryant, Edwin F., and Laurie L. Patton, editors. *The Indo-Aryan Controversy: Evidence and Inference in Indian History.* Routledge, 2005.

16. Bryant, Edwin. *The Quest for the Origins of Vedic Culture: The Indo-Aryan Migration Debate.* Oxford University Press, 2001.

17. Chakrabarti, D. K. *India, an Archaeological History: Palaeolithic Beginnings to Early Historic Foundations.* Oxford University Press, 1999.

18. Chatterjee, B. K., and G. D. Kumar. *Comparative Study and Racial Analysis of the Human Remains of the Indus Valley Civilization with Particular Reference to Harappa.* Self-Published.

    a. National Library, Kolkata, acquisition no. DB 5299 dated 30.06.1964

19. Chatterji, Suniti Kumar. *Indianism and the Indian Synthesis: Delivered before the University of Calcutta and Visva-Bharati University in August, 1959.* University of Calcutta, 1962.

20. Chatterji, Suniti Kumar. *The Ramayana Its Character, Genesis, History, Expansion and Exodus; a résumé.* Prajna, 1978.

21. Childe, V. Gordon. *The Aryans: A Study of Indo-European Origins.* Routledge, 1996.

22. Dalmia, Vasudha, et al. *Charisma and Canon: Essays on*

     Prosenjit Dasgupta

the Religious History of the Indian Subcontinent. Oxford University Press, 2001.

23. Dandekar, R. N. *Insights into Hinduism.* Ajanta Publications, 1979.

24. Dandekar, R.N. *Vaishnavism and Saivism – A Fresh Look, Pandita Atombapu Sharma Lectures.* 1976.

25. Dasgupta, Shashi Bhushan. *Obscure Religious Cults: As Background of Bengali Literature.* University of Calcutta, 1946.

26. Deshpande, Madhav, and Peter Edwin Hook, editors. *Aryan and Non-Aryan in India.* Center for South and Southeast Asian Studies, The University of Michigan, 1977.

27. Djilas, Milovan. *The New Class: An Analysis of Communist System.* Frederick A. Praeger, 1957.

28. Durrani, Farzand Ali. *Rehman Dheri and the Origins of Indus Civilization.* Temple University, Pennsylvania, 1986.

29. Elst, Koenraad. *Decolonizing the Hindu Mind: Ideological Development of Hindu Revivalism.* Rupa, 2018.

30. Embree, Ainslie T. *Sources of Indian Tradition.* 2nd ed., Colombia University Press, 1988.

31. Fairservis, Walter Ashlin. *The Roots of Ancient India: The Archaeology of Early Indian Civilization.* 1st ed., Macmillan, 1971.

32. Gandhi. *Communal Unity.* Navajivan Publishing House, 1949.

33. Ghate, Vinayak Sakharam., and V. S. Sukthankar. *Ghate's Lectures on Rigveda.* Oriental Book Agency, 1959.

34. Ginsburg, Tom, and Aziz Z. Huq. *How to Save a Constitutional Democracy.* Oxford University Press, 2019.

35. Gupta, Swarajya Prakash. *Mahabharata, Myth and Reality – Differing Views.* Agam Prakashan, 1976.

36. Gupta, Swarajya Prakash., and V.A. Ranov. *Archaeology of Soviet Central Asia and the Indian Borderlands.* Vol. 2, B.R. Publishing Corporation, 1979.

37. Habib, Irfan. *The Indus Civilization: Including Other Copper Age Cultures and History of Language Change till c. 1500 B.C.* Tulika Books, 2002.

38. Haksar, A. N.D. *Jatakamala.* Harper Collins, 2003.

39. Hazra, Rajendra Chandra. *Studies in the Puranic Records on Hindu Rites and Customs.* The University of Dacca, 1940.

    a.   PhD thesis, 1936, University of Dacca

40. Hiuen-Tsiang. *Buddhist Records of the Western World.* Translated by Samuel Beal, Oriental Book Reprint Corporation, 1983.

41. Ilaiah, Kancha. *Why I Am Not a Hindu: A Sudra Critique of Hindutva Philosophy, Culture and Political Economy.* Samya, 2005.

42. Jaffrelot, Christophe, editor. *Hindu Nationalism: A Reader.* Permanent Black, 2007.

43. Jayaswal, Vidula. *Palaeohistory of India: A Study of the Prepared Core Technique.* Agam Kala Prakashan, 1978.

44. Jha, Shefali. "Secularism in the Constituent Assembly Debates, 1946-1950." *Economic and Political Weekly,* 27 July 2002.

45. Jones, Kenneth W. *Arya Dharm: Hindu Consciousness in 19th Century Punjab.* University of California Press, 1976.

46. Kirkpatrick, Jeane J., editor. *The Strategy of Deception: A Study in World-Wide Communist Tactics.* Farrar, Strauss & Cudahy, 1963.

47. Kochhar, Rajesh. *The Vedic People: Their History and Geography.* Orient Longman, 2000.

          Prosenjit Dasgupta

48. Kosambi, D. D., and R. S. Sharma, editors. *Indian Society: Historical Probings, in Memory of D.D. Kosambi*. People's Publishing House, 1974.

49. Kosambi, Damodar Dharmanand. *Myth and Reality Studies in the Formation of Indian Culture*. Popular Prakashan, 1962.

50. Kumar, Ashutosh, and Yatindra Singh Sisodia. *How India Votes: A State-by-State Look*. Orient BlackSwan, 2019.

51. Lal, B. B, and S. P. Gupta, editors. *Frontiers of the Indus Civilization: Sir Mortimer Wheeler Commemoration Volume*. Books & Books on Behalf of Indian Archaeological Society Jointly with Indian History & Culture Society, 1984.

52. Lorenz, Konrad. *Behind the Mirror a Search for a Natural History of Human Knowledge*. Methuen & Co., 1977.

53. Lorenz, Konrad. *Studies in Animal and Human Behaviour*. Methuen, 1971.

54. Malkani, K. R. *The RSS Story*. Impex India, 1980.

55. Mallory, J.P, and D.Q Adams, editors. *Encyclopedia of Indo-European Culture*. Fitzroy Dearborn, 1997.

56. Marshall, John. *Mohenjo-Daro and the Indus Civilization: Being an Official Account of Archaeological Excavations at Mohenjo-Daro Carried out by the Government of India between the Years 1922 and 1927. Edited by Sir John Marshall. In 3 Volumes, with Plan and Map in Colours, and 164 Plates*. Arthur Probsthain, 1931.

57. McCrindle, John Watson, and E. A. Schwanbeck. *Ancient India as Described by Megasthenês and Arrian: Being a Translation of the Fragments of the Indika of Megasthenês Collected by Dr. Schwanbeck, and of the First Part of the Indika of Arrian by J.W. McCrindle*. Edited by R. C. Majumdar, 2nd ed., Chuckervertty, Chatterjee & Co., 1960.

58. Mishra, Dina Nath. *RSS: Myth and Reality*. Vikas Publishing House, 1980.

59. Muir, J., Trübner and Co &. *Original Sanskrit Texts on the Origin and History of the People of India: Their Religion and Institutions*. Trübner And Co., 1871.

60. Mukhopadyay, Manisha. *Brahmanical Mythology in Sanskrit Inscriptions*. Writers Workshop, 1981.

61. Nandi, Ramendra Nath. *Social Roots of Religion in Ancient India*. K.P. Bagchi & Co., 1986.

62. Paddayya, K. *Recent Studies in Indian Archaeology*. Munshiram Manoharlal Publishers Pvt., 2002.

63. Pearsall, Deborah Marie, editor. *Encyclopedia of Archaeology*. Elsevier/Academic Press, 2008.

64. Piggott, Stuart. *Prehistoric India to 1000 B.C.* Cassell, 1962.

65. Popper, Karl R. *The Poverty of Historicism*. Routledge, 2002.

66. Possehl, Gregory L., editor. *Ancient Cities of the Indus*. Vikas Publishing, 1979.

67. Possehl, Gregory L., editor. *Indus Civilization*. American Institute of Indian Studies, 1982.

68. Puri, Geeta. *Bharatiya Jana Sangh Organization and Ideology Delhi: A Case Study*. Sterling Publishers, 1980.

69. Pusalkar, Achut Dattatraya. *Studies in the Epics and Puranas*. Bharatiya Vidya Bhavan, 1963.

70. Radhakrishnan, S. *Religion and Culture*. Hind Pocket Books, 1968.

71. Radhakrishnan, S. *The Hindu View of Life: The Famous Upton Lectures of 1926*. George Allen and Unwin, 1957.
    a.   10th impression

72. Ragozin, Zénaide Alexeievna. *Vedic India: As Embodied*

Principally in the Big Rig-Veda. Munshi Ram Manohar Lal, 1961.

73. Renfrew, Colin. *Archaeology and Language: The Puzzle of Indo-European Origins*. Jonathon Cape, 1987.

74. Renou, Louis, editor. *Hinduism, Edited by Louis Renou*. Prentice-Hall, 1961.

75. Richman, Paula, editor. *Questioning Ramayanas: A South-Asian Tradition*. Oxford University Press, 2000.

76. Rodrigues, Valerian, editor. *The Essential Writings of B.R. Ambedkar*. Oxford University Press, 2002.

77. Sachau, Eduard, editor. *Alberuni's India*. Vol. 1, K. Paul, Trench, Trübner, 1914. Internet Archive. https://archive. org/details/AlberunisIndia/page/n4.

78. Sampurnanand. *Cosmogony in Indian Thought*. Benares: Kashi Vidyapitha, 1942.

79. Sankalia, H. D. *Prehistory and Protohistory in India and Pakistan*. Bombay University Press, 1963.

    a.   Based on Dr. Bhagwanlal Indraji Lectures, 1960

80. Sarup, Lakshman. *The Nighantu and The Nirukta: The Oldest Indian Treatise on Etymology, Philology, and Semantics*. London: Oxford University Press, 1920.

81. Sen, D., and Asok K. Ghosh, editors. *Perspectives in Palaeoanthropology: Professor D. Sen Festschrift*. Firma K.L. Mukhopadhyay, 1974.

82. Shastri, Gaurinath. *A Concise History of Classical Sanskrit Literature*. Oxford University Press, 1960.

83. Singer, Milton, editor. *Krishna: Myths, Rites, and Attitudes*. East-West Center Press, 1966.

84. Singer, Milton, editor. *When a Great Tradition Modernizes – An Anthropological Approach to Indian Civilization*. Praeger Publishers, 1972.

85. Singh, Karan. *Essays on Hinduism.* 2 revised ed., Ratna Sagar, 1990.

86. Sircar, D. C. *Indian Epigraphy.* Motilal Banarsidass, 1965.

87. Sircar, D. C. *Some Problems of Indian History and Culture (Three Lectures).* B.J. Institute of Learning and Research, 1974.

88. Sircar, D. C. *The Bharata War and Puranic Genealogies.* University of Calcutta, 1969.

89. Sleeman, William Henry. *A Journey through the Kingdom of Oude – 1849-50.* Cambridge University Press, 1971.

90. Thapar, Romila. *Cultural Pasts: Essays in Early Indian History.* Oxford University Press, 2000.

91. Thapar, Romila. *History and Beyond.* Oxford University Press, 2000.

92. Tod, James. *Annals and Antiquities of Rajasthan.* Vol. 2, Munshiram Manoharlal, 2001.

93. Upadhyay, Govind Prasad. *Brahmanas in Ancient India a Study in the Role of the Brahmana Class from c. 200 BC to c. AD 500.* Munshiram Manoharlal, 1979.

94. Watters, Thomas. *On Yuan Chwang's Travels in India.* Edited by T. W. R. Davids et al., Munshiram Manoharlal, 1961.

95. Whaling, Frank. *The Rise of the Religious Significance of Rāma.* Motilal Banarsidass, 1980.

96. Wheeler, Robert Eric Mortimer. *Early India and Pakistan.* Thames and Hudson, 1959.

97. Williams, Monier. *Hinduism.* Sushil Gupta India Ltd., 1955. Re-print of the 1877 edition.

98. Williams, Monier. *Religious Thought and Life in India: An Account of the Religions of the Indian Peoples Based on a Life's Study of Their Literature and on Personal*

     Prosenjit Dasgupta

Investigations in Their Own Country. Oriental Books Reprint Corporation, 1974. Re-print of the 1883 edition published by John Murray.

     Prosenjit Dasgupta

     Prosenjit Dasgupta

Acknowledgements

This work would not have been possible without access to the vast treasure trove of knowledge and wisdom that numerous scholars in India and abroad have recorded in their various books about this country, its history and civilization. These works bring one face to face with a search for knowledge that, at times, consumed four to five decades of a scholar's life on a single field of research. This encounter was a humbling experience.

It was a revelation to me that the oldest extant sacred text that we have, the *Rigveda* (referred to as RV in some parts of the preceding text), would have been largely lost to us, had not the scholar Yaska around the 6th century BCE compiled the *Nirukta*, or the etymology of words in the Rigveda (relying on the earlier dictionaries, the *Nighantu*). This, in turn, became the subject of a detailed commentary by Sayanacharya of Vijayanagar in the 14th century CE. The aforementioned commentary, and some scattered fragments (some in the *Brahmi* script), then formed the corpus of the Rigveda as is commonly accepted today. The Bhandarkar Oriental Research Institute in Pune has about thirty copies of a number of versions of the Rigveda.

The work of the Bhandarkar Institute, and that of some great scholars in Pune and elsewhere, such as R.N. Dandekar, B.S. Sukthankar, V.S. Ghate, V.S. Agrawala, H.D. Sankalia and others, have been both seminal and monumental (as may be seen in the Bibliography), and have been an inspiration to the author. The thoughts and words of Swami Vivekananda, Gurudev Rabindranath Tagore and Mahatma Gandhi, quoted out of context at times, repeatedly restored the perspective of the author and helped brush aside the recurring doubts.

In addition, some of the works on key topics by Dr Sarvepalli

Radhakrishnan and Dr Suniti Kumar Chatterji, and of yet later scholars like Dr R.C. Hazra and Professor Sukumari Bhattacharji, have provided substantial material for thought and research to the author. These may well be commended to students of such and similar topics.

As to a key part of the ancient history of India, that is, the Indo-Aryan phase (from which much else of Indian history and self-appreciation proceeds), I can do little better than invite attention to the book, "The Indo-Aryan Controversy (Evidence and Inference in Indian History)", edited by Edwin F. Bryant and Laurie L. Patton, running into thirteen chapters and some five hundred pages. Another "must see" is Edwin Bryant's wide-ranging work, "The Quest for Origins of the Rigvedic Culture". Both these works provide a wealth of information representing a wide cross-section of learned views.

Acknowledgement must be made of the information available so readily on the Internet, and especially on Wikipedia, for checking updates, some basic information, some of the quotations, and so on. The three books relied on in this text, "The Indo-Aryan Controversy", "Alberuni's India", and "India as Known to Panini", were downloaded from the Internet, as they were not readily available in libraries.

I am only too aware of the adage: "Fools rush in where angels fear to tread." But fools also need to learn at some point of time so as not to remain as fools for all time to come. This study represents the effort to learn from betters. Errors and omissions in this work, of course, necessarily remain the responsibility of the author.

Prosenjit Dasgupta